John Thomas Ball

**The Reformed Church of Ireland**

1537-1886

John Thomas Ball

**The Reformed Church of Ireland**
*1537-1886*

ISBN/EAN: 9783337162412

Printed in Europe, USA, Canada, Australia, Japan

Cover: Foto ©ninafisch / pixelio.de

More available books at **www.hansebooks.com**

# THE REFORMED CHURCH

OF

IRELAND.

(1537–1886.)

BY THE RIGHT HON.
J. T. BALL, LL.D., D.C.L.

*LONDON:*
LONGMANS, GREEN, AND CO.
*DUBLIN:*
HODGES, FIGGIS, AND CO.
1886.

# PREFACE.

OF THE CHURCHES in which during the sixteenth century, either by legislative interference or their own voluntary action, the principles of the Reformation were introduced, none can claim attention more justly than the Church then established in Ireland. Its history has been traced to the time of the Union with accuracy and minuteness; but of subsequent events, although some (for instance, Disestablishment and the construction of a new Constitution) are of the highest importance, a narrative is yet wanting. The following pages are an attempt to supply this deficiency; they also aim at recalling what has been already discussed by others, but in a compressed form, and without details which no longer instruct or interest. Opinions, as they have prevailed within the Church, the eminent persons by whom they have been supported, and the reasons which have been assigned for them, necessarily come under consideration, but merely historically, and with no design of taking part in the controversies which have arisen in reference to theological questions. Other denominations of religion contemporaneously existing in Ireland, their systems and proceedings, and in like manner the general history of the country, are noticed only so far as was required for the purposes of the narrative.

*December*, **1886**.

# CONTENTS.

## CHAPTER I.

### INTRODUCTION.

|  | PAGE |
|---|---|
| Scope of the present Treatise, | 1 |
| Ecclesiastical policy in Ireland in the reign of Henry VIII. directed from England, | 1 |
| Reformation Movement in England at that time, | 2 |
| Condition of Society in England at that time, | 2 |
| Improved condition and increased power of the English Laity, | 3 |
| Discontent caused by the internal condition of the Church in England, | 3 |
| State of the Parochial Clergy in England, | 3 |
| State of the Religious Houses in England, | 4 |
| The Laity become estranged from the Clergy in England, | 5 |
| Wolsey's policy, | 6 |
| Henry VIII. takes part with the Reformers, | 7 |
| Ecclesiastical Legislation of the English Parliament, | 8 |
| Previous ecclesiastical statutes, | 8 |
| The King claims to be "Supreme Head of the Church," | 9 |
| Admission of "the Headship" with a qualification by the two English Convocations, | 10 |
| English Statute "in Restraint of Appeals," | 10 |
| English Statute in relation to Convocation, | 11 |
| Decision of the Convocations of Canterbury and York as to the Jurisdiction of the Pope, | 12 |
| English Supremacy Act, | 13 |
| Effect of Henry's ecclesiastical statutes (English), | 14 |
| Down to 1535, no legislation in England as to doctrine, | 14 |

## CHAPTER II.

### [1535–1547.]

|   | PAGE |
|---|---|
| The Reformation Movement of the Sixteenth Century did not extend itself to Ireland, | 15 |
| Relations then supposed to exist between England and Ireland, | 15 |
| The Supremacy of the Crown in the Church in Ireland held to be a consequence of the Supremacy in England, | 15 |
| In 1535, Henry VIII. proceeds to have the Supremacy acknowledged in Ireland, | 16 |
| Henry appoints George Browne Archbishop of Dublin, | 17 |
| Commission to Archbishop Browne and others, to induce admission of the King's Supremacy in Ireland, | 17 |
| Opposition in Ireland to the King's Ecclesiastical Policy, | 17 |
| Letter from Archbishop Browne to Cromwell recommending a Parliament to be called, | 18 |
| Separation of the Irish People into two divisions, | 18 |
| Constitution of the Irish Parliament, | 19 |
| No Convocation as yet in Ireland, | 19 |
| Proctors sent by the Clergy to attend Parliament, | 20 |
| Irish Parliament met in May, 1536, | 20 |
| Statute to declare the Proctors had no right to vote, | 20 |
| The Commons favourable to the Supremacy, | 20 |
| Opposition to the Supremacy among the Lords, | 20 |
| Speech of Archbishop Browne in the House of Lords, | 21 |
| Irish Supremacy Act passed, | 21 |
| Other Ecclesiastical Statutes also passed, | 22 |
| Effect of this Legislation confined to the English districts, | 23 |
| Condition of the Irish districts, | 23 |
| Condition of the Pale, | 24 |
| Act to change the King's style from "Lord" to "King" of Ireland, | 25 |
| After this Act a policy of conciliation adopted, | 25 |
| Influence of the Crown in Ireland increased, | 26 |
| Neglect of missionary exertions to introduce the Reformation among the native Irish, | 26 |
| The Bishops in the Pale favoured the Reformation, | 27 |
| How far there was Doctrinal Reformation in England in Henry's reign, | 28 |
| How far in Ireland, | 28 |
| Archbishop Browne's "Form of Beads," | 28 |
| First Fruits and Twentieths in Ireland given to the Crown, | 29 |
| Religious Houses in Ireland dissolved, | 30 |
| No Legislation at this time as to Convocations or Synods in Ireland, | 30 |
| Appointments to vacant Bishoprics in Ireland after the Supremacy Act, | 30 |

# CHAPTER III.

[1547-1558.]

|  | PAGE |
|---|---|
| Accession of Edward VI., | 31 |
| The King educated in Protestantism, | 31 |
| No Parliament in Ireland in this King's reign, | 31 |
| Various Latin Services in use in England, | 32 |
| Services in use in Ireland, | 32 |
| An English Prayer Book enacted by the English Parliament, | 33 |
| The English Prayer Book introduced into the Church in Ireland under the authority of a Letter from the King, | 34 |
| St. Leger, the Lord Deputy, summons an Assembly of Bishops and Clergy to consider the King's Letter, | 35 |
| Meeting and proceedings of the Assembly, | 35 |
| Proclamation to require the use of the Prayer Book, | 36 |
| Edward's first Prayer Book differs from the present English Prayer Book, | 37 |
| Sources from which the Services adopted in the Prayer Book were derived, | 38 |
| St. Leger recalled and replaced by Crofts, | 39 |
| Conference of Crofts with Archbishop Dowdall, | 39 |
| Primacy transferred from Armagh to Dublin, | 39 |
| Archbishop Dowdall leaves the country, | 39 |
| Goodacre appointed in the room of Dowdall, | 39 |
| Consecration of Goodacre as Archbishop of Armagh, and of Bale as Bishop of Ossory, according to the English form, | 40 |
| Appointment of other Bishops in Ireland by the King, | 40 |
| Edward's first Prayer Book printed in Dublin, | 40 |
| Irish Version ordered, but not made, | 40 |
| Second English Prayer Book of Edward VI., | 41 |
| Accession of Mary, | 42 |
| Restoration of Dowdall to the See of Armagh, | 42 |
| Some Bishops deprived: others fled, | 42 |
| Appointments in the room of Bishops deprived, | 43 |
| Death and character of Archbishop Browne, | 43 |
| Bull of Paul IV. pronouncing absolution of the separation from Rome, | 44 |
| Repeal of the ecclesiastical statutes of Henry VIII., | 44 |
| No persecution in Ireland for religion, | 45 |
| Commission alleged to have been issued, | 45 |
| Civil affairs in Mary's reign in Ireland, | 45 |
| The "Plantation" system introduced, | 46 |
| King's and Queen's Counties formed and planted, | 46 |
| Statutes to facilitate the formation of counties, | 47 |
| Effect of the civil policy initiated at this time, | 47 |

## CHAPTER IV.

### [1558–1603.]

| | PAGE |
|---|---|
| Accession of Queen Elizabeth, | 49 |
| Numerical proportion of Roman Catholics and Protestants in England, | 49 |
| Superior energy of the Protestants, | 50 |
| Protestant influence in Elizabeth's first English Parliament, | 50 |
| English Supremacy Act of Elizabeth, | 51 |
| Elizabeth's objection to be called "Head of the Church," | 51 |
| Substitution in the Oath of Supremacy of the words "Governor," &c., for "Head of the Church," | 51 |
| Heresy defined, | 51 |
| Supremacy explained, | 52 |
| Elizabeth's English Prayer Book, | 53 |
| Alterations in this Prayer Book from former Prayer Book, | 53 |
| Irish Parliament summoned, and met in 1560, | 54 |
| Acts of the Irish Parliament, | 55 |
| Irish Supremacy Act, | 55 |
| Irish Act directing the use of Elizabeth's English Prayer Book, | 56 |
| Other Irish Ecclesiastical Acts, | 58 |
| Meeting of Clergy in Ireland called by Lord Sussex, the Deputy, | 59 |
| Proceedings at the meeting of Clergy, | 60 |
| Leverous, Bishop of Kildare, and Walsh, Bishop of Meath, deprived, | 61 |
| Conduct of other Bishops, | 61 |
| Appointments of Bishops, | 62 |
| How far the Statutes relating to religion were enforced, | 64 |
| The Thirty-nine Articles enacted in England, | 65 |
| In Ireland a different set of Articles, Eleven in number, enjoined, | 66 |
| Nature of "the Eleven Articles," | 66 |
| "Free Schools" established, | 68 |
| Foundation of Trinity College, Dublin, | 68 |
| Establishment of the English power in Ireland in Elizabeth's reign, | 69 |
| Additional Counties formed, | 70 |
| Plantation of Munster, | 71 |
| Other Colonization in this reign, | 73 |

## CHAPTER V.

### RETROSPECT.

| | PAGE |
|---|---|
| Organization of the Church of Ireland in 1536, | 74 |
| Monastic Institutions in Ireland, | 74 |
| Their condition at the era of the Reformation, | 76 |
| The Parochial system at the era of the Reformation, | 77 |
| Evil effect of the system of Appropriations upon the Parochial Clergy, | 78 |
| Other causes depressing at this time the condition of the Clergy, | 79 |
| Measures adopted in relation to Monastic property, | 79 |
| The interests of the Church neglected, | 80 |
| Injudicious ecclesiastical policy adopted, | 83 |
| Effect of the policy adopted on the Clergy, | 83 |
| Letter of Sir Philip Sidney to Queen Elizabeth in relation to the state of the Church, | 84 |
| How far Protestantism made progress, | 85 |
| Difficulties in the way of Protestantism among the Irish part of the people, | 85 |
| Neglect to introduce Protestantism among the Irish, | 86 |
| Progress of Protestantism in the Pale and English districts, | 87 |

## CHAPTER VI.

### [1603–1625.]

| | |
|---|---|
| Accession of James I., | 89 |
| General submission in Ireland to the authority of James, | 89 |
| Change of policy in civil affairs, | 90 |
| Division of the Island into counties completed, | 90 |
| Circuits of the Judges enlarged, | 91 |
| Irish Chieftains accept grants from the Crown, | 91 |
| Tyrone and Tyrconnell leave the Kingdom, | 91 |
| Forfeiture of the territories of Tyrone and Tyrconnell, | 92 |
| Plantation of Ulster, | 92 |
| Majority of the new settlers Scotch, | 94 |
| Parliament summoned, and met in 1613, | 95 |
| Constitution of the Parliament of 1613, | 95 |
| Sir John Davis elected Speaker, | 96 |
| His Address to the Deputy, Sir Arthur Chichester, | 96 |
| Repeal of Statutes which oppressed the Irish, | 97 |
| First Convocation in Ireland, | 97 |
| Convocation proceeds to frame Articles of Faith, | 98 |

## CONTENTS.

|   | PAGE |
|---|---|
| The Thirty-nine Articles not adopted, | 99 |
| Reasons for this course, | 100 |
| Irish Articles of 1615, | 100 |
| Less religious toleration in Ireland under James than under Elizabeth, | 104 |
| Proceedings of James in reference to ecclesiastical affairs, | 105 |
| Episcopal appointments by James, | 105 |
| Hampton, Archbishop of Armagh, | 105 |
| Downham, Bishop of Derry, | 107 |
| Effect of the King's measures, | 108 |

# CHAPTER VII.

### [1625-1660.]

|   |   |
|---|---|
| Religious controversies in England at the Accession of Charles I., | 110 |
| Increased power of the Puritan party in Parliament, | 112 |
| Hostility of Elizabeth, James I., and Charles I., to the Puritans, | 112 |
| Mode in which the ecclesiastical patronage of Charles was exercised, | 112 |
| Dissolution of Charles's third English Parliament, | 112 |
| Fourth Parliament of Charles (1640), | 113 |
| Discontent of the Laity, | 113 |
| In Ireland there was not at this time religious dissension, | 114 |
| Letter of Charles reproving the condition of the Church in Ireland, | 114 |
| Strafford appointed Lord Lieutenant of Ireland, | 114 |
| Bramhall accompanies Strafford to Ireland, | 114 |
| Condition of the Church in Ireland, | 115 |
| Measures of Strafford for the benefit of the Church, | 116 |
| Strafford and Bramhall desire to introduce the English Articles in Ireland, | 117 |
| Irish Convocation of 1634, | 117 |
| Bramhall proposes the adoption of the English Articles, | 117 |
| Adoption of the English Articles by the Irish Convocation, | 118 |
| The Irish Articles of 1613 not expressly repealed, | 119 |
| Course pursued by Convocation as to the Canons, | 120 |
| Statutes affecting the Church, | 121 |
| Removal of Strafford (1640), | 121 |
| Rebellion of 1641, | 122 |
| Effect of the Rebellion of 1641 on the Church, | 123 |
| Westminster Assembly, | 124 |
| The Solemn League and Covenant, | 124 |
| The Westminster Directory, &c., | 125 |
| Prohibition in Ireland of the use of the Prayer Book, | 126 |

## CHAPTER VIII.

### USSHER AND BEDELL.

| | PAGE |
|---|---|
| Death of Archbishop Ussher, | 128 |
| Incidents of his life, | 128 |
| Character of Ussher as a Bishop, | 129 |
| Ussher's defence of Episcopacy, | 130 |
| Ussher's opinions as to the nature of the Episcopal office, | 131 |
| Compromise of the controversy as to Episcopacy suggested by Ussher, | 131 |
| Learning and opinions of Ussher, | 133 |
| Ussher's personal character, | 135 |
| Bishop Bedell, | 136 |
| State of Bedell's Dioceses, | 136 |
| Bedell's character, &c., | 137 |

## CHAPTER IX.

### [1660–1685.]

| | |
|---|---|
| Rule of the Commonwealth in Ireland, | 139 |
| Transplantation of the Natives to Connaught, | 139 |
| Colonization, | 140 |
| Effect of colonization on the interests of the Church, | 140 |
| Re-establishment of the Church by Charles II., | 142 |
| Bramhall appointed Archbishop of Armagh, | 142 |
| Consecration of two Archbishops and ten Bishops, | 143 |
| Jeremy Taylor, | 143 |
| Taylor preaches the Consecration Sermon, | 144 |
| The Irish Parliament meets, | 145 |
| Taylor preaches before Parliament, | 146 |
| Proceedings of the House of Commons, | 146 |
| Claims of the Presbyterian Clergy, | 147 |
| English and Irish Uniformity Acts, | 148 |
| Position of the Presbyterian Clergy in Ireland before the Uniformity Act, | 148 |
| Revision of the English Prayer Book, | 149 |
| The Prayer Book as revised in England adopted in Ireland, | 149 |
| Changes introduced in the Prayer Book, | 149 |
| Additions in Ireland to the English Services, | 150 |
| Influence of Bramhall; his character, | 150 |
| Political measures affecting the Church, | 151 |

## CHAPTER X.

### [1685-1702.]

| | PAGE |
|---|---|
| Policy of the English Government in Ireland before 1685, | 152 |
| Policy of James II., | 152 |
| Different results of his policy in England and Ireland, | 153 |
| Abdication of James, | 153 |
| The Crown conferred in England upon William and Mary, | 153 |
| Ascendency of the Roman Catholic interest in Ireland, | 153 |
| Parliament called by James in Ireland (1689), | 154 |
| Acts of the Parliament called by James, | 154 |
| Protestant Ascendency restored in Ireland, | 155 |
| The Established Church restored to its former position, | 156 |
| Vacant Bishoprics filled, | 156 |
| The Irish Convocation not summoned by William and Mary or by William, | 157 |
| The Clergy taxed by Parliament in Ireland, | 157 |
| Non-Jurors in England and Ireland, | 157 |
| Charles Leslie, | 158 |
| Acts of the Irish Parliament relating to ecclesiastical affairs, | 159 |
| Primate Boyle, | 159 |
| Bishop Hacket deprived, | 159 |
| Beginning of the Penal Code, | 160 |
| Assertion by the English Parliament of a right to legislate for Ireland, | 161 |
| Discontent in Ireland, | 161 |
| Molyneux's "Case of Ireland," &c., | 162 |
| Molyneux's Treatise condemned by the English Parliament, | 162 |
| Effects of the Controversy raised by Molyneux, | 163 |

## CHAPTER XI.

### [1702-1714.]

| | |
|---|---|
| Penal Code for Ireland as enacted in the reign of Queen Anne, | 164 |
| Provisions of the Irish Penal Code, | 164 |
| Injurious effects of the Penal Code upon the Interests of Protestantism in Ireland, | 165 |
| Impolitic laws as to Protestant Dissenters in Ireland, | 166 |
| Neglect of the real interests of the Church by the Irish Parliament, | 167 |
| First Fruits and Twentieths restored, | 167 |
| Swift represents to the Queen the depressed condition of the Church, | 167 |
| Convocation meets along with Parliament in 1703, | 169 |

## CONTENTS.

|   | PAGE |
|---|---|
| Resolution of the Lower House in reference to the conversion of the native Irish, | 169 |
| Proceedings of Convocation in 1705, 1709, 1711, | 170 |
| The Crown ceases to summon Convocation in Ireland, | 171 |
| Considerations which discouraged exertions to convert the Natives, | 171 |
| Measures adopted for the purpose of converting the natives, | 172 |
| Vacancies in Bishoprics filled, | 173 |
| Primates Marsh and Lindsay, | 173 |
| Archbishop King, | 173 |
| Swift, | 174 |
| Bishop Stearne, | 175 |
| Neglect of duty by many Bishops, | 175 |
| Effects of the Penal Code, | 176 |
| Protestant Ascendency completely established, | 176 |

## CHAPTER XII.
### [1714–1760.]

|   | |
|---|---|
| Social condition of Ireland during the reigns of George I. and George II. | 177 |
| Religious condition of England and Ireland at the commencement of the eighteenth century, | 177 |
| Prevalence of Infidelity, | 178 |
| Standard of opinion in society irrespective of religion, | 179 |
| English and Irish clergy, | 180 |
| Peculiar circumstances injuriously affecting the Irish Clergy, | 180 |
| Mode in which the ecclesiastical patronage of the Crown was exercised in Ireland, | 181 |
| Merit of some of the Irish Clergy, | 181 |
| The questions debated at this time related to the truth and authority of revealed religion, | 181 |
| Archbishop King's writings, | 182 |
| Bishop Peter Browne's writings, | 183 |
| Bishop Berkeley, | 184 |
| The writings of Berkeley, | 186 |
| Policy of Swift and of Berkeley contrasted, | 187 |
| Abbadie, Dean of Killaloe, | 188 |
| Treatise of Abbadie on the Truth of the Christian Religion, | 188 |
| Controversy between Bishops Browne and Berkeley on the moral attributes of a Supreme Being, | 189 |
| English and Irish parties in the State and the Church, | 190 |
| English policy in Ireland, | 190 |
| Swift, | 190 |
| Swift's "Sentiments of a Church of England Man," and Sermons, | 191 |

## CHAPTER XIII.

### [1760–1800.]

|  | PAGE |
|---|---|
| Revival of a religious spirit before the accession of George III. | 194 |
| The revival of religion principally due to Wesley and his associates, | 194 |
| Wesley adhered to the Church both in England and Ireland, | 195 |
| Introduction and progress of Methodism in Ireland, | 196 |
| The Evangelical party in the English Church, | 197 |
| Improvement of manners in England and Ireland, | 197 |
| Improvement of the clergy, | 198 |
| Patronage of the Crown in Ireland guided by political motives, | 198 |
| Primate Stone, | 199 |
| Bishop Hervey (Earl of Bristol) | 200 |
| Character of other Irish Bishops, | 201 |
| Non-residence of many of the beneficed clergy, | 202 |
| Parliament relaxes the Penal Code, | 203 |
| Parliament neglects legislating for the Church, | 203 |
| Primate Boulter, | 204 |
| Primate Robinson (Lord Rokeby) | 205 |
| Bishop Law, | 206 |
| Bishop Rundle, | 208 |
| Bishop Percy, | 208 |
| Bishop O'Beirne, | 209 |
| Bishops Hamilton and Young, | 209 |
| Kirwan, | 210 |
| Primate Newcome, | 211 |

## CHAPTER XIV.

### THE UNION.

| | |
|---|---|
| Union of the Kingdoms of Great Britain and Ireland, | 212 |
| Union of the Churches of England and Ireland, | 212 |
| Act 6 George I., declaring the right of the English Parliament to legislate for Ireland, | 213 |
| Effects of the Act 6 Geo. I. and of Poyning's Law, | 213 |
| Swift revives Molyneux's protest against the English Parliament legislating for Ireland, | 215 |
| Molyneux's protest renewed by Lucas at a later date, | 215 |
| New Parliament at the accession of George III. | 216 |
| Discontent of the Irish Parliament with its subordinate position, | 216 |

## CONTENTS.

| | PAGE |
|---|---|
| The Volunteers (1778), | 216 |
| Concessions to the popular party, | 217 |
| Grattan's motion in the Irish Parliament asserting its independence (1780), | 217 |
| Act 6 Geo. I. repealed, | 218 |
| The exclusive right of the Irish Parliament to legislate for Ireland conceded, | 218 |
| Effects of the concession, | 218 |
| Disagreements between the English and Irish Parliaments, | 219 |
| The policy of uniting the kingdoms of England and Ireland favoured by the Government, | 221 |
| Union of the Churches of England and Ireland approved, | 221 |
| Bishop O'Beirne's proposal as to the union of the Churches, | 221 |
| Act of Union (1800), | 222 |
| No national Synod or Convocation summoned either in England or Ireland to consider the union of the Churches, | 223 |

## CHAPTER XV.*

[1800–1871.]

| | |
|---|---|
| Relations of the State to the Churches of England and Ireland, | 224 |
| The union of the Churches continued for seventy years, | 225 |
| In 1871 the union of the English and Irish Churches terminated, | 225 |
| The Irish Church disestablished and disendowed, | 225 |
| For thirty years after the Union the question of the Irish Church not raised, | 225 |
| Until 1829 the question of Catholic Emancipation occupied attention, | 225 |
| Mr. Pitt and Lord Castlereagh intended that Emancipation should accompany the Union, | 225 |
| Successful opposition of George III. to Emancipation, | 226 |
| Emancipation Act of 1829, | 226 |
| Effect of delay in granting Emancipation, | 226 |
| Emancipation Act preceded and followed by agitation, | 226 |
| Tithe system, | 227 |
| Agitation is turned against the Establishment, | 227 |
| Tithe Composition Act, | 228 |
| Royal Commission to inquire into the revenues of the Established Church in Ireland (1832), | 228 |
| Royal Commission to ascertain the number of persons in communion with the Church, | 229 |
| Church Temporalities Act (Ireland) (1833), | 229 |

---

* This and succeeding Chapters, have been erroneously numbered in the treatise as XVI., XVII., XVIII., XIX., XX.

|                                                                                          | PAGE |
| ---------------------------------------------------------------------------------------- | ---- |
| Tithe Rentcharge Act (Ireland) (1838),                                                   | 230  |
| Act abolishing Ministers' Money in Ireland (1854),                                       | 230  |
| Objections made to the Irish Church Establishment,                                       | 231  |
| Arguments of those who opposed the establishment of any Church,                          | 231  |
| Answer of those who supported Establishments,                                            | 232  |
| The question of endowment distinct from the question of establishment,                   | 233  |
| Benefits from the Established Church in England,                                         | 234  |
| Inadequacy of the voluntary system to meet the religious needs of society,               | 234  |
| The Establishment in Ireland exposed to objections peculiar to itself,                   | 235  |
| Considerations which operated to prevent the objections to the Irish Establishment being acted upon, | 237  |
| Opposition to the Irish Establishment for about twenty years makes little progress,      | 239  |

## CHAPTER XVI.

[1800–1871.]

|                                                                                          | PAGE |
| ---------------------------------------------------------------------------------------- | ---- |
| Internal condition of the Irish Established Church from the Union to Disestablishment,   | 239  |
| General reaction in Europe from the prevalence of Infidelity which had characterized the end of the eighteenth century, | 239  |
| Improvement in religious feeling of the Clergy and Laity of the Church of Ireland,       | 239  |
| Tendency in the members of the Established Church in Ireland to recur to the opinions in favour during its early history, | 240  |
| A party which received the name "Evangelical" formed within the Church of Ireland,       | 241  |
| Opinions of the Clergy of the Evangelical party,                                         | 241  |
| Progress of Evangelical opinions in Ireland,                                             | 242  |
| Primary education in Ireland,                                                            | 243  |
| In 1831 a new system of primary education founded and supported by the State,            | 243  |
| Controversies within the Established Church as to the new system of education,           | 244  |
| Controversies in relation to theological and educational questions diminish,             | 244  |
| Improved exercise of ecclesiastical patronage by the Crown in Ireland,                   | 245  |
| High estimation in which, at the period of Disestablishment, the clergy of the Established Church in Ireland were held, | 246  |
| Some theological writings of members of the Established Church in Ireland after the Union, noticed, | 246  |
| Archbishop Magee's work upon the Atonement,                                              | 247  |
| Differences of opinion within the Church in Ireland as to the question of "Justification by Faith only," | 248  |

## CONTENTS.

xvii

| | PAGE |
|---|---|
| Downham's "Treatise of Justification," | 248 |
| Jeremy Taylor's Sermon entitled *Fides Formata*, | 249 |
| Opinions of the Evangelical Party upon the question of Justification, | 249 |
| Bishop O'Brien's "Sermons upon the Nature and Effects of Faith," | 250 |
| Alexander Knox's opinions upon the question of Justification, | 251 |
| Alexander Knox's general religious system, | 252 |
| Bishop Jebb's works, | 252 |
| The Tractarian party in England, | 253 |
| Tractarianism not favoured by the Laity or Clergy of the Church of Ireland, | 253 |
| "Cautions for the Times," | 253 |
| Archbishop Whately's writings, | 254 |
| Theory of the "Cautions for the Times" as to Apostolical Succession, | 256 |
| Professor Archer Butler's Sermon on Church Principles, | 257 |
| Archbishop Laurence and Bishop Mant, | 257 |

# CHAPTER XVII.

## DISESTABLISHMENT.

| | |
|---|---|
| Census of the people in 1841, 1851, and 1861, | 259 |
| Census of 1861 ascertained the religious profession of the people, | 259 |
| Disproportion between the number of members of the Established Church and that of the whole people, | 260 |
| Disproportion between the aggregate of all Protestant denominations and the whole people, | 261 |
| Arguments against the Establishment in Ireland founded on the Census, | 261 |
| Census of 1861 exhibited the predominance of three religious systems, | 262 |
| The members of each of the three chief religious systems for the most part of a distinct race, | 262 |
| Failure to convert the Irish, | 263 |
| Delay in proceeding against the Church in Parliament after the Census of 1861, | 265 |
| Question of the Irish Church moved in the House of Lords (1867), | 266 |
| Royal Commission to inquire into the condition of the Irish Church issued (1867), | 267 |
| In 1868 the question of the Irish Church brought forward in the House of Commons, | 267 |
| Resolutions and a Bill to suspend appointments in the Church of Ireland, carried in the House of Commons, | 269 |
| Bill to suspend appointments in the Church moved in the House of Lords, and rejected, | 269 |
| Report of the Commission to inquire into the Irish Church, | 269 |
| Dissolution of Parliament (1868), | 271 |
| Irish Church Act (1869), | 271 |
| Provisions of the Irish Church Act, | 272 |

*b*

## CHAPTER XVIII.

[1869-1871.]

|  | PAGE |
|---|---|
| Necessity of making provision to secure the continuance of the Disestablished Church, | 275 |
| Operation of the Irish Church Act in rendering the holding of Convocation or a General Synod legal without licence from the Crown, | 275 |
| The Archbishops summon Convocation, | 277 |
| Meeting of Convocation, | 277 |
| Arrangement of the Episcopate at this period, | 277 |
| Constitution of the Upper and Lower Houses of Convocation, | 278 |
| Proceedings of Convocation, | 278 |
| Resolution passed by Convocation to invite the co-operation of the Laity, | 279 |
| Convocation makes rules to regulate the representation of the Clergy in a Convention of Clergy and Laity, | 279 |
| Influential Laymen request a Lay Conference to be summoned by the Archbishops, | 280 |
| Lay Conference summoned, | 280 |
| Meeting and proceedings of the Lay Conference, | 281 |
| Convention, or General Synod of Clergy and Laity summoned, | 281 |
| Subjects requiring immediate decision by the Convention, | 281 |
| Meeting of the Convention (February, 1870), | 282 |
| Constitution of the Church framed by the Convention, | 282 |
| Preface to the Constitution, | 283 |
| Provisions of the Constitution, | 284 |
| Charter granted for incorporation of the Representative Body, | 288 |
| Provisions of the Constitution regulating the General Synod, | 288 |

## CHAPTER XIX.

[1871-1886.]

|  | |
|---|---|
| Power given by the Irish Church Act for ecclesiastical persons to commute their life estates and annuities, | 290 |
| The Bishops and Clergy commute, | 291 |
| The Commissioners pay over to the Representative Body the value of the life estates of the commuting Clergy charged with annuities, | 291 |
| Annual subscriptions towards future maintenance of the Clergy, | 291 |
| Power given by the Irish Church Act to the Representative Body to contract for retirement of the Clergy from duty, | 292 |

## CONTENTS.

| | PAGE |
|---|---|
| Retirement of the Clergy permitted on condition that a proportion of the commuting capital of a retiring incumbent shall be left for the Church, | 292 |
| Management of the property of the Church by the Representative Body, | 293 |
| Purchase of the Glebe Houses and portions of the Glebes by the Representative Body from the Commissioners, | 293 |
| Proceedings of the Synods, | 294 |
| Changes in the organization of the Church, | 294 |
| New code of Canons enacted by the General Synod, | 295 |
| Revision of the Prayer Book by the General Synod, | 297 |
| Observations upon the present position of the Disestablished Church, | 303 |

## APPENDIX.

NOTES AND ILLUSTRATIONS, . . . . . . . . . 307

" IT is very true that these ecclesiastical matters are things not properly appertaining to my profession, which I was not so inconsiderate but to object to myself; but finding that it is many times seen that a man that standeth off, and somewhat removed from a plot of ground, doth better survey it and discover it than those which are upon it, I thought it not impossible but that I, as a looker-on, might cast mine eyes upon some things which the actors themselves, especially some being interested, some led and addicted, some declared and engaged, did not or would not see."—BACON.

# THE
# REFORMED CHURCH OF IRELAND.

## CHAPTER I.

### INTRODUCTION.

NEARLY three hundred and fifty years have elapsed since the legislation which, in the reign of Henry the Eighth, separated the Church of Ireland from the See of Rome. It is proposed in the following pages to examine the nature of this legislation, the circumstances connected with it, and the more important incidents in the subsequent history of the Church, as it was thenceforward constituted. These matters cannot, however, be adequately estimated, or even understood, without reference to the laws which were previously enacted in relation to the Church of England, and to the causes and transactions out of which those laws originated. Irish ecclesiastical policy was then directed from England; it followed and repeated what was approved in that country, and was influenced by the relations supposed to exist between the two kingdoms, rather than by local conditions of society. Accordingly, the events which in England preceded the commencement of the period with which we are now concerned will be considered (briefly, since they are generally well known) in the remainder of this chapter.

The movement, which in the sixteenth century was directed to obtain a reformation of the religious system then established in most European kingdoms, commenced in Germany, and thence extended itself to England. There it found controversies in relation to the Church, its discipline, and doctrine, already prevalent. These had been originated about one hundred and fifty years before by Wycliffe and his followers. Subsequently repressed, but never entirely extinguished, they owed their revival at this period to conditions of society which some time previously had come into existence.

During the reign of Henry VII. changes were effected in the circumstances of the different classes of the English people, and in their relations between themselves. It was the interest of this monarch to depress the power of the nobility, and his legislation was therefore in some important respects directed to that object. One of his statutes gave increased facilities for barring entails of land, and thereby enabled its alienation and its consequent subdivision. New owners of this species of property were thus introduced. At the same time commerce extended itself, and diffused opulence among the merchants and traders. Contemporaneously education improved. This was especially the case in the two universities, where the range of instruction, long narrowed from excessive reverence for the schoolmen, became liberalized and expanded by study of the great writers of antiquity. A lay middle class, remarkable for its energy, enterprize, and intelligence, gradually rose into importance.

Formerly the nobles and the ecclesiastics of high rank altogether predominated in English social life. They had no desire to see what was established by law or practice either in the State or the Church altered, and discouraged innovations which, if commenced, might reach themselves. The persons who at this time advanced upon the stage were animated by very different sentiments. A spirit of inquiry, a desire to try received opinions by the tests of reasoning, and of the more accurate information which research was daily bringing to light, had grown up among them, and through their influence pervaded the community. Existing institutions began to be scrutinized, and were subjected to acute criticism.

Increase of power and of mental activity on the part of the laity came in contact with an ecclesiastical system which it was impossible to observe without dissatisfaction. In the lapse of time abuses had grown up and inserted themselves in the administration of the Church. The monasteries appropriated the revenues of numbers of valuable parishes, and left the cure of souls in them to an inferior class of clergy inadequately paid. Pluralities abounded. The disproportion between the incomes of the dignified and of the parochial clergy was extreme. The few were inordinately rich, the many depressed and impoverished. In the monasteries, in the colleges, and among the dignitaries, were persons of ability and attainments, but the mass of the clerical order reached only to a low standard; they did not share in the progress of the period. Discipline was relaxed among them, and their general habits and manners were altogether unsuited to their calling.*

The condition of the Monastic Orders excited equal dissatisfaction. They had accumulated an amount of property in lands, tithes, and personalty, conferred upon them by the bounty of successive generations, or obtained through appropriations of parochial endowments, which to the laity seemed excessive. This feeling particularly existed in reference to their landed property, which, being inalienable, was withdrawn from the operation of the laws that in other instances were multiplying the number of proprietors. Discontent and envy followed wealth, and were not appeased by compensating services. The Religious Houses at this time made no adequate return to the community for the benefits they had received. Originally designed to form the retreats of learning and piety, they no longer answered the ends of their foundation. In every part of Europe the popular estimate of the monks, of their character and conduct, was unfavourable.†

At the same time, and while thus declining in the

---

* The need of reform of the English clergy formed the subject of a remarkable sermon preached by Colet, Dean of St. Paul's, before the Convocation of Canterbury in 1511 (Knight's *Life*, App.). With this should be compared a Commission issued in 1455, by Archbishop Bourchier, "Ad reformandum crimina et excessus clericorum et laicorum dioeceseos Cantuariensis," and a pastoral of Archbishop Morton in 1486, "Epistola continens statuta de vitâ et moribus clericorum in provinciali synodo edita" (Wilkins, *Concilia*, vol. iii., 573, 619).

† The writings of Erasmus represent the prevalent notions of the age respecting monastic persons. It is a different question how far specific charges afterwards made against the English religious houses were actually established in proof. (See on the one hand Lingard, *Hen. VIII.*, ch. ii., and on the other, Froude, *Hist.*, ch. x.; also the recent observa-

estimation of the people, the whole clerical order demanded for themselves rights and privileges which, had there been no other cause, must necessarily have provoked complaint. Thus they asserted that they were to be tried only in the spiritual courts, and that for offences, even the most criminal, they were not amenable to the temporal. On the other hand, they insisted that the laity were subject to ecclesiastical judges for mere breaches of the moral law, and instituted prosecutions in respect of them, which were the more resented because of the great expenses attending proceedings before the Church Courts.*

Owing to these various circumstances, estrangement had manifested itself in England between the clergy and laity before the Reformers in Germany made any move. When they did, at first their example, afterwards their success, attracted imitation. As they advanced, the English laity, sympathizing with the objects which they professed to seek, advanced also; and it became obvious that the prevailing discontent, unless it were in some way appeased, would manifest itself in action hostile to the ascendency claimed by the clergy.†

---

tions of Canon Perry, *Hist.*, 2 ser., ch. viii.). That complaints were made of the monasteries before Henry VIII. or his time is certain. In 1489 Pope Innocent VIII. issued a Bull, *Pro reformatione monasteriorum et locorum exemptorum*, in which these complaints are referred to (Wilkins, iii. 631).

* The complaints made of the ecclesiastical courts are collected in a petition of the House of Commons, A.D. 1528 (cited by Froude, *Hist.*, ch. iii.).

† In 1515 the Bishop of London, speaking of the trial of an ecclesiastic by a jury, said to Wolsey, "The citizens of London so favour heresy, that they would find any clerk guilty, though he were as innocent as Abel" (Burnet, *Ref.*, vol. i. p. 35). Colet, in the sermon already cited, speaks of the contradiction of lay people.

At this period Wolsey was Henry's chief minister. To the sympathies of an ecclesiastic he added the ideas of a statesman; and perceiving the danger which threatened the ecclesiastical system, sought to avert revolution by reform. Possessing legatine powers, which enabled him to visit the monasteries, he proceeded to examine such of these institutions as had poor endowments and few inmates, being those respecting which there was most censure, and obtaining Bulls for the suppression of some of them, used their property towards founding new educational institutions. The object which he sought by these establishments seems to have been the improvement of the clergy, to remove from them the reproach of ignorance which the Lutheran party brought against them, and in accordance with advice, which he is said himself to have given the Pope, " to set up learning against learning."\*
But before he could further develop his designs came his fall from power, and with his fall his policy terminated. No one took his place or persevered with his measures. Even had his authority continued, they came, as is often the case with the policy of reform both in civil and ecclesiastical affairs, too late to have operated effectively. Matters had advanced beyond the stage when they might have availed, and the progress of opinion in the direction of extensive change could not be stayed. Germany had rejected mere internal amendment, and by this time wholly severed connexion with

---

\* Lord Herbert's *Henry VIII.*, p. 148. Hallam judges Wolsey severely; Froude regards him more favourably; Brewer, the able editor of the *State Papers*, thinks that had he served a different master, he would have effected extensive reforms.

Rome. Less than Germany attained would not then have satisfied the demands of the time.*

At this crisis of ecclesiastical affairs the king intervened. He had determined to obtain a divorce from Catherine of Arragon, upon the ground that she was the widow of his deceased brother, and that therefore his marriage with her was illegal. He had for the purpose instituted proceedings before the court of Rome. These were designedly delayed both by the Pope and his legates who were sent to try the case. Henry, meeting from them only procrastination and indecision, and foreseeing ultimate failure, unless he could come before some other tribunal, resolved to repudiate the Papal jurisdiction.

This decision cast the whole weight of the Crown (always in English social life of preponderating influence) into the scale of those who, discontented with the state of the Church, advocated alteration of the existing system. They had for some time been steadily gaining ground. This support accelerated their progress. That without it they would not ultimately have succeeded there is no reason to think; but certainly their success would not have been equally rapid; possibly

---

* Erasmus represented in Germany an unsuccessful minority, who advocated reform of the Church, without separation from Rome. That, with or without separation, reform was urgently needed is admitted by the ablest adversaries of the Reformation. (See Cardinal Bellarmine, *Concio.* xxviii. ed Colon Agr. 1617, vi. 296; Bossuet, *Histoire des Variations des Eglises Protestantes*, liv. i. s. i.). Bellarmine's words are: "Annis aliquot ante quam Lutherana et Calviniana heresis oriretur, nulla ferme erat (ut ii testantur qui etiam tunc vivebant), nulla (inquam) prope erat in judiciis ecclesiasticis severitas, nulla in moribus disciplina, nulla in sacris literis eruditio, nulla in rebus divinis reverentia, nulla propemodum jam erat religio."

also the result might not have assumed exactly in all respects the same shape and form. As it was, the king and the people advanced together, sought the same objects, and concurred in the same measures.

These measures were directed to assert the independence of the national Church, to repudiate the jurisdiction and authority of the Pope over it, and to establish the supremacy of the Crown within it. The policy on which they are founded cannot be said to have been then wholly new; it was in a considerable degree indicated in the statutes of previous reigns. So early as the time of Edward III. parliament had begun, and under subsequent kings it continued, to impose limits on the authority of the See of Rome, and to restrict its interference with the English Church. It declared that Church to have been founded and endowed by the ancestors of the king and of his nobles, and that their descendants ought therefore to have the right of presenting to its dignities and benefices. It repudiated the claim of the Bishop of Rome (for it is by this title he is described) to encroach upon the seigniories of these preferments and benefices as if he were patron or advowee thereof, and enacted that the appointments to them should be free according to the manner in which they were originally established. It condemned interference with the sentences of the king's courts in cases relating to rights in ecclesiastical property, and declared that the Crown of England had been so free at all times, that it was in no earthly subjection, but immediately subject to God in all things touching its regalty, and to none other, and that it was not to be submitted to the Pope, nor should the laws and statutes of the realm be by him defeated. Lastly, it prohibited the purchasing or bringing from Rome of translations, processes, sentences of excommunication, Bulls, or any other matters touching the king, his regalty, or his realm.*

The mode adopted to establish the supremacy of the Crown in the Church was by claiming that the king should be acknowledged to be its " supreme head." In assuming the title it is probable that more was aimed at than displacing the supremacy of Rome, for which, and indeed for repudiating its ecclesiastical system, a denial of its pre-eminence would have sufficed.† The title of "head," while it effected this object, gained the further advantage that it prevented any power within the realm being set up in rivalry of the king, and reduced into subordination all other authorities, including the convocations or synods of the clergy, from whom interference might be apprehended.

In 1531 the clergy were in Henry's power. They had violated the law which forbade the Bulls of the Popes to be introduced into the country, or to be acted upon if introduced. The offence was primarily Wolsey's in obtaining his appointment as " legate " from Rome. He had made no defence when arraigned for it; and now the clergy were involved in the consequences,

---

\* 16 Ric. II. c. 5 (2), A. D. 1392; and see also 25 Edw. III. st. 5, c. 22; 25 Edw. III. st. 6; 38 Edw. III. st. 11; 13 Ric. II. st. 11, c. 2; 13 Ric. II. st. 11, c. 3; 7 Hen. IV. c. 8; 3 Hen. V. c. 8.

† De quâ re agitur cum de primatu Pontificis agitur? brevissime dicam—de summâ rei Christianæ. Id enim quæritur, debeatne Ecclesia diutius consistere, an vero dissolvi et concidere.—Cardinal Bellarmine, *Præf. in libros de summo Pontif.*, vol. i. p. 189, G. (ed. 1615).

as they had recognized the appointment. Advantage was taken of the circumstance to press for an admission by the Convocations of Canterbury and York of the king's supremacy; and ultimately their liability was compromised by giving the required acknowledgment with a qualification, and by paying to the king large sums of money. The qualification attached to the acknowledgment was, that it was made only so far as it agreed with the law of Christ.*

This seems to be the first occasion on which the title, "Head of the Church," was claimed by any king of England, or that it was by any parliament, convocation, or synod of the clergy, acknowledged to belong to him. The title of "Vicar of God, who defends and rules the Church," is, however, ascribed to the office of king in the laws of the Confessor.†

In the year next after the acknowledgment of the title of Head of the Church had been made by the convocations, the king obtained from parliament the statute "for the restraint of appeals." This remarkable enactment treats the king as "head of the realm, unto whom a body politic divided by the names of spiritualty and temporalty were bound to bear obedience." It then recites that he was furnished with plenary and whole

---

* Cujus (*i. e.* ecclesiæ et cleri Anglicani) singularem pretectorem, unicum et supremum dominum, et, quantum per Christi legem licet, etiam supremum caput ipsius majestatem recognoscimus (Wilkins, *Concil.*, iii. 742).

† The passage ascribing this title is cited in Cawdrey's Case, reported by Lord Coke (5 Rep.) It is more fully in Thorpe's *Laws of Edward the Confessor* (p. 193): Rex autem, qui vicarius Summi Regis est, ad hoc constitutus est, ut regnum et populum Domini, et super omnia, sanctam ecclesiam regat et defendat ab injuriosis.

power and jurisdiction, to render and yield justice and final determination to all residents or subjects within his realm, in all causes and contentions occurring within the limits thereof, without restraint or provocation to any foreign prince or potentate. And after these recitals it provides that all causes testamentary, causes of matrimony and divorce, rights of tithes, oblations and obventions (the knowledge of which causes, it declares, by the goodness of the princes of the realm and the laws and customs of the same appertained to the spiritual jurisdicdiction), shall from thenceforth be heard and adjudged within the king's jurisdiction and authority, in such courts spiritual and temporal as the nature and qualities of the cases and matters in contention shall require. Whoever should procure from Rome, or any other foreign court out of the realm, any manner of process, citation, appeal, or restraint, or execute the same, was to be liable to the punishment and penalties inflicted by the statute of *premunire* (so called from the first words of the writ issued under it), which amounted to loss of the king's protection, imprisonment, and forfeiture of goods.\*

This Act "in restraint of appeals," was followed in 1533 by another, prohibiting the convocations from legislating or acting without the king's leave. In pursuance of a submission made by these bodies in the previous year, it was now among other matters enacted that the clergy should not in time coming promulgate or execute any canons, constitutions, or ordinances, in their convocations (which it is declared shall always be summoned by authority of the king's writ), without

---

\* 24 Henry VIII. ch. 12 (Eng.), A. D. 1532.

the king's assent and licence. And preliminary to thus enacting, it was declared that the clergy had acknowledged, according (it adds) to the truth, that the convocation of the clergy is, always hath been, and ought to be, assembled only by the king's writ, and that they submitting themselves to the king had promised, *in verbo sacerdotii*, that they would not presume to enact or execute any new canons, constitutions, or ordinances, without the king's licence.*

About the time when this last statute was under consideration by parliament, the Convocation of Canterbury, at the request of the king, discussed whether the Roman Pontiff had any greater jurisdiction in the realm of England conferred upon him by God in Holy Scripture than any other foreign bishop. On the 31st of March, 1532, they returned the formal answer that he had not. And on the 5th of May subsequently the Convocation of York gave the same reply. These answers were given without any qualification, and were not obtained by the pressure which accompanied the admission of the supremacy, the liability in which the clergy then were having been condoned, and being now not capable of revival.

After the statutes relating to appeals and to the convocations, it only remained, in order to complete the assertion by the king of his supremacy, and place his position beyond controversy, that an acknowledgment of the title, which in 1531 he had claimed from the convocations, should be also obtained from parliament. In order to effect this, a bill containing the provisions

---

* 25 Henry VIII. ch. 19 (Eng.), A. D. 1533.

requisite for the purpose was in 1534 brought forward, and in the month of November of that year became law.*

The statute† then passed is entitled "the King's Grace to be authorized Supreme Head." Its extreme importance demands that its exact language should be quoted. It commences by a recital in the following terms: "Albeit the king's majesty justly and rightfully is and ought to be the supreme head of the Church of England, and so is recognized by the clergy in their convocations, yet nevertheless for corroboration and confirmation thereof, and for increase of virtue in Christ's religion, and to repress and extirpate errors, heresies, enormities, and abuses heretofore used in the same, . . ." After this preamble thus declaring the existing law, and the motives for legislating in respect of it, the statute proceeds to enact, "that the king our sovereign lord, his heirs and successors, kings of this realm, shall be taken, accepted, and reputed the only supreme head in earth of the Church of England, called *Anglicana ecclesia;* and shall have and enjoy, annexed and united to the imperial Crown of this realm, as well the style and title thereof as all pre-eminences, jurisdictions, privileges, authorities, and immunities, to the said dignity belonging." Also it provides that he and they may visit, order, reform, correct, restrain, and amend all errors, enormities, and abuses, which by any manner of spiritual jurisdiction ought or might lawfully be reformed, ordered, restrained, corrected, or amended.

---

\* This is the date adopted by Bishop Stubbs in his very learned Paper printed in the Appendix to the Report of the Royal Commission to inquire into the Ecclesiastical Courts (A.D. 1883).

† 26 Henry VIII. ch. 12 (Eng.), A.D. 1534.

In this manner, before the commencement of the year 1535, the supremacy of the Crown in the Church was recognized in England both by the convocations and by parliament. The Sovereign was declared to possess a visitatorial power; the right to convene and dissolve the convocations, and to control their proceedings; he was also admitted to be the source of ultimate appellate jurisdiction from the ecclesiastical courts. It was at the time alleged as a reproach to this legislation that it was intended to go farther, and to confer something of a spiritual character upon the king, as if he were to be both Pope and King; but this was expressly denied, and does not seem well-founded.*

Down to this period (which it will hereafter appear is that from which the narrative of Irish ecclesiastical affairs, for the purpose of the present treatise, is intended to commence) no discussion or legislation in reference to any proposed alterations in the received system of theology, or connected with its teaching upon doctrinal questions, had arisen either in the convocations or in parliament; neither had the king made any declaration of his intentions respecting them. Whatever progress the religious views of the Continental Reformers attained before this time in England was exclusively due to the zeal and exertions of the first converts to them, and to independent investigation on the part of the people.

---

* This subject is considered in Note L of the Appendix, in connexion with the Supremacy Act of Queen Elizabeth, which for the words of Henry's Act ("Supreme Head in earth of the Church of England") substituted in the oath of supremacy the words, "supreme governor of this realm and of all other her highness's dominions and countries, as well in all spiritual or ecclesiastical things or causes as temporal."

# CHAPTER II.

[1535-1547.]

IN the historical records of the sixteenth century, so far as they have been preserved, nothing appears to indicate that the religious movement, which preceded the ecclesiastical legislation then enacted in England, extended itself to Ireland, or that any of a similar character originated at that period with its people. Nevertheless, from the time when the policy of separating the Church from the See of Rome was entered upon in England by Henry VIII. and his ministers, there could have been little doubt that they would seek also to introduce it in Ireland. According to the ideas then accepted, the latter country was dependent upon, and subordinate to, the former; bound to receive thence the principles of its laws. This was more especially the case in respect of questions relating to the prerogative, the King of England, although in Ireland having only the title of "lord" (*dominus Hiberniæ*), being supposed to possess in the two kingdoms the same pre-eminence. If he were declared supreme in the national Church of the superior country, such, the statesmen of that age held, he was and ought to be declared in the Church of the other also.

No proceeding, however, in furtherance of these views* was taken in Ireland before the commencement of the year 1535, nor if there had, could it have been expected to lead to any satisfactory result, the country being disturbed, and the attention of the local government engaged by its condition. Indeed even then the insurrection of Lord Thomas Fitzgerald still continued; but as advantages had been gained over his forces, its speedy suppression and the restoration of the English government to its former authority were to be anticipated. Under these circumstances the period seemed to be, and probably was, as favourable to interference with Irish ecclesiastical affairs as any likely to occur.

Accordingly, early in this year Henry determined to assert in Ireland the same rights and jurisdiction in connexion with the Church as he had succeeded in having acknowledged in England. In order to this it became indispensable (none of the Irish bishops or clergy manifesting any tendency in favour of the Reformation) to send over some English ecclesiastic of eminence who would in that kingdom act the part which Cranmer had performed for the king in England, and by his advocacy support the measures which it might be thought expedient to adopt. The person selected, owing, it is said, to the advice of Cromwell, whose influence was then in the ascendant, was George Browne, a monk of the Augustinian Order, and its Provincial in England. He had become noted in London for preaching,

---

* The views of the period as to the relations of the two kingdoms, and the consequences in reference to the ecclesiastical affairs of Ireland following from them, are indicated in the preambles of the Irish statutes of Supremacy and of Appeals, which will be subsequently stated.

which in many respects was adverse to the doctrines taught at Rome, and was supposed to sympathize with the opinions of the German Reformers. A vacancy in the See of Dublin, which had for some time been unfilled, gave the opportunity to confer upon him a position of eminence in the Irish Church; and the concurrence of the Dean and Chapter of St. Patrick's Cathedral, Dublin, and of the Prior and Canons of the Church of the Holy Trinity (afterwards known as the Cathedral of Christ-Church), Dublin, having been obtained in his appointment to fill the vacant office, he was, at London, on the 19th of March, 1535,* pursuant to a mandate from the king, consecrated Archbishop of Dublin, by Archbishop Cranmer, assisted by two suffragan bishops.

This appointment was followed by the issue of a Commission directed to Browne, along with other persons of eminence, by which they were directed to confer with "the nobility and gentry" in Ireland, and endeavour to procure their support for the king's ecclesiastical policy, and in particular to induce them to admit his supremacy. In conjunction with his colleagues, the archbishop during some months persevered in exertions for this purpose, not unaccompanied by danger to himself personally, but without attaining any success. From the clergy generally he met opposition. In this they were led by Cromer, Archbishop of Armagh, a prelate highly esteemed, and possessing much influence. Whatever (they argued) might be elsewhere alleged against

---

* The dates always assume the year to begin on the 1st of January. If it were reckoned, according to the English practice of the time, to begin 25th March, the year of Browne's consecration should be expressed 1534–5.

the authority of the Roman See, it was not in Ireland that it should be denied by a king of England, for to this source he owed his own title to rule the island. "The Pope's predecessors," said Cromer, "gave it to the king's ancestors."

In the autumn of 1535 (the Commissioners having come to recognize that it was useless for them to proceed further), Browne addressed a letter to Cromwell, in which, after explaining the failure of their proceedings and the causes of it, especially adducing as such the ignorance of the clergy, the predilection of the people for the religion to which they were accustomed, the small value set on the king's Commission, he recommended that a parliament should be called to enact the supremacy.*

At this time, notwithstanding that nearly four centuries of English rule had elapsed, the Irish people were separated into two great divisions, forming, in effect, distinct nations, differing in language, sentiments, and interests. One was composed of descendants of the English, who had from time to time settled in the country, principally in Dublin and a district round it, termed the Pale, composed of portions of the four counties, Dublin, Kildare, Meath, and Louth. The other consisted of the native population, who occupied the provinces of Ulster and Connaught, almost all of Munster, and the greater part of Leinster. Parliament represented only the English race, and legislated with a view solely

---

\* This letter is printed in full in Note B of the Appendix. The principal authorities for the transactions of the period are this letter, and a *Life of Browne*, compiled by Sir James Ware's son, and published by him along with the English version of the *Annals* of his father.

to their interests. It was composed of two Houses—a House of Lords and a House of Commons. The former consisted of laymen, who had received or inherited peerages conferred by the English Crown, of the bishops, and of the superiors of twenty-four Religious Houses. As yet no Irish had been made lay Peers. The House of Commons was returned from counties, then not more than twelve in number,\* and from cities and boroughs situate in those counties. The number of members did not, it is said, reach one hundred. None came from any place exclusively inhabited by the Irish; and a native, if elected, was not allowed to sit.†

In England, with every parliament assemblies of the clergy for the provinces of Canterbury and York, known as the Convocations, and consisting of the bishops, certain dignitaries, and representatives of the clergy, called Proctors, who were returned from the different dioceses, were summoned. The bishops and clergy sat together in one house in the Convocation of York, and in separate houses in that of Canterbury. These assemblies were the authorities empowered to tax the clergy for the needs of the State. In Ireland no assembly of the character of the English convocations was, down to this time, summoned with parliament,‡ or had assumed, like them, the

---

\* These counties were the same as King John formed, A. D. 1210, viz. Waterford, Dublin, Kildare, Meath, Uriel or Louth, Catherlough or Carlow, Kilkenny, Wexford, Cork, Limerick, Kerry, Tipperary. In 1543 Meath was divided into two shires, Meath and Westmeath. See, as to the formation of the other counties, Note C of Appendix.

† The constitution of the Irish Parliament is further considered in Note D of the Appendix.

‡ As will subsequently appear, an Irish convocation was convened by the Crown, first in the reign of James the First, and last in the reign of Queen Anne. A summary history of Irish convocations will be

right to levy a subsidy. Usually, however, with the bishops attending an Irish parliament there came proctors representing the clergy of their dioceses, who were entitled to sit in the House of Commons along with the lay members, but whether as a constituent part thereof, and with the right to vote, or as assessors and advisers, and if so, whether with a veto, does not seem to have been as yet definitively settled.

After Browne's advice had been given to convene parliament, there appears to have been some delay, for its first subsequent meeting was not until the month of May in the next year (A.D. 1536). It was then found that the proctors claimed to vote, and that if their claim was admitted, they were likely to obstruct the king's measures. An Act was therefore passed which, professing to be in accordance with the opinions of the judges and other learned men, declared that the proctors were only counsellors and assistants, and not members of the House of Commons.

When the proctors were thus excluded from voting, the House of Commons was, for legislative purposes, wholly lay; also it was entirely English. Accordingly, its members appear not to have made any objection[*] or difficulty as regards the question of the supremacy. It was otherwise in the House of Peers, where the Spiritual

---

found in a Paper on the subject read by Dr. Reeves, now Dean of Armagh in the disestablished Church of Ireland, at a meeting of the Church Congress in Dublin, A.D. 1868. It is much to be desired that Dr. Reeves's contributions to Irish ecclesiastical history, made on this and similar occasions, were published in a collected form.

[*] Justice Brabazon writes to Cromwell that "the Commons' House is marvellous good for the king's causes, and all the learned men within the same be very good." 17th May, 1536.—*State Papers,* ii. p. 316.

Lords were numerous.* A summary of the arguments used by Archbishop Browne in that assembly, when answering his brethren, has been preserved. They rest, first upon the king's authority in the State—" He that will not (he says) pass this Act, as I do, is no true subject to his Highness"; and next upon precedents of similar concessions by Rome itself—" Rome and her bishops in the Fathers' days acknowledged emperors, kings, and princes, to be supreme over their dominions, nay, Christ's own vicars."†

Ultimately an Irish Supremacy Act,‡ modelled upon the English, and of exactly the same effect, was obtained from this parliament. It declares that the King our Sovereign Lord, his heirs and successors, Kings of the realm of England, and Lords of this land of Ireland, shall be accepted, taken, and reputed the only supreme head in earth of the whole Church of Ireland, called *Hibernica ecclesia*, and shall have and enjoy, annexed and

---

* The number does not appear, but Lord Gray and Justice Brabazon say of the Spiritual Lords "they sought an occasion to deny all things that should be presented to the Upper House, where they were the most in number."—*State Papers*, Hen. VIII., ii. p. 438.

† The report of Browne's speech, which has been preserved, is given in Note E of the Appendix.

‡ 28 Hen. VIII. ch. 5 (Ireland), A.D. 1537. The Acts of this parliament are not numbered in the order in which they were passed. The Supremacy Act is ch. 5; the Act as to the proctors, which preceded it, is ch. 12. The parliament commenced to sit in May, 1536, at Dublin; was adjourned to Kilkenny, 25th July following; afterwards it was adjourned and prorogued, meeting at various places successively; and finally, on 13th October, 1537, meeting at Dublin, it was there terminated and concluded 20th December, 1537. The date assigned for the Acts in the editions of the Statutes is 1537, being the year which corresponded with the end of the parliament when the roll of its transactions was completed.—See statement prefixed to the Acts of 28 Hen. VIII., in the edition of the Statutes, 1765.

united to the Crown of England, as well the style and title thereof, as all jurisdictions, &c., to the same dignity belonging.

The preamble which prefaces the enacting part deserves attention. It differs entirely from the English; and a comparison of the recitals contained in the two statutes will illustrate how distinct the principles were upon which the legislation of each country proceeded. The English founds itself upon what is assumed to be the previous law of the kingdom (that the king was and ought to be head of the Church), and upon the acknowledgment of this by the clergy in their convocations: the Irish makes no allusion either to Irish law or the Irish clergy, but states that the king was head of the Church of England, had been so recognized by the English clergy and parliament, and that Ireland was depending and belonging to the Imperial Crown of England; thus clearly announcing the Act to be a corollary and consequence of the English.*

The Irish Supremacy Act was, like the English, accompanied by a statute† prohibiting appeals being taken to Rome, and substituting a tribunal of delegates, to be appointed under the Great Seal of Ireland, to hear

---

\* The preambles of the Irish Supremacy Act and of the Statute of Appeals are in the following words. Of the first—" Like as the king's majesty justly and rightfully is and ought to be supreme head of the Church of England, and so is recognized by the clergie, and authorized by an Act of Parliament made and established in the said realm: so in like manner of wise, forasmuch as this land of Ireland is depending and belonging justly and rightfully to the imperial Crown of England." Of the second—" Forasmuch as this land of Ireland is the king's proper dominion of England, and united, knit, and belonging to the imperial Crown of the same realm."

† 28 Hen. VIII. ch. 6 (Ir.), A.D. 1537.

them. It recites that the land of Ireland is united, knit, and belonging to the Crown of England, which Crown (it declares) is endowed with power and pre-eminence sufficient to yield full and plenary remedies in all causes. Another Act of this time declares that the king's majesty, the lords spiritual and temporal, and the commons, were forced of necessity, for the public weal, to exclude any foreign pretended power or jurisdiction within the land; and enacts that any person, by writing, act, or deed, obstinately and maliciously maintaining the authority of the Bishop of Rome or of his See, shall incur the penalties of the English statute of *premunire* (16 Ric. II.); and that an oath acknowledging the king's supremacy shall be taken according to the form, and upon the occasions, therein prescribed, an obstinate refusal by anyone bound to take it to amount to treason.[*]

That this legislation had, or was expected to have, any practical effect outside the districts inhabited by the English colonists is not probable. In the Irish country, that is, in much the greater part of the island, English law was not acknowledged; the king's writ did not, as it was expressed, run; the natives adhered to their own ancient customs and usages. They were nominally subjects of the Crown of England, but were in fact governed either by chieftains of their own race, or by Anglo-Norman lords, to whose ancestors estates acquired by forfeiture or conquest had from time to time been granted, and who in manners and sentiments were as Irish as the Irish themselves. Too powerful to be controlled by a weak central executive government, these chieftains and nobles, the real rulers of the country,

---

[*] 28 Hen. VIII. ch. 13 (Ir.), A.D. 1537.

assumed the position of independent princes, making peace and war between themselves, as their interests or enmities prompted, without reference to the Crown.*

Even in the Pale at this period the English interest was weak. It had declined during the civil wars of the houses of York and Lancaster, when the resources of the mother country were engaged at home, and assistance could not be spared elsewhere. From the depression then caused it had not as yet recovered. During its continuance the Irish of the tribes which surrounded the Pale crossed with impunity its borders, and gained possession of much land near them: while the colonists inadequately protected, and subject to spoliation and violence, became dispirited, and either left the country or took refuge in the immediate neighbourhood of Dublin. At this time the English language, habits, and manners, seem to have reached only a limited distance from the seat of Government.†

With such difficulties surrounding the introduction of a new policy, it became of importance to remove whatever tended to diminish the royal authority, or hinder the admission of its pre-eminence by all the king's subjects. These consequences were attributed to the title of "Lord," borne by the kings of England in Ireland.

---

\* In a remarkable State Paper written in, or not long before, 1515, the names of the Irish chieftains possessing "regions, some as big as half a shire, some a little less," described as " chief captains who live by the sword," and of the Anglo-Irish, described as "captains of the English noble folk, who follow the same Irish order," are given. The former are twice as numerous as the latter. See Note F of Appendix.

† In 1535 an important representation of the state of the Pale was made by official persons through Allen, Master of the Rolls, to the king. See Note G of Appendix.

It was considered to denote inferiority, and its origin was referred to the circumstance of a grant of the island from Pope Adrian IV. to Henry II.* If that monarch and his successors had other right, if their title was original, and not derived from another power, why (it was argued) were they not kings? To take away the grounds on which this reasoning rested, and confer upon the Crown such additional influence as it was thought would accompany the appellation of higher dignity, parliament was summoned; and that its decisions might possess more than ordinary weight and importance, Irish chieftains were induced to attend it. An Act was passed which, after reciting that under the name of lords the kings of England had all the jurisdiction of a king, but that for lack of the name of kings, Irishmen and inhabitants within the realm of Ireland had not been so obedient to his highness and his progenitors as they, according to their allegiance, ought to have been, provided that the king, his heirs and successors, kings of England, should be always kings of Ireland.†

This measure was followed by exertions to conciliate the most important of the Irish and Anglo-Irish chieftains, who had hitherto stood apart from the king's government in Ireland. Peerages were conferred upon

---

* The prevalence of this supposition among the native Irish was expressly asserted by Allen, Master of the Rolls, when he recommended to the king's Commissioners a change in the king's title: "Irishmen, of long continuance, have supposed the regal estate of this land to consist in the bishop of Rome, and the lordship of the kings of England here to be but a governance under the obedience of the same, which causeth them to have more respect of due subjection unto the said bishop than to our sovereign lord."—*State Papers*, ii. p. 480. Bishop Staples, in 1538, advised to the same effect: *State Papers*, iii. 30.

† 33 Hen. VIII. ch. 1 (Irish), A. D. 1542.

several of the former; and Desmond, the most powerful of the latter, was placed upon the Council. Partly owing to this policy, and partly to success in some encounters with the natives of a previous date, the influence of the Crown steadily gained ground during the remainder of Henry's reign; the disaffected submitted; and at the time of his death, about six years later, there appeared a general acquiescence in his authority.

These circumstances, if taken advantage of, might have in some degree facilitated missionary exertion in favour of Protestant tenets among the Irish. In England the Bible was translated and placed in the churches for the congregations to read; and the theology of the Reformers was taught by preaching and by writings extensively circulated. In Ireland neither of these means of instructing the people were at this time adopted; the Bible was not translated into the Irish tongue, nor were Irish-speaking teachers of the new religious system sent among the natives. Acknowledgments of the supremacy were, in important instances, obtained from persons of eminence, both lay and clerical, in the Irish districts,* but such acknowledgments were consistent with their not conforming on other points, and were not followed by any efforts on their part to gain over converts even upon the question of the supremacy.

It must therefore be pronounced that the Reformation was at this time presented only to the English

---

\* As many as two archbishops and eight bishops took the oath of supremacy at Clonmel before Archbishop Browne, the Lord Chancellor, and other dignitaries, when the latter were upon a progress through the country (*State Papers*, Hen. VIII., vol. iii. p. 117). The agreements of submission between Henry and the Irish chieftains contain admissions that the king was head of the Church of Ireland (Leland, vol. ii. p. 168).

portion of the people. To them it came not merely from the Government, but from the teaching of those members of the clerical order who followed Archbishop Browne, and gave their support to the opinions approved in England. No difficulty caused by difference of language, or want of respect for the source whence these opinions came to them, distracted the attention of the colonists from the topics submitted for their consideration. They had never ceased to sympathize with the mother country, to reverence its authority, and follow its lead in politics and manners.

Much the greater proportion of those who were of English descent dwelt in Dublin and the part of the Pale which surrounded it. The Pale was situate in four dioceses, Dublin, Meath, Kildare, and Armagh. The bishop of the first-named diocese was Archbishop Browne; of the second, Staples, who adopted the opinions of the Reformers as decidedly, and advocated them as strenuously, as Browne. In 1540, a vacancy enabled the king to nominate to Kildare an Irish ecclesiastic, Miagh, who immediately acted with Browne and Staples. The part of the Pale within Armagh diocese was small. Thus episcopal influence among the English was substantially on the side of the new ecclesiastical policy.

It requires to be kept in mind, when examining the events of this reign, that neither in England nor Ireland had doctrinal teaching assumed the form it took under Edward VI. and Elizabeth. In Ireland no Act of Parliament or proclamation of the Government gave an authoritative exposition upon the subject. In England a statute was passed, and publications were sanctioned by the king, which expressly deal with questions of theology, and which show that much of the old tenets were to be still retained. Thus "the Act of the Six Articles" (A. D. 1539) affirmed transubstantiation, the celibacy of the clergy, private masses (*i.e.* for the dead), and auricular confession; and the book called "the Erudition of a Christian man" adhered to the Roman Catholic view of the sacraments as to number and nature. The subjects respecting which in both countries distinctly Protestant opinions were pronounced, were "the remission of sins," and the graven images and relics in the churches. The first, it was declared, could not be given by the Pope, or any other ecclesiastical authority; the images and relics were to be completely removed.

A document of importance, indicating, so far as it extends, the ideas approved in Ireland at this time by the reforming party, has been preserved,* and may properly be now referred to in connexion with the subject of doctrinal teaching. It consists of directions issued by Archbishop Browne to his clergy to be read in the parish churches, as a guide for the prayers of the congregations. It is entitled "the Form of the Beads."† It commences by directing them "to pray for the universal Catholic Church, both quick and dead, and especially for the Church of England and Ireland, and first for the king, supreme head on earth immediate under God of the said Church." It then declares that the jurisdiction usurped by the

---

\* *State Papers*, vol. ii. p. 564, Hen. VIII. pt. iii., A. D. 1538.

† The "Form of Beads" is printed in full in the *State Papers*. The word "beads" was at first used to signify prayers, afterwards what they were counted by.

Bishop of Rome is now, by the authority of parliament, and by the consent and agreement of the bishops, prelates, and both universities of Oxford and Cambridge, and of the clergy both of England and Ireland, extinct, and ceased for ever; and directs this to be published to their children and servants. This, the clergyman is to say he himself knows to be true, and that it is certified to him by his ordinary, the Archbishop of Dublin, under his seal. It then exhorts to have no confidence in the Pope, or his letters of pardons (since "no man can forgive sins but God only"), and to put all their confidence and trust in our Saviour, Jesus Christ, "which is gentle and loving, and requireth nothing of us, when we have offended him, but that we should repent and forsake our sins, and believe steadfastly that he is Christ the Son of the living God, and that he died for our sins, and soforth, as it is contained in the *Credo;* and that through Him, and by Him, and by none other, we shall have remission of our sins, *a pœnâ et culpâ.*" Prayers for the royal family and persons in authority, as specified, are then enjoined; as they are also "for the souls departed out of this world in the faith of our Saviour Christ, which sleep in rest and peace, that they may rise again and reign with him in eternal life." Lastly, it directs that "for these and for grace every man say a Paternoster and an Ave."

Beside the legislation which has been narrated, measures affecting the property of the Church also came into operation during this reign. Thus, the First Fruits and Twentieths were added to the revenues of the Crown. The former was a tax of one year's emoluments of a bishopric or benefice levied from the incumbent on his appointment, and heretofore paid to the Pope; the latter was a proportion of his annual income, thenceforth made payable to the king. The Religious Houses, except such as were situate in the remote Irish districts of the north, were dissolved, and their property confiscated. The entire of their possessions were either retained for the benefit of the Crown or granted to laymen; nothing was restored to the Church.

There was not in this reign any legislation relating to convocations or national synods: none respecting the former, because they had never been convened in Ireland; none respecting the latter, because they had long fallen into disuse, very probably in consequence of the clergy being, like the laity, divided asunder according to the races from which they were respectively descended, and therefore declining to meet together. Legislation was, of course, not needed in respect of provincial or diocesan synods, which were summoned by archbishops and bishops, and which met from time to time; but, it is said, were attended only by the English, and held, as it was expressed, *inter Anglicos.**

At the period of the Supremacy Act no prelate then in office was removed, neither were the incumbents of the benefices disturbed. Between that date and Henry's death some vacancies occurred in the bishoprics. One of these was in the See of Armagh: to this and to others the king appointed directly; in some instances he confirmed appointments made by the Pope.†

---

\* Leland, vol. ii. p. 159.

† The particulars of these appointments will be found in Mant's *History*, vol. i. pp. 167–172.

# CHAPTER III.

[1547–1558.]

WHEN, upon the death of Henry VIII. (January 28, 1547), his son Edward succeeded to the throne, he was a child nine years old. From the guardians appointed by his father's will, the Earl of Hertford, brother of Jane Seymour, the king's mother, was selected to act as Protector. This nobleman, long suspected of holding the opinions of the Reformers, now manifested his decided adherence to Protestantism; and finding in the young king a mind singularly precocious, and naturally inclined to religious inquiries, he placed around him persons likely to communicate the sentiments he himself approved. Under these influences, as well as from his own reflections, Edward, as he advanced in years, became more and more favourable to the Reformers; gave them, especially Cranmer, his confidence, and encouraged every measure calculated to promote their views. Accordingly, during his reign, various statutes recommended by them, and having relation to the Church and ecclesiastical affairs, were passed. These were not re-enacted in Ireland, no parliament being there summoned from the death of Henry until the third year of Queen Mary; but some of them, now to be noticed, were, notwithstanding, put in force in the Irish Church.

The most important of Edward's measures was the English Prayer Book. Until this was completed, the existing Latin services continued to be used. They varied in different dioceses, the principal varieties being the uses of Sarum, York, Bangor, and Lincoln: among which that of Sarum, prevailing in the province of Canterbury, was the most generally adopted.*

What were the liturgies of the Irish Church at this time is not stated by historians. At the Synod of Cashel (1172), held by order of Henry II., it was directed that "all divine matters shall for the future, in all parts of Ireland, be regulated after the model of Holy Church, according to the observance of the Anglican Church."† Whether this was ever completely carried into practice is very doubtful: the English and Irish portions of the clergy lived for the most part separate from each other; and it is not improbable that usages varied in different parts of the country. It may, however, be with confidence assumed, that in Dublin and its neighbourhood the example of the English Church would have decisive influence: and as the intercourse from these places with England was with the dioceses where the use of Sarum

---

* It appears from Lyndwood, a canonist of authority, that in the province of Canterbury the use of Sarum was followed. The following reason was assigned for it: Episcopus namque Sarum in collegio episcoporum est precentor, et temporibus quibus archiepiscopus Cantuariensis solenniter celebrat divina, præsente collegio episcoporum, chorum in divinis officiis regere debet, de observantiâ et consuetudine antiquâ (Prov. de fer. ii. 4). The composition of the use is attributed to Osmund, Bishop of Salisbury, 1078.

† Omnia divina ad instar sacrosanctæ ecclesiæ, juxta quod Anglicana observat ecclesia, in omnibus partibus Hiberniæ amodo tractentur. Cited by Ussher (iv. 275) from Giraldus Cambrensis.

prevailed, that the services were according to the Sarum use.*

The preparation of an English Prayer Book was entrusted to Commissioners over whom Cranmer presided. The draft prepared by them was approved by the Convocations of York and Canterbury,† and then was finally enacted in a statute which required it to be read at common and open prayer, in every cathedral or parish church, or other place within the realm of England, Wales, Calais, or other the king's dominions.

The words just cited, it will be observed, refer not only to England and Calais, but to "other the king's dominions," and are therefore wide enough to include Ireland. Similar language had been used in the English Acts of Appeals, of First Fruits, and of Faculties, in the reign of Henry VIII.; but in none of these instances was English legislation considered sufficient; statutes to the same effect as the two first Acts had been passed, and the third Act had been extended to Ireland, by the Irish Parliament.

Whether it was supposed by the English Government that the words of the enactment relating to the new Prayer Book obliged its use in the Irish Church does not appear. At a later period the legal authorities, who upheld the power of the English Parliament to make laws binding in Ireland,‡ conceded that general

---

\* Henry de Loundres, Archbishop of Dublin under John, came from Sarum diocese, A.D. 1212. See Note H of Appendix.

† Procter on the *Book of Common Prayer*, p. 22.

‡ Acts of Parliament including Ireland by express words were before this period, and one was at this period, passed by the English Parliament. Its claim of authority to legislate for Ireland was not abandoned until 1782. That it was ever admitted by the Irish people was at that time

D

words did not suffice for the purpose: that Ireland should be expressly named. But this may not have been thought at this time. Accordingly Edward and his ministers relying, it is probable, upon the English Act, but possibly also considering that the royal supremacy in the Church gave jurisdiction to direct forms of worship, proceeded as if the sanction of the Irish Parliament could be dispensed with, and that it was enough to issue an order from the Crown.

Upon the 6th February, 1551, a letter was addressed to Sir Anthony St. Leger, who was then the Deputy, by the king, in which, after reciting that his father had translations of the Bible placed in the parish churches, and that he himself had caused the liturgy and prayers to be also " translated* for the general benefit of his subjects' understandings, wherever assembled in the parish churches, either to pray or to hear prayers read, and in order that they might the better join therein in unity, hearts and voice," he directed notice to be given to the bishops and clergy "to perfect, execute, and obey his royal will and pleasure accordingly."

---

denied; but whether the claim was or was not legally just, it is obvious that its existence tended to dispose the Irish Parliament to accept the measures proposed by the English Government; since, if the claim were well-founded, opposition was useless, as there remained the ultimate resource of the English Parliament; and if ill-founded, yet being advanced by the stronger power, who might proceed to maintain it by force, prudence would suggest to obviate controversy by voting for what was desired.

* It has been suggested that the word " translated " was used in consequence of the amount of the old Sarum services which (as will subsequently be seen) were actually translated and retained; but it is more probable that it merely means, have been expressed in English: translation referring to the language, not the contents. The full words are, " translated into our mother tongue of the realm of England according to the assembly of divines lately met within the same."

Soon after he had received this communication, St. Leger summoned an assembly of bishops and clergy, in order to submit it for their consideration, and to induce them to act in conformity with its directions. Henry does not seem to have consulted any synod or merely ecclesiastical assembly in respect of his measures, or to have communicated them to any such, after they had been enacted by parliament. The present is the first recorded occasion subsequent to the Supremacy Act on which reference was made by the Crown or by any Deputy to a body composed exclusively of persons of the clerical order, in connexion with a measure or proceeding of an ecclesiastical character.*

On the 1st March, 1551, the assembly summoned by the Lord Deputy met. The See of Armagh, to which at this time was attached the Primacy in the Church, was filled by Dowdall, who had been appointed by Henry VIII. upon the death of Cromer. He had previously been Prior of a monastery, which he surrendered, and had also been Cromer's official. Pope Paul III., not recognizing the king's right to nominate, conferred the office upon another ecclesiastic, Waucop, who, relying upon this title, attended the Council of Trent, and subscribed himself Armachanus. Dowdall, however, being consecrated in Ireland by Staples, Bishop of Meath, and other bishops, gained and kept possession of the See, and was acknowledged by the suffragan bishops and by the clergy of the province to be the archbishop. When the king's directions had been

---

* Both Sir Richard Cox and the *Life of Browne*, by Ware, state that the persons summoned were the archbishops, bishops, together with other of the then clergy.

brought before the assembly by the Deputy, the Primate, who, notwithstanding the events connected with his appointment, adhered to Rome, at once opposed the adoption of the Prayer Book, particularly objecting that the most ignorant could then say mass. A discussion ensued between him and St. Leger; and ultimately Dowdall, with all his suffragan bishops, except Staples, Bishop of Meath, retired from the meeting. Upon this occurring, the Deputy, it is reported, turned to Archbishop Browne, who in the absence of the Archbishop of Armagh, was the highest in rank, and handed him the king's order. Browne then addressed those who remained, and urged upon them the duty of obedience to the king, very much in the same manner as he had formerly expressed himself in the House of Lords during the debate upon the supremacy in the late king's time. With those who continued present he appears to have been successful, and to have obtained from them acquiescence in his propositions.*

After this meeting a proclamation was issued to carry the king's directions into effect, and a service in English was first publicly performed in Christ Church Cathedral, Dublin, on Easter Day, 1551, in the presence of the Deputy, Archbishop Browne, and the Mayor and Bailiffs of the city. Subsequently English services came into use in many churches of the Pale.

The Prayer Book, which was at this time introduced into the churches of England and Ireland, differs from that

---

* The *Life of Browne* says that "after this" (but whether after Browne's speech or after the meeting is not clear) "several of the meeker or most moderate of the bishops and clergy cohered with Browne." See the full narrative extracted from the *Life*, in Note I of Appendix.

now in use in the English Church in various particulars, of which the following are the most important. In the former the Morning and Evening Prayer began with the Lord's Prayer; the Exhortation, the General Confession, and the Absolution, which now precede it, being all subsequent additions. In the Litany there was a suffrage praying deliverance from the Bishop of Rome, and the clergy were described as bishops, pastors, and ministers, and not as bishops, priests, and deacons. In the Communion Service (which was entitled, "The Supper of the Lord and the Holy Communion, commonly called the Masse"), the men and women were separate; the sign of the cross was used in consecrating the elements; water was mixed with the wine; the Ten Commandments were not read; and to the present prayers, when consecrating the elements, were added the words, "with thy Holy Spirit and word vouchsafe to bless and sanctify these thy gifts, and creatures of bread and wine, that they may be unto us the body and blood of thy most dearly beloved Son Jesus Christ." The sign of the cross was made when repeating the words " bless and sanctify these thy gifts, and creatures," &c. When delivering the elements only the first of the two clauses now said by the officiating minister was to be used. In the Baptismal Service there was a form of abjuration directing the unclean spirit to come out of the child and depart; and two ancient ceremonies were retained—investing the child with a white garment called the chrisom, and anointing. In the Burial Service there was a prayer that the sins of the deceased should not be imputed to him, and a collect, epistle, and gospel were appointed for a communion at that time. In the prayer for the estate of Christ's Church there was contained a thanksgiving for the grace and virtue declared in the saints, and chiefly in the Virgin Mary, who was described as "glorious and most blessed"; and also a commendation to the mercy of God of those who had departed "with the sign of faith, and now do rest in the sleep of peace." In the Visitation of the Sick, the sick person, if he desired it, was to be anointed, and there was a prayer referring to the ceremony.

The instruction to the Commissioners who prepared the Prayer Book was, according to the statement in the recitals of the English statute enacting it, "to have as well eye and respect to the most sincere and pure Christian religion taught by the Scripture, as to the usages in the primitive Church." In preparing the forms much use was made of the existing services, particularly those of Sarum; but of what was thus derived a large proportion can be traced to a still remoter antiquity. The collects for Morning and Evening Prayer, and more than half those then appointed and still retained for Sundays and Holidays, are contained in collections upwards of twelve hundred years old.*

The prayers adopted from the ancient liturgies have at all times been regarded as presenting admirable models for public worship. A severe sim-

---

\* The collects for Morning and Evening Prayer, and fifty-four of the collects read with the epistles and gospels, were taken from the Sarum Missal. These can be traced, some to the Sacramentary of Leo (Pope 440-461), some to that of Gelasius (Pope 492-496), and the rest to that of Gregory the Great (Pope 590-604). The Missal now in use in the Roman Catholic Church is formed from a revision of the former services, made after the Council of Trent, under the authority of Pope Pius V., and from additions of Popes Clement VIII. and Urban VIII.

plicity of thought and expression characterizes the originals, and the translations were made at a period when the English language exhibited a strength and majesty not since surpassed. To the influence of their example it must be attributed that the portions of the present services which were added to, or substituted for, omissions from the old, have attained an elevation of sentiment and diction not unworthy to be placed beside what was preserved, so that nowhere is there perceptible inequality or want of harmony.

St. Leger, being recalled, was succeeded as Deputy by Sir James Crofts, who being desirous to induce acquiescence in the views of the English Government, invited Dowdall to a conference. This afterwards took place at St. Mary's Abbey, and after much debate was terminated by the latter saying, "It was all in vain when two parties so contrary met; and that the Lord Deputy's pains were only lost." The bishops of Meath (Staples) and Kildare (Lancaster) attended Crofts at this interview. The discussion was carried on between Dowdall and Staples. The former urged the antiquity of the Mass; the latter that the Prayer Book was but the Mass reformed.

In consequence of the course taken by Archbishop Dowdall, an Act of the King and Council of England deprived Armagh of the Primacy, and transferred it to the See of Dublin. Subsequently, Dowdall left the country, whether voluntarily, in resentment of this treatment, or being banished, is not certain; but whichever was the case, the king, dealing with the bishopric as vacant, appointed to it an English ecclesiastic named Goodacre, who, together with Bale, another Englishman nominated to Ossory, was consecrated (February, 1553) by Archbishop Browne, assisted by the bishops of Kildare and Down, in Christ Church Cathedral, Dublin. For this consecration an English service, which had been sanctioned some time after the Prayer Book, was used, Bale having insisted upon it, although no proclamation to authorize it in Ireland had been issued by the Viceroy.

Besides Goodacre and Bale, Edward, during his short reign, appointed the following bishops: Lancaster, Dean of Ossory, to Kildare, vacant by the death of Miagh; Travers to Leighlin, on the death of Sanders; Casey, a clergyman of the diocese, to Limerick, upon the death of Coyn or Quin; and Walsh, a person of native descent, to Waterford.

In 1551 an edition of the English Prayer Book was printed in Dublin. It professes to be issued by commandment of St. Leger, late Lord Deputy, and of the Council. It contains at the end a prayer for Crofts by name, who is described as "now governor over this realm, under our most dread sovereign Lord Edward VI."*

In the instructions given to this Deputy when he came to Ireland, it was directed that the services of the Prayer Book should be translated into Irish for use in those places which needed it. Unfortunately this injunction was not carried out, and no Irish version was then made either of the Bible or Prayer Book.

In England, during this reign, the doctrinal opinions

---

* A copy of this edition of the Prayer Book is in the Library of Trinity College, Dublin. It was the first book ever printed in Dublin. Its title-page is, "The Book of the Common Prayer and Administration of the Sacraments and other Rites and Ceremonies of the Church: after the use of the Church of England."

of the Reformers were extensively adopted. One result of this was, that various matters in the English Prayer Book were objected to as not consistent with them; and, as these were also disapproved by some eminent divines of the foreign Protestant Churches, the services were again subjected to revision. A second Prayer Book, the result of this proceeding, was enacted by parliament. It was never, either by statute or order, introduced, nor was it at all used, in the Irish Church; but as it formed the basis of that which under Elizabeth was authorized for Ireland, some of the more important changes therein made require notice. In it, for the first time, were introduced in the Morning and Evening Services the prefatory Sentences, the Exhortation, the General Confession, and the Absolution. The Abjuration, investing with a chrisom and anointing in Baptism, directed in the first Prayer Book, were omitted: so also anointing in the Visitation of the Sick. Prayers for the Dead were left out of all services where they occurred. In the Communion Service, the words in the title, " commonly called the Masse," were omitted: the prayer at Consecration was changed into—" Grant that we, receiving these thy creatures of bread and wine, according to thy Son our Saviour Jesu Christ's holy institution, in remembrance of his death and passion, may be partakers of his most blessed body and blood": the direction to use water with the wine was expunged; so were the words in the first book at delivering the elements, and in lieu of them the second of the clauses now used on that occasion substituted. In the Burial Service, the suggestion of a Communion was omitted. Offices for Ordination were annexed.

The ecclesiastical policy pursued by Edward's Government in Ireland was terminated by his death (1553). Mary, who succeeded him, resolved to re-establish the power and influence of Rome in all her dominions. Notwithstanding that her religious opinions were well known, she was described in the letters from the English Privy Council, upon her accession, as "on earth supreme head of the Churches of England and Ireland."

One of her first acts in Ireland was to restore Dowdall, who had been dispossessed under Edward, to the Archbishopric of Armagh, and to uphold the primacy of that See. This act must be referred to her supremacy, for Dowdall had never been recognized by the Pope, who acknowledged Waucop, nominated from Rome. Goodacre having died before the queen's accession, no conflict arose with his claims. Then steps were taken both in England and Ireland to proceed against such bishops as favoured Protestantism, the ground of offence put forward being their having married. The result was that Browne, Archbishop of Dublin; Lancaster, Bishop of Kildare; and Travers, Bishop of Leighlin, were deprived. Two other bishops anticipated removal by flying from the country—Bale, Bishop of Ossory, and Casey, Bishop of Limerick.* In their room Curwin, a native of West-

---

* Casey was restored by Queen Elizabeth in 1571, when the person appointed by Mary in his place died. Some writers consider Lancaster a different person from Lancaster, afterwards Archbishop of Armagh, but from Cal. S. P. Ir. 1509–1573, p. 371, he seems the same. Why others were not restored has not been explained. Bale was one of the prelates named in the warrant for the consecration of Archbishop Parker in England, and is supposed to have objected to return to Ireland.

moreland, and then Dean of Hereford, was appointed to the See of Dublin; Walsh, a Cistercian monk, to Meath; Leverous, who had been a chaplain to the Earl of Kildare, to Kildare; O'Fihil (anglicized Field), a Franciscan friar, to Leighlin; Lacy or Lees, a canon of Limerick, to Limerick; and Thonory to Ossory. For the Archbishopric of Cashel, which, though vacant before Edward's death, had remained unfilled, Roland Fitz Gerald, called Le Baron, was, pursuant to a Queen's Letter, elected by the Dean and Chapter. Such appointments as were made by the Crown had the sanction of the Pope. All the new prelates, except Curwin, were of Irish race, and unfriendly to the Reformation. Curwin, to judge by his subsequent conduct, seems not to have been of any very decided opinions.

Browne, soon after he was deprived, died. He was unquestionably the most able agent concerned in the introduction of the Reformation into Ireland. He is described as "a man of a cheerful countenance, in his acts and deeds plain and downright, to the poor merciful and compassionate, pitying the state and condition of the souls of the people." He has not, however, escaped censure. He was reproved by Henry VIII. for negligence of duty, "elation of mind and pride." Staples, Bishop of Meath, who was of his own party in ecclesiastical affairs, also at one time complained of him. On the other hand there exist contemporary testimonies to his zeal and to the merits of his preaching.* By writers of a later period he has been condemned for unduly

---

\* See especially a letter of Lord James Butler to Henry VIII., 1538, printed in *State Papers*, Henry VIII., vol. ii. p. 563.

exalting the authority of the Crown, resting the case against Rome too much upon it. But this was not peculiar to him: similar ideas were popular with many of the Protestant party in England, and Cranmer himself went great lengths in the same direction.

In the third year of the queen's reign a parliament was convened at Dublin, when a Bull from Pope Paul IV., pronouncing absolution for the separation from Rome, was read by Archbishop Curwin to the Lords Spiritual and Temporal. It, however, confirmed the dispositions of benefices, the dispensations, and other ecclesiastical proceedings, and the dealings with Church lands, that had taken place during the separation. An Act was then unanimously passed repealing all "statutes and provisions made against the See Apostolic of Rome since the twentieth year of King Henry VIII.; and also for the establishment of spiritual and ecclesiastical possessions and hereditaments conveyed to the laity." The queen also made gifts to laymen of lands derived by the Crown from the monasteries. The loss to the Church occasioned by Henry's grants of monastic property was not redressed; and the practical effect of the measures of this reign extended little beyond restoring the use of the Latin Liturgies instead of the English Prayer Book.

Notwithstanding the persecution of Protestants in England at this time, there is no record of anyone having suffered for religion in Ireland; and it is related that, so far as questions of that character were concerned, the social condition of the country was sufficiently tranquil to induce English Protestants from Cheshire to come and reside in Dublin.

It is said that shortly before Mary's death it was intended to put in force laws against heresy, which had been revived, and that a Commission for the purpose was issued by the queen. The failure of the design is attributed to the abstraction at Chester of the document which contained the Commission from the person who had charge of it.* There is no doubt that a story to this effect was in the next reign current. The narrative does not, however, suggest that the Commission was sought by the Irish Government, or that it had any other origin than the policy of the queen and her English ministers, with whose other proceedings it would have been in perfect consistency.

During the reign of Edward no events of importance connected with civil affairs occurred. The peace which his father had established over the country was maintained; but only externally, no substantial progress towards uniting together the English Government and the native Irish being in reality made. The agreement of Mary with the latter upon religious questions did not lead to any alteration in the political relations of the two countries. The old disturbances revived; the old proceedings to put them down were resumed.† But upon

---

* The story, and the authorities for it, are published with much circumstantiality of detail in Ware's *Life of Archbishop Browne*. See Appendix, Note K.

† Sir Richard Cox having remarked the zeal of Queen Mary for her religion, observes: "Yet the Irish were not quieter during her reign than they were under her brother; but, on the contrary, their antipathy against Englishmen and Government induced them to be as troublesome then as at other times, and prevailed with Mr. Sullevan to give this severe character of her reign—that although the queen was zealous to propagate the Catholic religion, yet her ministers did not forbear to injure and

success an entirely new mode of dealing with the vanquished was initiated. The territories of the defeated septs, and not merely the seigniories and rights of their chieftains, were held to be forfeited to the Crown, which therefore was entitled to dispose of them as if they were its own possessions, and to allot them among English settlers.

The first example of plantation (as colonization in this manner came to be called) was upon the subjugation of the tribes known as the O'Moores, O'Connors, and O'Dempseys. They occupied districts not far from the Pale, of which the chief were then known as Leix and Offaly. These were confiscated and converted into two counties, named thenceforward, from Mary and her husband Philip king of Spain, the Queen's and King's Counties, in each of which a fort was erected, and by degrees around the forts small towns formed, the fort and town in the former being designated Maryborough, and in the latter Philipstown.

Contemporaneously a statute* was passed by the Irish Parliament which empowered the Lord Deputy to grant the lands situate in these counties for estates in fee-simple, or of more limited tenure, as, in order to "the more sure planting and strength of the countries with good subjects, should be thought in his wisdom and discretion

---

abuse the Irish. Quæ tametsi Catholicam religionem tueri et amplificare conata est, ejus tamen præfecti et conciliarii injuriam Ibernis inferre non desistiterunt."—*History*, p. 309.

   \* 3 & 4 P. and M., ch. 1 (Irish). The preamble of this Act recites— "Whereas the countries of Leix, Slewmarge, Offallie, Irrie, and Glynmalier, which belong of right to the King and Queen's most excellent Majesties, were of late possessed by the Moores, the Connors, the Dempseys, and other rebels, and now by the industrious travaile of the Earl of Sussex,

meet and convenient." The statute was acted upon until the queen's death, but not to any considerable extent; the number of new inhabitants brought upon the confiscated lands being, when compared with their dimensions, small. Those who came were scattered too much apart, and were consequently exposed to the incursions of the former owners who had been removed to make way for them, without being able to combine together for mutual protection.

Another statute, also affecting the position of the native Irish, was passed about the same time as that relating to Leix and Offally. It enabled what were termed in it "waste grounds," that is, lands not then being shire land, to be divided into counties, shires, and hundreds.*

Both this statute and the policy of plantations which was commenced along with it were calculated to effect great social changes. To convert a territory into counties was the preliminary to enforcing English law, and an English mode of administering justice. To plant, was to substitute entirely new owners and occupiers. Heretofore the course pursued had been to leave the Irish parts of the island without interfering with their inhabitants, or abrogating their customs or regulations as to the possession of land. When any portions of

---

now Lord Deputy of Ireland, be brought again to be in the possession of their Majesties, and so remain, to be disposed as to their Highnesses shall be thought good : forasmuch as the well disposing of the aforesaid countries and planting of good men there shall not only be a great strength to those quarters, but also a wonderful assurance of quiet to all the rest of the English countries, and a great terror to all the Irish countries bordering upon the same."

\* 3 & 4 P. and M. (Irish), ch. 3.

them fell, after an unsuccessful rebellion or otherwise, within the power of the Crown to dispose of, it was deemed sufficient to set over them new paramount Chieftains. Anglo-Normans ruled in place of native Irishmen; inferior rights were not touched; the old services and duties continued to be rendered; the change was only in the persons who were to receive them. Henceforward all titles, whether original or derivative, came to be regarded as involved in the consequences of a forfeiture; and all claiming through them were liable to be dispossessed.

That the Irish districts sent no members to parliament; that neither directly nor indirectly was their assent given to this mode of proceeding, formed no objection to it in the minds of English statesmen of the sixteenth century. They held that the superior and victorious nation had the right to legislate for the defeated and subordinate; to take their lands, and, when they had been taken, to distribute them. Looking solely to the interests of their own country, they perceived the advantage of introducing in Ireland allies instead of enemies, civilization in lieu of barbarism, and of effecting these improvements by means which provided for those who, unemployed, were troublesome at home: they overlooked, or, if they saw, they disregarded, the consideration that arbitrary acts of this character alienate the affections of the subject race from the governing, spread through the community a sense of insecurity, and finally create the impatient discontent that predisposes to disloyalty and rebellion.

# CHAPTER IV.

[1558-1603.]

ELIZABETH, when, upon the death of her sister Mary, she came to the throne, proceeded after a slight delay, which was employed with judgment in conciliating popularity and strengthening her own influence, to determine what course it was proper to pursue in reference to ecclesiastical affairs, and ultimately resolved that the policy which had been adopted in the reigns of her father and of her brother Edward should be revived.

In what proportion the people of England were, at the accession of the queen, divided between the old and the new religious systems there are no satisfactory modes of determining; and, as might under these circumstances be anticipated, historians disagree upon the question; some holding that those who favoured Protestantism formed a majority of the people: others that the Roman Catholics were the more numerous: and others that there was a zealous Protestant party, a zealous Roman Catholic, and an intermediate, which, according to events and the political considerations arising from them, might be swayed to either side.*

---

* See Hallam, *Const. Hist.* vol. i. 137, note. Lingard, *Hist.*, *Reign of Elizabeth*, ch. 7. Macaulay, *Essay on Lord Burleigh*.

But whatever may have been the number of those who adhered to each religion, circumstances and the position which the Reformers occupied in the country aided the progress of Protestantism, and tended to procure for it superior influence. The strength of the Roman Catholic interest lay partly in the northern counties, which, remote from the seat of government, were then the least important; and partly in the agricultural districts, where the population was scattered over a wide surface. On the other hand, in London and the other towns the principles of the Reformation were in the ascendant, especially among the trading and manufacturing classes, who were the most active and intelligent portion of the people, and had for some time been acquiring wealth and power.

It was probably owing to these causes that, when the Queen's first Parliament met, and measures repealing the ecclesiastical statutes of the preceding reign were brought forward, the House of Commons was found (although not without division of opinion) willing to pass them; and that in the end, notwithstanding opposition from the bishops, legislation was obtained which a second time severed the connexion of the English Church with the See of Rome, and permanently impressed a Protestant character upon its constitution and formularies.

Of this, the most important enactment was a new Supremacy Act. It substantially agreed with the former statutes in relation to this subject, and, like them, prohibited any foreign prince, person, prelate, or potentate from exercising any manner of jurisdiction, authority, pre-eminence, or privilege, spiritual or temporal, within the realm, or any other Her Majesty's dominions. There was, however, one important particular in which the Act varied from the Supremacy Act of Henry VIII. In the oath of supremacy which was now imposed, the queen was described, not as before by the terms " head in earth of the Church of England," but by the words, " the only supreme governor of this realm, and of all other Her Highness's dominions, as well in all spiritual and ecclesiastical things or causes as temporal."

The substitution of the word " governor " was made in deference to the objections which had from the first been by many urged against the use of the word " Head of the Church," and were now again raised and renewed. Among those who objected was Elizabeth herself. " She is unwilling," Jewel wrote to Bullinger, " to be addressed in speaking or in writing, as head of the Church of England, for when the title was proposed, she earnestly answered that this honour is due to Christ alone, and cannot belong to any human being whatever."*

The Statute also contained a provision not before enacted, which confined " heresy " to what had been adjudged such by the authority of the canonical scriptures, or by the first four General Councils, or any of them, or by any other General Council wherein the same was so declared by the express and plain words of the said canonical scriptures, or as should thereafter be

---

*Juellus ad Henricum Bullingerum. " Regina non vult appellari aut scribi caput ecclesiæ Anglicanæ; graviter enim respondit, &c."— *Jewell's Works*, published by Parker Society, p. 1211. It appears, from the correspondence of the Spanish Ambassador, that Elizabeth told him she would not be called "Head of the Church."—Froude, *Hist.*, vii. 67, 69.

adjudged such by Parliament, with the assent of the clergy in their convocation.

Notwithstanding the alteration in the oath of supremacy, considerable misunderstanding of the meaning and effect of the statute continued; and accordingly it was deemed advisable to take advantage of "injunctions" which were issued from the queen to persons selected to hold visitations through the country, and publish in them "that the queen's subjects were not to give ear to those who said that any power of ministry in divine things might be challenged under her laws for kings and queens; that only the same authority was claimed that had been used under her father and brother, and is and was due to the queen, that is, under God to have the sovereignty over all manner of persons within the queen's realms and dominions, of what estate, ecclesiastical or temporal, they be, so that no foreign power should have superiority over them."

Again, at a later period of her reign, when the Articles of Religion were framed for the Church, the subject of the Supremacy was explained in one of them (xxxvii.): this being the last time at which, either by the English Parliament or Convocation, any declaration was made in reference to the subject. The language of this Article agrees with the "injunctions"; and it states that the queen's majesty hath the chief power in the realm of England and other her dominions, unto whom the chief government of all estates of this realm, whether they be ecclesiastical or civil, doth appertain; and that where we attribute to the queen's majesty the chief government, we give not to our princes the ministering either of God's word or of the sacraments; but that only prerogative which we see to have been given to all godly princes in Holy Scriptures by God himself, that is, that they should rule all states and degrees committed to their charge, whether they be ecclesiastical or temporal."*

The same Parliament, which passed the Supremacy Act, re-established English Services in the churches, instead of the Latin that had been restored by Mary. The second Prayer-book of Edward VI. revised, and in some respects altered, was ordered to be used. Of these alterations the most important were in connexion with the Communion service. For the first time the two clauses now used in administering the elements were joined together, the first only having been in the First Prayer-book of Edward VI., and the second only in his Second Book. The Communion was directed to be received kneeling, and a further rubric, explaining that adoration was not thereby intended, was omitted. This change aimed at conciliating the Roman Catholic party; so did also an omission from the Litany of the suffrage, which had been in both Edward's Prayer-books, for

---

* In Protestant monarchical countries, where the supremacy of the Pope is repudiated, there are reasons of policy for asserting such a supremacy for the Crown, as is explained in the thirty-seventh Article; otherwise, there is great risk of disunion, of empire within empire. The Crown's greatness is the greatness of the nation; and being, according to the explanation given in the Articles, secular in character, it expresses the power of the laity, and their authority in the Church.

Bishop Browne (commenting on Article xxxvii.) says the Eastern Church admits the Supremacy of the Crown. At a synod of bishops held in Greece in 1833 it was resolved that spiritually the Head is Christ, but with respect to the administration of the Church, the king of Greece is head (Neale, *Eastern Church*, Introduction, p. 60.)

See further as to the question of the Supremacy, Note L of Appendix.

deliverance from the Bishop of Rome. Prayers were added for the queen and clergy.* Dress and habits were to be as they were allowed at the time of Edward's first Prayer-book, until order should take place therein, under the authority of the queen, with the advice of the commissioners for causes ecclesiastical."

When the supremacy of the Crown and the use of the new Prayer-book in the Church of England had been established, a Parliament was called in Ireland, in order that by its assistance similar results might be there attained. This Parliament met in the month of January, 1560. It was constituted in the following manner: The House of Lords was composed of lay peers and bishops, the House of Commons of lay representatives from counties, cities, and boroughs. If all bishops who seem to have been entitled attended, they would number twenty; if all Lords temporal, twenty-three. The names of fifty-six citizens and burgesses from twenty-eight cities and boroughs are preserved; so also are the names of twenty knights from counties. They were returned from ten counties, viz., Dublin, Meath, Westmeath, Louth, Kildare, Carlow, Kilkenny, Waterford, Tipperary, and Wexford.†

Of the proceedings of this Parliament, except the Acts which were passed by it, there is no record. These

---

\* These were derived from Pope Gregory's Sacramentary.

† The dissolution of the monasteries reduced the number of Peers by twenty-four, this being the number of abbots and priors who used to sit. Leland says that in the towns from which the citizens and burgesses came the royal authority was predominant. *History of Ireland*, vol. ii., p. 225. See further as to the constitution of this Parliament, Note M of Appendix.

Acts related to the Supremacy, the Prayer-book, the First Fruits and Twentieths, and the appointment of Bishops. The Supremacy Act followed the English, and, like it, in the oath which it prescribed, omitted in speaking of the queen the phrase "head of the church," and substituted that of "the only Supreme Governor of this realm, and of all other Her Highness's dominions and countries, in all spiritual or ecclesiastical things or causes as well as temporal." The oath was to be taken by every person then or afterwards holding ecclesiastical or civil office, on pain of not being admitted to the office, or, if in possession, of forfeiting it. Persons advisedly and maliciously speaking or writing in defence of the pre-eminence or jurisdiction, spiritual or ecclesiastical, of any foreign prince or potentate, were guilty of offences, punished in some cases by forfeiture of goods, in others by imprisonment, on a second repetition by the penalty of the statute of Premunire, and on a third as for treason.*

The preamble of this statute recites, that in the queen's father's reign divers good laws were made for the extinguishment of foreign powers and authorities, and for restoring and uniting to the imperial crown of this realm the ancient jurisdictions, authorities, superiorities, and pre-eminences to the same of right belonging, and that these had been repealed by an Act of Parliament of King Philip and Queen Mary, by reason of which repeal the queen's subjects were brought under an

---

* 2 Eliz., chap. 1 (Irish), A.D. 1560, entitled: "An Act restoring to the Crown the ancient jurisdiction over the State ecclesiastical and spiritual, and abolishing all foreign power repugnant to the same."

usurped foreign power and authority. The Act is then declared to be for repressing the said usurped foreign power, and for restoring the rights, jurisdictions, and pre-eminences appertaining to the imperial crown of this realm. It does not, like the Irish Supremacy Act of Henry VIII., refer to the relations between England and Ireland, or found itself upon them.

The Act* relating to the Prayer-book introduced into Ireland the book which, as has been mentioned, had been enacted by the English Parliament in the first year of the queen. Its principal provisions are the following: It recites, that at the death of King Edward VI. there remained one uniform order of common service, prayer, and administration of the Sacraments and other Rites and Ceremonies in the Church of England, set forth in one book, authorised by Act of Parliament of the fifth and sixth years of the same king, which was repealed and taken away by an Act of Mary. It then enacts that all and singular ministers in any cathedral or parish church, or other place within the realm of Ireland, shall say and use the matins, even-song, celebration of the Lord's Supper, and administration of each of the sacraments and all other common and open prayer, in such order and form as in said book mentioned, with such alterations and additions as are therein set forth.

The use by the clergy of the services thus authorised is ordered under severe penalties. Preaching or speaking, in derogation of the Prayer-book or of any part thereof by the clergy, is prohibited. This last provision, so far as open words, is extended to all persons.

---

\* 2 Eliz., chap. 2 (Irish), A. D. 1560.

Punishments are also to be inflicted for compelling, causing, or procuring other services to be performed, and for interrupting those prescribed. Persons not having reasonable excuse shall resort to their parish church or chapel accustomed, or upon reasonable let thereof to some substituted place, upon every Sunday and other days ordained and used to be kept as holy days, upon pain of punishment by the censures of the Church; and also upon pain that every person so offending shall forfeit for every such offence twelve pence, to be levied by the churchwardens of the parish where the offence shall be done, to the use of the poor.

This Act contains the singular provision that, if the minister or priest had not knowledge of the English tongue, he might say the new services in Latin. The reason assigned in the Act for this was, that in most places there could not be found English ministers to serve in the churches, and that if those who did serve were to use such language as they understood, the due honour of God would be advanced; and "that the same may not be in their native language, as well for difficulty to get the services printed in Irish, as that few in the whole realm could read the Irish letters."

It is also to be noticed that the Act did not leave the character of the ornaments of buildings, or the dress of the clergy, to be determined by a rubric, but expressly provided that such ornaments of the Church and of the ministers thereof should be retained, and be in use, as were in the Church of England by the authority of Parliament, in the second year of the reign of Edward VI., until other order should be therein taken by the authority of the queen's majesty, with the advice of her commissioners appointed and authorised under the Great Seal of England or of Ireland for causes ecclesiastical; or by the authority of the Lord Deputy or other governor or governors of the realm of Ireland for the time being, with the advice of the Council of said realm under the Great Seal thereof, with power to the same authority with the like notice, and in the circumstances therein mentioned, " to ordain and publish such further ceremonies or rites as may be most for the advancement of God's glory, the edifying of His Church, and the due reverence of Christ's holy mysteries and sacraments."

This statute is the first enactment by an Irish Parliament which enjoined the use of an English Prayer-book. When the first Prayer-book of Edward VI. was introduced in the Irish Church, it had the sanction only of a direction from the Crown; and it is very doubtful to what extent even in English districts that direction had practical effect. The statute is framed according to the notions of the statesmen who were then in favour with Elizabeth, upon the assumption that the State had a right to regulate forms of religion, especially matters relating to public worship, and that all its subjects must externally conform to its orders.

With respect to the First Fruits and Twentieths, which were by Henry VIII. given to, and by Mary withdrawn from, the Crown, they were now again added to its resources. And along with them, were also re-annexed to its possessions the emoluments of such rectories as, having belonged to the monasteries and having been retained by the Crown, had been by the late queen relinquished.

The Act regulating appointments to bishoprics provided that they were to be made by patents under the Great Seal, consequent upon instructions or letters missive from the queen and her successors, instead of, as in England, by the deans and chapters of the sees, who, when electing, had to act in obedience to recommendations from the Crown, which, as they might not be disobeyed, were in effect mandates.* It was felt that in the unsettled state of the Irish Church, and with the opinions accepted by much the greater proportion of its clergy, any reference to the Chapters might lead to conflicts between the queen and these corporations; and that it was better the office of Bishop should be granted directly from the Crown.

The Deputy, when the Parliament of 1560 met, was Lord Sussex. By him, as soon as the legislation he desired had been obtained, it was dissolved: he himself returning to England. After a short time Sussex was again sent back as Lord Lieutenant, and in about three weeks after he had been sworn into office he received a letter from the queen, "signifying," as it is reported, "her pleasure for a general meeting of the clergy of Ireland, and the establishment of the Protestant religion through the several dioceses of that kingdom."†

In pursuance of these directions, and summoned by

---

* 2 Eliz., chap. 4 (Irish), A. D. 1660. This Act recites that, "elections of archbishops and bishops, by deans and chapters within the realm of Ireland, were to the delay and costs of such persons" as the queen appointed; and that these elections were "in very deed no elections, but only by a writ of *congé d'elire*, had colours, shadows or pretences of elections, serving to no purpose, and seeming also derogatory and prejudicial to the queen's prerogative royal, to whom appertaineth the collation of all archbishoprics and bishoprics within her said realm."

† Sir James Ware's *Annals*, A. D. 1560.

Lord Sussex for the purpose of carrying them out, a meeting of bishops, or more probably of bishops and clergy, took place in the third year of the queen's reign;* but no record remains of the names of the persons actually attending, or of the precise nature of the proceedings which took place when the assembly met, further than that one of the bishops, Walsh of Meath, is reported to have been " enraged with her majesty's proposals," and " after the assembly had dispersed themselves," to have preached against the new Prayerbook. As he alone of the bishops is mentioned to have dissented, the acquiescence of such others as were present in the Deputy's proposals may not unreasonably be inferred. When introducing his ecclesiastical policy Lord Sussex received the assistance of Curwin, who had been appointed Archbishop of Dublin and Lord Chancellor by Mary, and who now conformed, retaining both his offices. Leverous, bishop of Kildare, seems to have at once, and before the meeting, which has been described, was held, gone into opposition, refusing to take the oath of supremacy. His objections were, he represented, increased by its being required for a queen, for as ecclesiastical authority had not been conferred upon the Virgin, the supremacy could not be meant for any other of her sex.† He, and Walsh who persevered in his

---

\* Ware calls this meeting " an assembly of the Irish clergy." In the Loftus MSS. it is termed " a convocation of bishops." See Note N of Appendix.

† Leverous's argument is mentioned in Mason's *History of St. Patrick's Cathedral*, p. 163. It was first related in Bishop Rothe's *Analecta*, part iii., entitled, *de processu martyriali*, which has been lately reprinted at Dublin in a volume edited by Dr. Moran, Roman Catholic Archbishop of Sidney, N.S.W. The Article relating to the

hostility to the new Prayer-book, were deprived of their offices.

What was the conduct of the bishops who were in possession of the other sees, at Elizabeth's accession to the throne, has been a subject of controversy. Some of them owed their appointment to Mary: the rest had been allowed by her to remain when others were removed; all must have at least professed adherence to her views. These circumstances have been urged to prove, not merely that these prelates were not Protestant in opinion (for which purpose they furnish most legitimate topics), but that none of them conformed. How little they can be relied upon to support the latter inference, Curwin is a decisive example. He served Mary and he served Elizabeth. No one can doubt that, both in England and Ireland, many beside Curwin did the same;* nor has there ever been a period of change and transition

---

Supremacy was later in date than Leverous's objection. In 1580, Lord Baltinglass repeats Leverous's ideas. "Questionless" (he says), "it is great want of knowledge, and more of grace, to think and believe, that a woman, uncapax of all holy orders, should be the Supreme governor of Christ's Church : a thing that Christ did not grant unto His own mother." (Letter to Lord Ormonde, July, 1580, *Cal. Carew* MSS., 1575-1588, p. 289.

* St. Leger was Deputy of Edward and Deputy of Mary. Lord Sussex was Deputy of Mary and Lieutenant of Elizabeth. The truth is, that many, both in England and Ireland, had no decided opinions on the matters in controversy, and readily obeyed whatever was, for the time being, directed by the authority of the Crown. Nor under a Tudor sovereign were there wanting those who would say with Erasmus, " Non omnes ad martyrium satis habent roboris; vereor autem, ne si quid inciderit tumultus, Petrum sim imitaturus. Pontificis ac Cæsaris bene decernentis sequor quod pium est : male statuentis fero quod tutum est. Id opinor etiam bonis viris licere, si nulla sit spes profectûs."—ad Ricm. Pacæum, vol. iii., 651 d. (ed. Lugd. Bat. 1703).

in which conduct of this character has not extensively prevailed. Why, too, if there was not compliance, was there not deprivation? Bishops of remote dioceses might have escaped notice or interference from the government, but if those within its reach imitated Walsh and Leverous, it is in the highest degree improbable that they would not have met the same punishment.

The vacancies in Meath and Kildare, caused by the deprivation of Walsh and Leverous, were filled by the queen, who selected for the latter Craik, Dean of St. Patrick's Cathedral, Dublin, and for the former, Hugh Brady, a native of the diocese, whose merits afterwards gained for him from Sir Henry Sidney the character of "an honest, zealous, and learned bishop, a holy minister for the gospel, and a good servant to the queen."

Elizabeth found the Archbishopric of Armagh vacant, delayed long in appointing to it, and finally conferred it upon Adam Loftus,* to whom she had previously given the Deanery of St. Patrick's when vacated by Craik. Brady and Craik were appointed by patents; Loftus, for some reason not satisfactorily explained, by writ of *congè d'elire*. In 1567 Curwin, Archbishop of Dublin, induced Elizabeth to translate him to the bishopric of Oxford in England, and Loftus was by the queen moved to Dublin. The vacancy thus caused in Armagh, and three succeeding vacancies in that see, all occurring during this reign, were filled by the queen, the appointments being by patents. She also conferred

---

* Adam Loftus came over from England as chaplain to Lord Sussex. His graceful manners, attractive personal appearance, logical and rhetorical abilities, had previously attracted the notice of the Queen, who became herself his patron, and made him one of her chaplains.

the Archbishopric of Cashel in 1567 and 1570, and of Tuam in 1573 and 1595; all which offices were likewise granted by patents. Vacancies in the other dioceses, with the exceptions now to be stated, were filled in a similar manner.* The exceptions were in Derry and Raphoe, Killaloe, Kilfenora, and Emly, in none of which dioceses did the queen ever exercise patronage: also in Kilmore, in which she exercised it only on one occasion. In Down one vacancy was filled by the Pope, the others by the Crown.

The exercise by the queen of the right to collate to bishoprics is not to be regarded as proof that when appointments were made in such dioceses as were not in or immediately near the Pale, Protestantism had been accepted by their inhabitants, or that even the English services were in use. They were assertions of political power. If the ecclesiastics appointed admitted the supremacy, the object which was esteemed most important was gained. It was not their theological opinions, but their profession of allegiance unqualified by any reservation in favour of a foreign power, to which consequence was attached. Also, it is not to be assumed that the clergy in such dioceses were, to any extent, guided by the bishops placed over them. Irish for the most part, they were as little disposed to yield obedience to an ecclesiastical ruler nominated from England, as the laity of their race were to a civil.

---

* Abstracts of the queen's letters or patents for these appointments will be found in Morrin's *Calendar of the Patent and Close Rolls of Chancery in Ireland*, vols. i. and ii. See further, as to the bishops who held office under Queen Elizabeth, Note O of Appendix.

How far the law relating to attendance at church was enforced is doubtful. In the next reign the Roman Catholic party, seeking indulgence from James and desirous to present Elizabeth to him as an example, said attendance was not compelled: the Protestants replied, true, but this was because everyone, whether in opinion Roman Catholic or Protestant, readily went to church. It is, however, certain that in Dublin, whatever may have been the case elsewhere, at one time fines for non-attendance were levied.* Notwithstanding, and although on several occasions ecclesiastics were treated with cruelty, the queen's government seems to have been tolerant when merely religion was in question If the instances which some writers allege to the contrary are examined, they appear to be connected with political transactions, and to have arisen from a supposition which, whether rightly or wrongly, was entertained, that the persons punished were engaged in the Irish confederacies.† Some commissions were issued to obtain acknowledgments of the supremacy, but even as to this the administration of the law was negligent.‡

---

\* Ware says that fines for non-attendance were levied in Dublin (*Annals*, A. D. 1563). Carte (*Ormonde*, i. 67) seems to say the people generally went to church at first. Compare also Leland's *History of Ireland*, vol. ii. p. 381, note.

† See Froude, x. 482; xi. 262; Bagwell, ii. 357. Plowden, a Roman Catholic historian, says, that "during the whole reign of Elizabeth in Ireland we read of no imprisonment, banishment, or execution of any priest for the sake of his religion," *History of Ireland*, vol. i. p. 331. There is no reason to think that a Roman Catholic of English race, supporting the English government, would have been molested because of his religion.

‡ The commissions are stated in Morrin, i. 497; ii. 252, 290. In the next reign, when the lords of the Pale complained to James that magistrates were deposed for not taking the oath of supremacy, they

Controversial discussion in relation to Roman Catholic doctrines, and the use of contemptuous or severe language in speaking of them, the Queen in every way discouraged: of which a singular illustration is recorded in the case of Jones, then bishop of Meath. This prelate was reported to her for having in a sermon "inveighed in sharp and vehement sort against those that were of the Romayn religion." She summoned him to London, and referred the sermon to the Archbishop of Canterbury, and not until this prelate certified that what was uttered in it ought not to minister any just cause of offence, did she excuse the preacher.*

The Prayer Book was, in England, followed some years after its use was enacted by the adoption in the Church of the standard of doctrine known as the "Thirty-nine Articles of Religion." These were not introduced into the Church in Ireland until the time of Charles I. In Elizabeth's reign, and for some portion of the next, a short collection of Articles, eleven in number, was prescribed to be read by parsons, vicars, and curates on first entering into their cures, and also on two days in each year afterwards. It was published in 1566, as is said on the title-page,† by the

---

say that "this was sparingly and mildly carried on in the time of your late sister of famous memory, Queen Elizabeth," Leland, ii. 444.

* Letter from the Queen to the Lord Deputy, May 12, 1587, Morrin, ii. 125. In this letter she says that her directions were that "such a sharp manner of proceeding should be forborne by our clergy in Ireland." Lord Mountjoy says his instructions from the council were, to deal moderately in the matter of religion, Leland, ii. 383.

† The title-page is "A breefe declaration of certein principall Articles of Religion, set out by order and aucthoritie, as well of the right Hon. Sir Henry Sidney, knight of the most noble order, Lord President of

authority of the Deputy and of the archbishops, and bishops. The Articles were a copy of some framed by Archbishop Parker and other English bishops, and used in the English Church before the Thirty-nine Articles were authorised. It has been asserted that the Irish clergy, along with them, used to subscribe the Thirty-nine Articles also; but, if so, it was without direction from the Deputy, the Parliament, or any Synod. If any did subscribe, it was to meet the wishes of the bishops who ordained or instituted them.

These eleven Articles being so long in use deserve to be briefly summarised. The first states the doctrine of the Trinity in explicit terms. The second asserts the Scriptures to contain all things necessary to salvation, and professes belief in the Nicene, Athanasian, and Apostles' Creeds. The third relates to the Church and its power to institute or vary ceremonies. The fourth defines who may lawfully take any office or ministry, ecclesiastical or secular. The fifth acknowledges the queen's prerogative and superiority of government of all estates and in all causes, as well ecclesiastical as temporal, within this realm, and other her dominions, as in the late statute was expressed. The sixth declares the Bishop of Rome to have no more authority than other bishops have in their provinces and dioceses. The seventh assents to the Prayer Book set forth by

---

the Councel in the principalitie of Wales, and marches of the same, and General Deputie of this realme of Ireland, as by the archbyshopes and byshopes and other Her Majestie's High Commissioners for Causes Ecclesiastical, in the same realme." Imprinted at Dublin by Humfrey Powel, the 20th of January, 1566. There is a copy in the Library of Trinity College, Dublin, supposed to be the only one extant.

the authority of Parliament. The eighth denies that certain ceremonies, which were formerly used at baptism, and had been then lately abolished, pertained to the substance of the rite. The ninth condemns private masses, and the doctrine that the mass is a propitiatory sacrifice. The tenth maintains the ministration of the Communion in both kinds. The eleventh disallows the extolling of images, relics, and feigned miracles, and exhorts all men to the obedience of God's law and to the works of faith, of which examples are enumerated.*

The Irish Supremacy Acts of Henry and Elizabeth, although varying in expression, were equally effective for the purpose of causing a separation from the Roman Catholic system. Both were inconsistent with the supremacy of the Pope, and with his being the paramount governor and ruler of all Christian Churches. But denial of his supremacy might coexist with retention of the doctrinal opinions upheld at Rome; and in point of fact for a long time many of them were not repudiated. Elizabeth's Prayer Book, especially when compared with the first Prayer Book of Edward VI., marked a line of decided dissent from former theological opinions. The divergence thereby manifested was made still more wide by the Articles which have just been cited. The Church in which they were brought into use was thenceforth in direct antagonism to the doctrinal teaching of Rome upon several distinct points of grave importance.

---

* A twelfth Article merely expresses assent to the others. Hence they are quoted by Hardwicke as "eleven." A reprint of the Dublin edition of 1566 is given in the Appendix to Elrington's *Life of Ussher*.

The want of schools which existed in every part of Ireland attracted, at an early period of Elizabeth's reign, the attention of her government, and led to an Act being obtained from Parliament, which required "a free school" to be maintained in every diocese. The nomination of masters for these schools was given in the dioceses of Armagh, Dublin, Meath, and Kildare, to their respective bishops; in the others to the Lord Deputy. The salary of the master of each school was to be provided by a tax levied upon the Ordinary and clergy of the diocese.*

At the period of the Reformation there was no University, nor was there even a collegiate institution of any importance, in Ireland. It was not until 1592 that this deficiency was supplied. The Queen then incorporated a college, to which she gave the name of Trinity College, with which an University was to coexist, supplied from the College with officers and students, and entitled to confer upon these students the usual academic degrees. There were to be a Provost, Fellows, and Scholars: there was also to be a Chancellor.† The first Provost and the first Chancellor were

---

* 12 Eliz. chap. 1 (Irish).

† The effect of Elizabeth's charter, as regards the constitution of an University, is far from clear. It is not exactly defined whether the College and University are identical or distinct; nor, if distinct, whether the University was at once created, or was to be subsequently developed. Whatever was intended, the result practically came to be the same; for as Lord Chancellor Blackburne, when Vice-Chancellor of the University, decided, by means of the agency of the Chancellor or Vice-Chancellor and proper officers, for whose perpetual appointment the Crown made ample provision, the power to grant degrees was ensured. In the next reign, when the right of sending burgesses to Parliament was conceded, the existence of the University as a separate body was assumed, and it has

named in the charter; the former was Archbishop Loftus, and the latter Lord Burleigh, Elizabeth's great minister. A building for the use of the College was erected near Dublin, the site and grounds around it being the gift of the Corporation of that city, to whom, with other property of the dissolved monastery of All Hallowes, they had been granted after the suppression of the religious houses. There is no doubt that to serve the Church, by educating those who were to be its future clergy, was a prominent object sought in establishing the College,* but this did not confine the range of study, which extended to every department of literature and science.

The scope of the present treatise admits only of a brief reference to the civil events of Elizabeth's reign. Wars and insurrections succeeded each other in an almost uninterrupted series. Shane O'Neill soon after its commencement, Desmond about thirty years later, and Tyrone for some years before the Queen's death, were in open rebellion against her authority; each at the head of forces which it needed armies from England to subdue. In the intervals between these wars occurred

---

ever since been acknowledged in the various charters and letters issued by the Crown. The charter describes the College as *mater universitatis*, a phrase which seems to indicate that there were two distinct bodies, and to refer, either to the College supplying the students to whom the University would grant its degrees, or to its supplying the persons who were to be its officers and members, or to both. See Todd's Preface to *List of Graduates*, published in 1869, and Sir Joseph Napier's observations in the Supplement. See as to the foundation of the College, also, Note P. of Appendix.

* " Ad bonas artes percipiendas colendamque virtutem et *religionem* " (Charter). The Fellows were to hold only for seven years. " ut alii in eorum locum suffecti, pro hujus regni et *ecclesiæ* beneficio, emolumentum habeant."

insurrections, on a less scale, but formidable. Of these contests the ultimate result was, that the English power became triumphant over the whole island, and that at the Queen's death there remained no adversary capable of further resisting it, Tyrone, the last and most powerful of the rebel chieftains, having then given in his submission.*

As the conflicts between the English and the natives, which have been referred to, were not all at the same time nor in the same place, opportunities would seem to have been presented after the termination of each for attempting conciliation of the defeated septs. But an exactly opposite course was pursued, and victory was followed by much severity and cruelty on the part of the Queen's soldiers. This was especially the case in Munster, where vast territories were laid waste, so that those who escaped the sword perished miserably by pestilence and famine.†

During this reign there was a considerable increase in the number of counties. At its commencement there were the twelve formed by King John, of which one was subdivided by Henry VIII. into Meath and Westmeath:

---

\* "Queen Elizabeth sent over more men and spent more treasure to save and reduce the land of Ireland than all her progenitors since the Conquest. During her reign there arose three notorious and main rebellions, which drew several armies out of England: the first of Shane O'Neill, the second of Desmond, the last of Tyrone; for the particular insurrections of the Viscount Baltinglass, and Sir Edmund Butler, the Moors, the Cavanaghs, the Birnes, and the Bourkes of Connaught, were all suppressed by the standing forces here." (Sir John Davis, *Discoveris*, &c., p. 17.)

† Spenser's description of the state to which Munster was reduced has been often cited. It is painful to read it. In addition, Lecky refers to other authorities, *History*, vol. ii. p. 96. During these wars Elizabeth seems to have sought to prevent religious animosities being infused into

there were also two more which had been made by Philip and Mary:* beside these, Thomond, then called Clare, had been formed ; and what is now Down was at that time in two divisions—Down or Lecale, and Ard. In 1565, Sir Henry Sidney added five more shires, viz., Longford, Galway, Sligo, Mayo, and Roscommon. Clare he transferred to Connaught from Munster. At a later date Sir John Perrot constituted Leitrim, Armagh, Monaghan, Tyrone, Coleraine or Derry, Fermanagh, and Cavan. In 1575 and 1585, the two divisions of Down were united into the county that now bears the name.† But these proceedings were followed by scarcely any practical effect. Until the time of the Queen's successor the Judges were not sent to any of the new counties.‡

The policy of colonising the country with English settlers, commenced by Mary, was continued by Elizabeth. She found the plantation of the King's and Queen's Counties, which had been begun by the former, incomplete; she therefore, after observing that "our countries of Leix and Offaly did yet remain unestablished and uninhabited, being peopled only with our

---

the controversies. "Your Highness" (says Lord Grey) "gave me a warning at my leave-taking for being strict in dealing with religion." See letter to the Queen, 22nd December, 1580, cited by Froude, xi. 242: who also there refers to a letter from Lord Grey to Walsingham, complaining that "rebellion and disobedience to the Prince's word was chiefly regarded, and reformation of God's cause made a second or nothing at all." It seems agreed that the Queen's armies were not entirely English, and contained Roman Catholic Irish. Plowden, i. 87 ; Lecky, ii. 101.

* See pp. 19 and 46.
† See Note C of Appendix as to the formation of counties, &c.
‡ See Sir John Davis's *Discoverie*, &c., pp. 53, 54.

men of war, whereby they lay waste, and that, therefore, our charge was likely to grow intolerable," gave directions to have castles and houses of strength built, and the lands peopled.* Notwithstanding that she incurred much expense in order to encourage this plantation, it was considered to have failed in attaining the objects for which it was undertaken. The English power was but slightly increased by it, only an insufficient number of colonists taking advantage of the opportunities it afforded, and those that did becoming mixed and assimilated with the natives among whom they were dispersed. The Queen, however, undeterred by the limited success of Mary's plantation, herself entered upon one of greater magnitude. When the last Desmond was subdued, she divided the territories which he and the subordinate chieftains who followed him had ruled over in Munster, and substituted for them English proprietors. Those who received grants from her were instructed to introduce English farmers, labourers, and artisans; but the size of the estates bestowed upon them rendered them independent of control, and emboldened them to regard more their own personal interests than the rules laid down for their guidance. It was attended with less expense and brought more profit, to retain the Irish occupier than to introduce the English settler; nor was the latter object always attainable. Hence the proposed plantation was carried out only to a small extent. English chiefs or proprietors were substituted for Irish; and by them, in places adjacent to their forts and

---

\* *Cal. Carew MSS.*, 1515–1574, p. 279.

castles, and along the coast, English colonists were induced to come and reside. But this was confined to the coast and to the neighbourhood of their residences; and at the close of Elizabeth's reign the Irish still formed the mass of the actual occupiers of the soil of the southern province.

Beside, however, the colonists who were brought over in pursuance of schemes of plantation, many English, animated by a spirit of adventure (about this time very prevalent), established settlements in the country. Enterprizing, not easily deterred by fatigue or danger, they added much to the strength of the Anglo-Irish population.

## CHAPTER V.

RETROSPECT.

THE termination of the reign of Queen Elizabeth—forty-five years after her accession to the throne, and sixty-six after the Irish Supremacy Act was passed—affords a convenient occasion to examine the condition of the Reformed Church of Ireland, and to estimate what were the effects of the measures that had been adopted in relation to its property and discipline, and what the progress which the religious system it represented had made among the people.

The organization of the Irish Church, at the time when the Parliament of 1536 was summoned to deal with its interests, was diocesan and parochial. It consisted of four archbishops, twenty-six bishops,[*] of cathedral chapters, of the incumbents of parishes (into which the whole island had been subdivided), and of curates. To these are to be added the clerical members of the religious orders, whose establishments were then numerous and spread over the entire country.

For centuries monasticism had prevailed in the Irish

---

[*] The number of Sees was thirty-five; but by the consolidation or union of some, the number of archbishops and bishops was always less. See Note Q of Appendix.

Church, and was especially venerated by the people. Of reverential and devotional temperament, they sympathised with the ceremonial and ritual observances of its system, and regarded with affectionate admiration those whose lives were dedicated to maintain them. Sentiments of this character were subsequently confirmed by the benefits which the religious houses conferred upon the community. In a period of barbarism civilization owed to them that it even existed. There were then neither educational nor charitable institutions; these associations supplied their place, and were the inns, hospitals, and colleges of the age.

At first the endowments of monasteries and convents in Ireland were of moderate amount: between the twelfth and sixteenth centuries they had immensely increased. The Anglo-Normans bringing over with them the ideas of their own more opulent country, enlarged and enriched many old foundations, and added others of greater magnitude. As the possessions of these corporate bodies were carefully preserved, whatever they at any time received was added to the previous amount, so that their lands and chattels now represented the accumulated gifts of successive generations, and the aggregate of all had come to be of large value. A third species of property —tithes—they derived from a practice which had been brought into England by the Normans, and afterwards introduced (probably by their descendants) into Ireland, whereby, under the name of appropriations, benefices were annexed to religious houses, and the emoluments which they produced became, after some provision for the discharge of parochial duties, the property of the societies to which the houses belonged.

The monks were both of English and Irish race; the former generally in the Pale and other English districts, and the latter in the Irish provinces. They were also of every class. The Superiors of twenty-four houses were spiritual lords, and with them were to be ranked others who, without being Peers, were not inferior in position to those who were. The mendicant friars touched the other extremity of the social scale. Between these were many of intermediate importance. Variety of circumstances was accompanied by a variety of discipline, which enabled the Orders to adapt their ministrations to every condition of society. While members of the greater monasteries were the guides of chiefs and nobles, and influenced the opinions of the higher classes, missionaries from the humbler penetrated the remotest districts, and preached to the most rude and uncivilized tribes.

Whatever education existed in the country was derived from the religious houses. Their teaching of the English portion of the people was aided by the intercourse which it maintained with England, and by the opportunity thus presented of obtaining and making use of the books which, after the introduction of printing, were published there. In the Irish districts no similar assistance was available; for English books could not be read by their inhabitants, a printing-press did not exist in the entire island, and neither English nor foreign printers employed their types on Irish writings.

In England the influence of the monasteries was diminished by the charges of misconduct and immorality brought against their inmates. The Irish were not free from allegations of a similar import, and in some instances authority may be cited to support them which is of weight; but there is no official declaration against them generally upon this ground, as there was in the case of the English, and in its absence the unfavourable representations cannot be accepted as by any means universally well-founded.*

In comparison with the monastic system, the parochial must be held to have been at the era of the Reformation depressed. The aggrandisement of the former was purchased by the impoverishment of the latter. The tithes which the religious houses owned came altogether from the revenues of benefices which had become vested in them by appropriations. They amounted to more than one-sixth of what were rendered by the entire island.† To make up such an amount, they were necessarily collected from an extremely large number of parishes. Thus, in Meath there were in all two hundred and twenty-four parishes, of which one hundred and fifty-

---

\* The number and condition of the religious houses at the era of the Reformation are further considered in Note R of Appendix.

† Tithes belonging to private owners (impropriate, as they are called, in order to distinguish them from appropriate, *i.e.* those belonging to ecclesiastical corporations) are all derived from monastic property. According to the reports of the Royal Commission appointed in 1834 to inquire into the revenues of the Church of Ireland, the amount of compositions for impropriate tithes then came to £108,877 a-year, while those for the tithes of incumbents of parishes were £486,783 a-year, and of appropriators, £48,032 a-year. See Reports of 1836 and 1837. To estimate accurately the tithes owned by the religious houses, additions should be made to this amount of impropriate tithes, to represent portions of them which after Elizabeth's reign were restored by the Crown to the parishes out of which they accrued, or which were given to them by private bounty.

seven were appropriate to the monasteries, fifty-two of them having vicars endowed, and one hundred and five being without vicars.*

Appropriations when made to monastic corporations still left the emoluments which were transferred by them available for religious uses; they therefore cannot be held to have been entirely without benefit for the Church. But to the parishes and the parochial system they were altogether injurious. From the former they withdrew a large revenue, which properly should have been expended in the localities whence it was derived: while for the most part they left only an inadequate remuneration for the resident incumbents, whether vicars or curates—enough to provide subsistence, and in some instances a few comforts, without any surplus for hospitality or the poor. From the latter they took away the richer benefices, these being generally those appropriated, as the poorer would not afford a surplus above the provision which was required to maintain the discharge of religious duties.

The impoverishment of the appropriated parishes acted injuriously upon the supply of clergy who were willing to serve in them. They were of an inferior

---

\* These are the numbers of benefices and impropriate rectories in the diocese of Meath, as they were reported to Queen Elizabeth by Sir Henry Sidney. The impropriate necessarily correspond with those which had belonged to the monasteries, as it was by the confiscation of their possessions the Crown acquired its power to dispose of them. This letter is dated 28th April, 1566. See Sidney's *Letters and Memorials*, i. 112. Other evidence of the extent of the appropriations will be found cited by Mant, vol. i. pp. 355-370; and also at pp. 358, 370-379, 389. See also "Report of the Royal Commission to inquire into the Unions in the Irish Church," dated 18th April, 1831.

grade, deficient in knowledge and attainments. From them the evil of the system extended much farther. The standard of intellectual cultivation could not be lowered for so numerous a portion of the order without reducing the level generally. The clerical calling fell in popular estimation, and its interests were neglected.

To the same result other causes contributed. A disturbed state of society subjected the benefices which were situated outside the Pale to loss and suffering from violence: in some places they were seized, and intruders, even, it is said, laymen, forcibly put in possession. In all, even the best districts, patronage was often improperly exercised, the bishops being not seldom overawed by the chiefs and nobles into injudicious selections, and many appointments by the Court of Rome (which, although prohibited by law, still continued) being obtained through private interest, and made in ignorance of the character of those promoted.*

Affected by these various unfavourable influences, and perhaps still more by the state of society as it existed everywhere outside Dublin and a limited circuit around it, the parochial organization was received by the Reformed Church in a condition of weakness and insufficiency. Unfortunately the remedies imperatively demanded were not applied, and the measures of Henry and his successors tended to aggravate, not to lessen, the hindrances to its efficacy. When the monasteries were dissolved, the appropriated parishes might fairly have expected that the tithes which were drawn away

---

* See Note S of Appendix.

from them would have been restored: the interests of the Church, indeed of society, demanded that, for the work of education heretofore conducted by the Religious Orders, schools and colleges should have been provided. But neither measure was approved. The tithes, being either retained by the Crown or granted to laymen, became mingled with the mass of private property, and were held to be under no more obligation than the rest of it was to contribute to ecclesiastical or charitable uses. An educational institution suited for either the gentry or the clergy was not established until about ten years before Queen Elizabeth's death, when Trinity College was founded. Some alleviation of these adverse circumstances might have been obtained from judicious redistribution of ecclesiastical revenues: but nothing of the kind was attempted. The division of parishes, the emoluments of dignitaries and incumbents, remained exactly as they had been, and no alteration was made to correspond with social changes. The only expedient employed in order to meet the case of ill-endowed benefices, such as the vicarages and impropriate curacies, was one from which many evils subsequently flowed—the creation of unions and pluralities.

Without redistribution the property which remained for ecclesiastical purposes, after the abstraction of what belonged to the monasteries, inadequately met the needs of the Church. This inadequacy was increased by subsequent events. Causes, some of which operated from without, and others of which arose from within, combined to lessen the amount and value of ecclesiastical endowments. Among the former were the continual wars and insurrections of Elizabeth's reign, which were attended by much waste and spoliation. Government, maintaining itself with difficulty in any part of the island, could afford little protection to districts outside the neighbourhood of Dublin. Glebes and See-lands were frequently seized by the insurgent chieftains; and, their former boundaries being defaced, they became confused with the adjoining private property. Of the internal sources of loss, the most serious was the law which permitted bishops to deal with episcopal property in an improvident manner. With the consent of their deans and chapters, often easily procured, they could lease their lands for any term and at any rent which they thought fit, or even alienate them. Such a power presented an opportunity of enriching themselves, and their relatives or friends, which in times of trouble, when the incumbents knew not of what opinions their successors might be, and were often far from favouring the system they professed to serve, was too frequently taken advantage of.*

If we turn from financial to other interests of the Church, here also the policy pursued on behalf of the Crown will be found to have been injudicious. The inmates of the religious houses, when deprived of their own establishments, were not provided with other places of retreat, and were scattered among the people over all parts of the country. They were, even more than

---

* Mant, in his *History of the Irish Church*, enumerates instances of improvident dispositions of the See-lands (vol. i. p. 279). He also mentions several cases where, owing to the poverty of the bishoprics, arising from this and other causes, their incumbents were allowed to hold benefices *in commendam* (vol. i. p. 282, &c.).

the secular clergy, opposed to innovation: and the treatment which their societies received deepened opposition into active hostility. They became the most decided, and from their ability and energy the most formidable, adversaries of the Reformed Church. More than any other agency they kept alive a spirit of unwavering allegiance to Rome. Nor did this cease with the generation which suffered; for although the Orders of a higher class could not well be maintained without endowments, this was not the case with those of an inferior. Upon "the begging friars" (as they were called) repressive statutes and confiscations had little effect. Subsisting upon alms, in reality as well as profession poor, they offered nothing to attract cupidity: as they were wanderers, without fixed settlements, interference with them was difficult, if not impossible; and, accordingly, their associations, although by law dissolved, practically escaped and continued to exist.*

While the monastic portion of the clerical order was thus arrayed against the new religious system no steps were taken to gain over to its' support such of the parochial clergy as were of Irish race. Indeed, one of the measures adopted was calculated to repel them. By a statute of the Parliament which met in 1536 it was provided, that if a benefice fell vacant it should be conferred upon a person who could speak English, unless, after proclamations in the next market town, none such could be had.† The policy in favour with English statesmen at this time (of which the enactment now

---

* See Brewer's Introduction to the 3rd volume of the *Calendar of the Carew MSS.*, p. xiv.

† 28 Henry VIII. (Ireland), chap. 15, sec. 7.

mentioned is an example) was to confine the Irish clergy to the Irish districts, and even there to discourage and supersede them whenever possible. The effect of this necessarily was to subject them to the exclusive influence of the uncivilized condition of society amid which they lived, and effectually to bar the possibility of their improvement.

With respect to the clergy of the Reformed Church in the English districts, the neglect to provide means of educating persons intended for the ministry produced consequences not less injurious than those which ensued in the case of the Irish. They were ignorant, of rude manners, negligent in the performance of their duties. In order to compensate for their defects, it was thought expedient to induce English clergymen to accept Irish benefices: some were therefore sent over; others came of themselves; but of either class there were few, and most of the latter were (it is said) either "unlearned, or men of some bad note, for which they had forsaken England."*

What was the result of the course thus pursued in relation to ecclesiastical affairs has been pictured in a contemporary representation, which is of such high authority that more than a passing reference to it seems called for. In the year 1566, Sir Henry Sidney, then Lord Deputy, addressed to Queen Elizabeth a letter, describing the state of the Church, and suggesting some remedies. The diocese of Meath, which he terms the "best inhabited country of the realm," he selects as an illustration, and from it (he observes) "it will be easy to conjecture in what case the rest is, where

---

* Spenser, *View of Ireland*, p. 570.

little or no reformation of religion or manners hath yet been planted." The parishes in this diocese, which had been vested in the monasteries, were now impropriate in the Crown: of these, as has been already mentioned, fifty-two had vicars, and one hundred and five none. The latter Sidney found to be under the care of curates, to whom he applies the epithets of "simple or sorry"; of whom only eighteen could speak English; "of little learning or civility, living on the bare altarages (that is fees for services connected with the altar); without a house standing for any of them to dwell in; the walls of many of their churches being down; very few chancels covered; windows and doors ruined and spoiled. The former class (in which vicars officiated) were (he mentions) better served and maintained than the others, "yet but badly." Having thus exhibited the condition of the parishes, he turns from them to what he terms "the spoil" of the bishoprics, occasioned "partly by the prelates themselves, partly by the potentates, their noisome neighbours"; and then as to the entire Church, he emphatically declares "your Majesty may believe it, that upon the face of the earth, where Christ is professed, there is not a Church in so miserable a case; the misery of which consisteth in these particulars: the ruin of the very temples themselves; the want of good ministers to serve in them when they shall be re-edified, and of competent living for the ministers being well chosen."*

---

* Sidney's *Letters*, &c., vol. i. p. 112. At a still later date, but also in Queen Elizabeth's reign, Spenser gives an even more unfavourable account of the condition of the Church and clergy. He describes the poverty of the benefices in the Irish districts, which often do not yield a

With a Church thus depressed, what progress was made by the religion which it was established to teach? This question requires to be answered separately for the English and the Irish portions of the people, so different were the proceedings adopted as to each, and the influences affecting them respectively.

To consider the case of the Irish first—there is no doubt that the hostile relations existing between them and the English Government raised great difficulties in the way of their accepting the Reformation. Protestantism, as it was presented to them, assumed a political, rather than a theological, character. The tenet most prominently put forward was the supremacy of the Crown in the Church; this was asserted to be a part of the royal prerogative, and was proclaimed by similar legislation, enforced by similar penalties, as other branches of it. To admit the supremacy was therefore to strengthen the regal authority, it gave what was supposed to be a religious sanction to the dominion claimed by each English Sovereign over Ireland—a dominion always submitted to with reluctance, and, when opportunity enabled, certain to be resisted. Any religious system which involved this doctrine came in conflict with national sentiment.

---

competent maintenance for any honest minister to live upon—scarcely enough to buy him a gown. The clergy (whether, it would seem, Irish or English) he charges with simony and other "enormities." The Irish (he says) are mere laymen, save that they have taken orders. — *View of Ireland,* pp. 508, 510.

In 1607, Sir John Davis accompanied Sir Arthur Chichester to some of the Ulster counties upon a progress to inquire into their condition. He reports the poverty of the livings in Cavan, and adds: "The incumbents were such poor, ragged, ignorant creatures we could not esteem them worthy of the meanest of those livings."—Davis's *Tracts,* p. 266.

Whether by judicious measures such Protestant opinions, as are not connected with the supremacy, might have been successfully introduced among the Irish, is uncertain, since none such were tried. The course actually pursued was calculated to raise only obstacles in the way of their acceptance. Not merely were the Irish clergy, as we have seen, neglected, and no effort made to conciliate them, but they were not even addressed by argument or persuasion. Bishops, when appointed by the Crown, and sometimes incumbents of benefices, were required to acknowledge the supremacy: in other respects, the Irish clergy were left to themselves, without its being proposed to reason with or instruct them. Under such circumstances, how could their conversion be expected? They had little knowledge of the Latin language, and less of the Greek or English, and until the reign of James I. there was neither an Irish New Testament nor an Irish Prayer Book; until as late as 1685 not an Irish Old Testament. *
In truth, Irish publications of any kind were then and long afterwards discouraged by English statesmen: they tended to preserve the language; and to preserve the language, it was held, would foster national sympathies and feelings.

To address the Irish laity separately from their clergy would have been useless. Always remarkable for attachment to their religious teachers,† they had never

---

\* See Note T of Appendix.

† Mommsen attributes to the Irish and the Gauls (both of Celtic race) that they see in the priest a father, "die kindliche Frömmigkeit, die in dem Priester den Vater sieht und ihn in allen Dingen um Rath fragt."— *History of Rome*, book v., chap. vii., near the end.

at any time initiated an independent religious movement. Of the knowledge requisite for the purpose they had absolutely none. They could not have acted by themselves, and they would not follow English guides. Laity and clergy took up the same position: both rejected what England dictated: both faithfully adhered to the Church and Court of Rome.

With the colonists of the English districts the same circumstances which predisposed the native Irish against the Reformation aided its progress. Their interests were bound up with the greatness of England: on that they depended for the retention of their own power in the midst of a hostile people, exceeding them altogether in number. They looked to the parent country as a guide, and inclined to follow its example. No difficulty arose with the Irish House of Commons, returned as it was from towns and counties with English inhabitants, in passing the Supremacy Acts of Henry or Elizabeth: afterwards, the constituencies which were represented expressed little dissatisfaction with its legislation.

The doctrinal teaching of Protestantism was therefore, in Dublin and the English districts, relieved from the difficulties which surrounded it in the Irish. It was promoted by reprinting or importing the various publications which in England advocated or served its cause. When the English Prayer Book was adopted, it was at once published also in Dublin; when the English Bible, after Elizabeth's accession, appeared in a convenient form in London, numerous copies were brought over to Dublin and circulated.* The impulse thus given was

---

* In Ware's *Annals*, Eliz. (p. 3, ed. Dublin, 1705), it is said that John Dale, a bookseller, sold seven thousand Bibles in two years' time

followed and assisted by the use in many churches of the Pale of the English Prayer Book and Bible. Under such influences a generation of English-speaking people grew up.* That many of these, especially of such as dwelt at a distance from the metropolis, still dissented from the Established Church is true; but on the other side are to be reckoned all the new colonists. It may therefore be affirmed with confidence, that at the period with which we are now concerned a large proportion of the English race were Protestant as well in opinion and belief as by profession.

---

for the booksellers of London, when they were first printed and brought over to Ireland, in the year 1566.

He also mentions that Heath, Archbishop of York (himself friendly to the Roman Catholic party in England), sent to the two Deans of Dublin (viz. of St. Patrick's and Christ Church) two large Bibles, to be placed in the middle of their choirs, which, he says, caused "a great rush of people on purpose to read them."

* Another matter, which in the diocese of Dublin aided the progress of the Reformation, is, that it was not until 1600 the Pope made an appointment to the See in opposition to the archbishop in possession. Thus the authority of Curwin, and for thirty-three years of Loftus also, was practically undisputed. When the Pope did appoint, he sent over Oviedo, a monk of Spain, who came with troops sent from that country to assist Tyrone—a circumstance not likely to make him acceptable to the Anglo-Irish.

# CHAPTER VI.

[1603-1625.]

JAMES THE FIRST, upon his accession to the throne of England, found in Ireland universal submission. He succeeded just when the prolonged struggle, which the native portion of the people maintained against English dominion during the reign of his predecessor, was terminated, and received a kingdom which, whatever may have been its real sentiments, professed obedience. Order had, however, not been completely established, and society still continued to exhibit the effects of the wars and disturbances through which for forty years before it had passed.

From the time when the native princes and chieftains submitted to Henry II., the Irish had been treated as enemies, against whom the colonists needed to be protected. The union of the two races was obstructed, and so far as legislation could promote the object, they were kept apart. For the English in Ireland to imitate the habits or manners of the natives, to take their names, to furnish them with horses or armour, were made punishable offences; to intermarry with them was, if the law were enforced, treason.* Measures of this

---

* See the provisions of the Statute of Kilkenny. This statute is not in the Statute-book. It has been admirably edited by Mr. Hardiman.

character avail little against the influence of neighbourhood and intimacy; but they are not the less mischievous in their effects. They proceed upon an assumption of superiority on the part of the nation imposing them, which the people against whom they are directed are certain to resent.

James, who had been brought up in Scotland, and was therefore not biassed by the prevalent English ideas, seems from the first to have proposed to himself a policy of a different character. All who lived in Ireland, natives as well as colonists, he professed to regard as subjects who, if obedient, deserved his paternal care. Distinctions of laws and customs in different provinces or districts were to be abolished, and the whole system of jurisprudence, the constitution of society, to be assimilated to what was established in England.

In order to accomplish these ends, the first matter entered upon was to extend everywhere the administration of justice in the English manner. The new counties, defined during Elizabeth's reign, facilitated this measure; and to them was now added another shire, formed from part of the county of Dublin, which was considered too large. The new shire was named Wicklow. It completed the division of the island

---

It was renewed by an Act of 10 Hen. VII., except as to some clauses which forbade the English to speak Irish among themselves, or to ride in the Irish manner. The Acts, 5 Edw. IV., c. 3; 25 Hen. VI., c. 4; 28 Hen. VI., c. 1, are dictated by the same policy: and as late as Henry VIII. it is continued by 28 Hen. VIII., c. 15, which prohibits the English from following the Irish habit of wearing long hair, or hair on the upper lip, and from using (as the natives did) linen dyed with saffron, and fixes prescribed dimensions for shirts and smocks.

into counties, which from that time to the present has, with some alterations, but merely of boundaries, continued the same. The circuits of the judges were enlarged, so as to take within their reach at first Ulster, and subsequently all parts of the country.

The next proceeding was to induce as many as possible of the Irish chieftains to surrender their existing titles, and accept grants from the Crown. On such occasions they were obliged to make new arrangements with those who held under them, and rents payable in money were required to be substituted for the services and duties that had been until then rendered.*

While these proceedings were in progress, either secret information, or some occurrences in Ulster, led the Irish Government to apprehend a renewal of disturbances, and to take precautions against it. Tyrone, who, although, as has been before mentioned, his rebellion was entirely subdued, had as yet not been interfered with, and Tyrconnell, another of the northern chieftains—either because they intended insurrection, or because, if innocent, they feared that in the event of an outbreak they would be treated as guilty—decided to consult for their own safety, and fled to the Continent. A short time afterwards, O'Dogherty, also a native chieftain, who had before been their ally, proclaimed war, and, being at first unchecked, seized and burned the town of Derry. Tyrone and Tyrconnell were at once treated as outlaws; O'Dogherty met his death from an accidental shot. Thereupon, the territories not only of these three

---

* See Sir John Davis's *Discovery*, &c., pp. 57, 58.

Chiefs, but also of their followers, were held to be confiscated to the Crown. Thus immense tracts of land, amounting to the entire, or nearly the entire, of the counties of Donegal, Tyrone, Derry, Fermanagh, Cavan, and Armagh, were placed at the disposal of the King.

James, notwithstanding the policy which he had laid down to guide his general conduct towards the natives, entertained upon the question of colonization precisely the same ideas as his predecessors, Elizabeth and Mary. So also did his ablest ministers.* It was, therefore, determined to plant the lands now subject to his control with English and Scotch settlers. As former proceedings for a similar purpose had been attended with little success, the causes of their failure were investigated, and the plan for the present occasion framed with provisions designed to obviate them. In devising it the King was aided by the great abilities of Bacon, at that time his Attorney-General in England, and by the experience in Irish affairs of Sir Arthur Chichester, then the Lord Deputy.

The scheme of plantation ultimately approved was upon a most extensive scale; the importation of settlers being intended to be numerous enough to ensure that they, and not the natives, should preponderate in influence over the planted counties. Lest the colonists might be induced to abandon their previous habits, and in order to prevent their assimilation with the Irish they were to be encouraged to live together in villages. No single

---

\* See, for instance, Lord Bacon's Tract entitled, *Considerations touching the Plantation in Ireland,* and Sir John Davis's *Discovery,* &c., p. 58.

proprietor was to have more than two thousand acres. Those who had this amount were to constitute one class. A second class might receive fifteen hundred acres, and a third one thousand. The first class were to build a castle and a fortified courtyard (called a bawn); the second a house and bawn; from the third a bawn only was required. The first class were to introduce twenty families, numbering forty-eight persons of English or Scotch birth; four of their farmers were to have one hundred and twenty acres, and to hold in fee-farm; to six, leases were to be made of one hundred acres each; and the residue of every allotment of two thousand acres was to be occupied by husbandmen and artificers. The other classes were to be under similar obligations proportioned to the dimensions of their grants. Large estates were to be assigned to the Companies of the Corporation of London.* Lands which had belonged to the Church were to be restored to it; and, in addition, portions of the estates forfeited by laymen were to be granted as glebes for parochial clergymen. In each county certain distinct and defined districts were to be reserved for the dispossessed natives.†

These rules, admirably calculated to promote the objects of those who prepared them, were (not, however, without considerable variations) carried out. The

---

\* When the lands were distributed, Trinity College also received a portion.

† Davis, however, says that "the king made a mixed plantation of British and Irish, that they might grow up together in one nation: only, the Irish were in some places transplanted from the woods and mountains into the plains and open countries, that being removed (like wild fruit-trees) they might grow the milder and bear the better and sweeter fruit."—*Discovery*, &c., p. 58.

result was, that a large number of English and Scotch emigrated from their own countries, and came and settled in the six forfeited counties. Of these the Scotch formed a majority: and as two other Ulster counties, Down and Antrim, were also in the early part of the seventeenth century peopled from the same kingdom, they gained a decided predominance of power and influence in the northern districts of the island.

The introduction of so many Scotch colonists added another to the races of which the Irish people were composed. From this time they must be classified in three divisions, each marked by its own peculiar characteristics. The distribution of these in the occupation of the soil, after the plantation had been carried out, was much as follows :—The principal part of the English dwelt in Dublin, the Pale, the Ulster settlements, towns in other parts of the country outside the Pale, especially the seaports; the Scotch were altogether in Ulster: the Irish everywhere else, numbers of them being also in the Pale and Ulster.*

When the plantation had been carried out, the course of the King's policy towards the natives was resumed, and partly in order to complete it, partly with the object of obtaining a confirmation of the attainder of the Ulster chieftains and of the confiscation of their territories, a parliament was summoned. To give weight to its enactments, to exhibit the impartial rule of the Sovereign, and in the hope of conciliating at least some

---

* Estimates of numbers, either of the people or of their subdivisions in this reign, are mere conjectures. It seems probable that persons of unmixed native descent continued to form the majority. Davis, however, seems to think they did not. *Discovery,* &c., p. 3.

discontented tribes, it was determined to extend the representation of the people in the House of Commons. The right to vote for its members, and the right to sit, if elected, were to be irrespective of any distinction of race or religion. It was also determined that not only should the entire number of counties (now for the first time) be represented, but that a number of new boroughs should be created. In selecting these, however, regard was had to the supposed tendencies of their inhabitants in favour of the English interest; and it was owing to this circumstance that most of the new towns which had been commenced by the settlers in Ulster were among them.

The parliament thus summoned met in the month of May, 1613. The House of Lords consisted of bishops and temporal peers, the latter about twenty-five in number; the members returned to the House of Commons amounted to two hundred and thirty-two, of whom two hundred and twenty-six attended. These were found to be divided into two parties, one on the side of the King's government, and ready to support their measures, the other adverse to them: the former English and Scotch, in religion Protestant, numbering one hundred and twenty-five; the latter composed of the other members, partly Irish, partly English by descent, all opposed to the Reformation, and, from refusing to conform, then termed Recusants.*

A contest for the office of Speaker, for which each of the two parties put forward a different candidate,

---

\* See as to this parliament, Leland, who refers to a MS. in the Lambeth Library.—*History of Ireland*, vol. ii. p. 447.

finally ended in the appointment of Sir John Davis, James's Irish Attorney-General, and one of the most eminent persons of the age. To this circumstance we are indebted for the most complete account extant of the differences between the constitution of this parliament and that of its predecessors, Davis having taken the opportunity of an address to Sir Arthur Chichester, when he as Deputy ratified his appointment, to enter at some length upon the subject.* In this he points out that former parliaments were summoned on special occasions, and for limited purposes; that the House of Commons came at first from a small number of shires, and even when the counties were increased, not from the remote shires of Ulster: whereas, the present parliament was (he observes) called not to repel a rebellion, or to reduce degenerate subjects to their obedience, but, as God hath blessed the whole island with an universal peace and obedience, together with plenty, civility, and other felicities, principally in order then to confirm and establish these blessings, and to make them perpetual unto posterity. The time at which it is convened is (he says) when the kingdom,

---

* Sir John Davis's address is preserved in the original journal of this House of Commons, from which it is printed in the Appendix to the second volume of Leland's *History*. Davis was sent to Ireland by James; but he had in the previous reign acquired distinction in England, especially by a philosophical poem, entitled *Nosce Teipsum*, of great merit, but scarcely deserving Hallam's judgment that "perhaps no language can produce a poem extending to so great a length, of more condensation of thought, or in which fewer languid verses will be found." His reputation now rests on the historical treatise in relation to Ireland, which has been referred to in previous notes to this chapter. Charles I., in 1626, appointed him Chief Justice of England, but he died suddenly before he could enter on this office.

wholly reduced into shire-ground, contains thirty-three* counties at large; when all Ulster and Connaught, as well as Leinster and Munster, have voices in parliament by their knights and burgesses; when all the inhabitants, English of birth, English of blood, the new British colony, and the old Irish natives, do all meet together to make laws for the common good of themselves and their posterity.†

In conformity with the King's general policy, and with the objects which were by their Speaker thus set before the House of Commons, an Act was obtained from this parliament which repealed all the statutes then in force that tended to keep separate the people of English and of Irish race. Its recitals were as important as its enacting provisions. They declared that "the cause of the former laws did now cease; in that all the natives and inhabitants of the kingdom, without difference and distinction, were taken into his Majesty's gracious protection; and that there were no better means to settle peace than to allow them to commerce and match together, that so they might grow into one nation, and former differences be forgotten."‡

Along with this parliament a Convocation of the clergy was, for the first time in Ireland, summoned. It met on the 24th of May, 1613. It was modelled after

---

\* This number seems to be obtained by regarding Tipperary as divided into two ridings.

† "I speak "—said Lord Clare in his celebrated speech advocating the Union—" I speak without incurring the hazard of contradiction, when I say, that Ireland never had an assembly which could be called a parliament until the reign of James the First."

‡ Act 13 James I., ch. 5.

the Convocation of Canterbury, except that it was for the entire island, whereas that was only for a province. It consisted of two Houses, sitting separately—an Upper, composed of bishops; and a Lower, of certain dignitaries *ex-officio*, and of two representatives, called proctors, elected for each diocese by its clergy. Jones, Archbishop of Dublin, and then also Lord Chancellor, presided in the former, and Barlow, afterwards Archbishop of Tuam, was Prolocutor of the latter.\* Although so few years had elapsed of James's reign, almost all the bishops of this date owed their appointments to him: they were by birth either English or Scotch.† Parliament and Convocation were not dissolved until 1615, there being in the interval adjournments and prorogations of both. Convocation assumed the same power of taxing the clergy which was enjoyed by the English Convocations, and not long before it was dissolved voted the King a subsidy.

In 1614, the attention of Convocation was directed to the Articles of Faith of 1566, then in use in Ireland. A consideration of their brief and imperfect nature led to a determination that others of a more extended and elaborate character should be framed and substituted for them; and accordingly a license to prepare articles of religion was obtained from the Crown.‡

---

\* Both Jones and Barlow were from Cambridge. Jones held the office of Lord Chancellor, from his appointment to the archbishopric, until his death in 1619. Barlow was recommended for the Archbishopric of Tuam to Charles I. by Ussher, in 1629 (Cotton's *Fasti*, iv. 14). He was probably, therefore, of theological opinions similar to those held by Ussher.

† See Note U of Appendix.

‡ This writ, Archbishop King informed Swift, in 1711, and Archbishop Wake, in 1717, that he had seen. (See Dr. Reeves's Paper "On

At this time in the English Church the Articles known as the Thirty-nine Articles of Religion were in use. They were dated as of 1562; but it was not until 1570 that their subscription was required from the clergy by Parliament.* These Articles had been so framed as to admit of some latitude in their interpretation, and were in practice assented to by persons of opposite opinions. This was especially the case in reference to the Article relating to the questions of predestination and election (XVII).

As the Irish Established Church had heretofore followed in the footsteps of the English, it might have been expected that for this reason, as well as from the advantage which the freedom of opinion conceded by the English Articles gave the clergy, they would have been at once adopted by Convocation; but it was decided otherwise: and accordingly Articles which, while making use of the Thirty-nine Articles, and of other standards of faith, should as a whole be an original composition, were directed to be prepared. That a motive to this course was a desire to act independently; to show that the Reformed Irish Church had for itself considered the doctrines respecting which it pronounced judgment, and had arrived in respect of them at its own conclusions, is certain; but there is reason also to think that with this was united a desire to speak upon the question of

---

Convocations", already referred to at page 20, note.) Some writers date the first meeting of this Convocation in 1615, but Dr. Reeves shows that it met nearly coincidently with the Parliament, and at the times mentioned in the text.

* 13 Eliz., ch. 12, A.D. 1570 (English).

predestination more exclusively in favour of the views of the German Reformers than the English Articles did.

This was the case more particularly in the Lower House, where circumstances gave a preponderance to what was afterwards termed "doctrinal Puritanism": a religious system which, in reference to predestination, if it did not adopt the opinions usually associated with the name of Calvin precisely in his own words, certainly differed from them only in a more mitigated form of expression. The circumstances which had this effect were, in the first place, the position of Irish Protestantism in the country engaging it in constant antagonism to the Roman Catholic creed, and as a result drawing it farther and farther from its tenets; and, in the second place, the influence which the new College, where Puritanism had been introduced by its first Provosts, began to exercise over the clergy.*

The tendency of Convocation soon manifested itself; for when the new Articles came to be framed, instead of adopting the language of the English Seventeenth Article, recourse was had to "the Lambeth Articles," a composition which had been drawn up to please the Puritan party by some English divines about

---

* The first Provost was Archbishop Loftus, who was so decidedly of the Puritan party, that he recommended for an Irish bishopric Cartwright, its most eminent champion in England (Shirley's *Letters*, &c., p. 321). The second was Travers, who had been Hooker's antagonist on the questions in controversy with the Puritans, and of whom Walton relates, that it was said, when Hooker preached *Canterbury* at the Temple Church in the morning, Travers preached *Geneva* at the same place in the afternoon. Alvey was the third, who was also a Puritan. See Elrington's *Life of Ussher*, pp. 15, 16. Sir Arthur Chichester, also, the Deputy at this time, is said to have belonged to the Puritan party.

four years before Queen Elizabeth's death, and which, although accepted by Archbishop Whitgift, she, with the concurrence of Burleigh, had rejected.

The Lambeth Articles deviated from the English Seventeenth Article by adding to what was contained in the latter a distinct affirmance of the doctrine of reprobation. Their first and third Articles say, "that God from eternity has predestinated some unto life, and has reprobated some unto death: that of the predestinated there is a predetermined and fixed number which can neither be increased nor diminished."*

The composition of the Irish Articles† is attributed to James Ussher, afterwards Primate, than whom no one had at that time, either in England or Ireland, a higher reputation for ecclesiastical learning. He then held the office of Professor of Divinity in Trinity College. His theological opinions were known to be of the Calvinistic school of divinity.

Whether the Articles as they were ultimately approved differed in any respect from Ussher's original draft does not appear. When completed they were one hundred and four in number. Their most important difference from the Thirty-nine Articles was in respect of the predestinarian question. They on this subject adopt the additions which were made by the Lambeth Articles to the English Seventeenth Article, and borrow the language as to reprobation which has been

---

\* i. Deus ab eterno prædestinavit quosdam ad vitam, et quosdam ad mortem reprobavit. iii. Prædestinatorum præfinitus et certus est numerus, qui nec augeri nec minui potest. Cited from Hardwick on *Thirty-nine Articles*, App., p. 344.

† See Carte, *Life of Ormond*, vol. i. p. 147.

cited. They, however, contain a clause apparently intended to mitigate the severity of the Article as to reprobation. It is expressed in the following terms:—
"All things (it proceeds) being ordained for the manifestation of his (*i.e.* God's) glory, and his glory being to appear both in the works of his mercy and of his justice, it seemed good to his heavenly wisdom to choose out a certain number towards whom he would extend his undeserved mercy, leaving the rest to be spectacles of his justice."\*

Their other differences from the Thirty-nine Articles were owing to the greater number of subjects entered upon, rather than to variance in doctrine. Among these subjects are some more usually dealt with in homilies, such as our duty to God, and our duty to our neighbour; and some which involve questions that other Churches have judged it wiser not to enter upon —such as the primeval state of man, the fall of angels, and the place of departed spirits after death.† It deserves to be noted that as regards the observance of Sunday the Articles lay down teaching directly contrary to the directions issued in England by James, who enjoined that in the intervals between the services in church the people should indulge in such sports

---

\* Among Ussher's MSS. preserved in the Library of Trinity College, Dublin, was found a Tract by Hooker, which discusses the question of predestination. It is printed in the Appendix to the second volume of Keble's edition of Hooker's works. The language of the Irish Articles in reference to predestination should be compared with what Hooker in this Paper describes as St. Augustine's "latter judgment" upon the subject. See Note V of Appendix.

† See Elrington's Observations upon the Articles in his *Life of Ussher*, p. 44.

and games as he enumerated. The Fifty-sixth Article expressly declares, that " the first day of the week, which is the Lord's Day, is wholly to be dedicated to the service of God: and that therefore we are bound therein to rest from our common and daily business, and to bestow that leisure upon holy exercises, both public and private."

From this circumstance, as well as from the general tendency of the Articles, it clearly appears that Convocation proceeded spontaneously, without the slightest dictation on the part of the Crown : and as it has never been suggested that the assembly was not duly summoned, its standard of doctrine may be taken fairly to represent what was generally approved by such portion of the Irish clergy as were really in communion with the Reformed Church. That the Articles as enacted were permitted by the King has excited surprise. Probably at a later period they would not have been accepted by him, for then his ecclesiastical policy was opposed to the theology which they represented ; and he altogether discouraged Calvinism, and was actively hostile to Puritans and Puritanism.*

The Articles, when completed by Convocation, were signed by the President of the Upper House, and by the Prolocutor of the Lower; and were then ratified by the Lord Deputy, pursuant, it is said, to the direction of the

---

* In 1620, James's hostility to the Puritans was well known. See a letter of Emanuel Downing to Ussher, of 24th October, 1620 (cited in Elrington's *Life*, p. 50), in which, among other things, he says, " which word (*i.e.* Puritanism), though not understood, but only known to be most odious to his Majesty, makes many afraid of joining themselves to the gospel, though in conference their consciences are convicted herein."

King.* They were not submitted to parliament, for what reason has not been explained; and, if the King authorised them, it is now impossible to conjecture.

Although James's political ideas in various respects favoured the native Irish, they were treated, so far as religion, with less toleration than in Elizabeth's time. Besides proclamations both at the commencement and near the end of this reign against seminary and other priests remaining in the country, attendance on the services at church was, in 1605, ordered "on pain of his Majesty's high displeasure, and of such further punishments as may be lawfully inflicted upon the wilful contemners of his royal commands and prerogatives." Nor did the matter rest in words and menaces; fines were imposed for disobedience of this order, and also for refusing to take the Oath of Supremacy.†

It is probable that in these proclamations and penalties the King was animated more by a desire to maintain his prerogative than by any consideration of a particular form of religion, or zeal to uphold it. He did not, however, neglect Irish ecclesiastical affairs.

---

* The official title of the Articles was—"Articles of religion agreed upon by the Archbishops and Bishops, and the rest of the Clergie of Ireland, in the Convocation holden at Dublin, in the yeare of our Lord God 1615, for the avoiding of diversities of opinion, and the establishing of consent touching true religion."

The Articles are printed at length in the Appendix to Elrington's *Life of Ussher;* in the Appendix to Hardwick on the *Thirty-nine Articles;* and also in the Appendix to the first volume of Dr. Killen's *Ecclesiastical History of Ireland.* It is therefore not thought necessary to repeat them in the Appendix to the present treatise.

† See the proclamations and instances of the proceedings to enforce them, cited by Dr. Killen from the *State Papers.—Ecclesiastical History,* vol. i. pp. 475-80.

Besides the grants which he made for the benefit of the Church out of the Ulster forfeited lands, restitution was compelled of property which had been forcibly taken from it; and in various instances when, by errors in previous patents, ecclesiastical estates were conveyed to laymen, a composition was obtained, it being intimated that unless this were conceded the patents would be vitiated, on the ground that the Sovereigns who issued them had been deceived in their grants.* Moreover, the condition of the Church was inquired into by Commissions† and otherwise, and exertions were used to improve the discipline of the clergy, but (as will appear from investigations made in the next reign) with little beneficial effect.

Besides the vacancies in the bishoprics which, as has been mentioned, were before the Convocation of 1613 filled with English and Scotch ecclesiastics, others occurred afterwards, in which the same system of appointing Englishmen or Scotch was continued. Ussher, who was Irish by birth and education, forms an exception. He was promoted first to Meath, in 1521, and thence to Armagh, in 1525, a few days before the King's death.

Ussher's predecessor in Armagh, Hampton, was also appointed by James. His character, attainments, and

---

\* Carte's *Life of Ormond*, vol. i. p. 35.

† The Reports as to the state of the dioceses of the Province of Armagh (except Dromore), given by their bishops in 1622, to a Commission issued by James, are preserved in the Library of Trinity College, Dublin; that for Dromore is in the Armagh Library. Mant summarises them in his *History*, vol. i., pp. 395–407. The number and evil effects of the impropriations clearly appear. Thus, in Armagh, while there were 46 rectories, there were 13 vicarages, and 33 impropriate curacies, which had only small allowances from the lay rectors.

exemplary discharge of the duties of his office deserve mention. Some time before he came to Ireland he had been sent by James on a mission to the Scotch, in the hope that his arguments might aid in reconciling them to episcopacy and to the ecclesiastical policy proposed for their Church; he had then preached a sermon on these subjects before the Assembly at Glasgow, which added to his previous reputation.* On one point—toleration and charity towards those who differed from him—he seems to have been in advance of his contemporaries. There has been preserved a letter of his to Ussher, occasioned by a sermon of the latter, which gave offence from language alleged to have been "harsh and sharp," and which was supposed to have recommended a more rigid execution of the laws against Recusants. In this letter Hampton counsels a milder interpretation of "the points offensive," and in reference to an expression which it was charged had been uttered in favour of drawing the sword uses the remarkable words, "of this spirit we are not nor ought to be".†

James's theological opinions varied at different periods of his reign. He was always strenuous for episcopacy, repeating as an undoubted maxim in statecraft, "no bishop, no king"; but when he first came to England this did not hinder his being content with Calvinistic divines; and he sent some of them to the Synod of Dort to represent the English Church. After that assembly had been held, he observed that the party which began then to be called Arminian, from its leader

---

\* A copy of his Sermon is in the Library of Trinity College, Dublin.

† The letter is printed in Ussher's works, vol. xv. p. 183. It is dated 17th October, 1622.

upon the Continent, and which was in direct opposition to Calvinism, was eminently zealous for the royal authority and prerogative, and he proceeded to give his confidence and support to them. When he appointed Ussher to Meath, he inclined decidedly to this party; nevertheless, the high reputation of this eminent man, and the personal esteem he had for him, entirely outweighed the objections which the doctrinal views he advocated might otherwise have caused.

Before James turned towards Arminianism, he collated to the See of Derry George Downham, or Downam, whose theological opinions in many respects resembled those held by Ussher. This divine had obtained high distinction at Cambridge, where he held the Professorship of Logic. He had also, with ability, taken part in the controversy respecting episcopacy,[*] which was commenced by the Puritans in the reign of Queen Elizabeth, and had ever since continued. The views which he advocated in reference to the office of bishop deserve attention. He holds it to be of apostolical institution, and that this is the opinion to which ascertained facts conduct—(1) because episcopal government was generally used in all Christian Churches for three hundred years after Christ and his Apostles, and there is no decree of any General Council to account for its adoption during that period; (2) because it was in use in apostolic times, and was not contradicted by the Apostles; (3) because in some instances the Apostles ordained bishops. In

---

[*] See "Sermon defining the honourable function of bishops, preached 17th April, A.D. 1608, at the consecration of the Right Reverend Father in God the Lord Bishop of Bath and Wells, by George Downham, D.D." Printed at London, A.D. 1608.

connexion with the apostolical origin of the institution, he refers to a distinction taken by some which he seems inclined to approve between things which are *divini juris*, and those which are *apostolici juris* :\* the former being generally, perpetually, and immutably necessary; the latter not so. With respect to the position of presbyters in reference to ordination, he holds that the right to ordain ministers is in bishops, yet he will not so appropriate it to them as that extraordinarily and in case of necessity it might not be lawful for presbyters to ordain.

The policy of the King in extending English rule

---

\* When the controversy respecting episcopacy first commenced, the defence of the order was largely rested upon the fact that the State had selected this form of Church government. Before the end of Elizabeth's reign a higher tone was adopted, and episcopacy was by some defended as being (what Downham thought) *apostolici juris*, and by others as being *divini juris* in the highest sense. Still the first line of reasoning continued to be urged by great names. Thus, Lord Bacon in his Tract on *Pacification of the Church*, addressed to James I., says :—" That there should be but one form of discipline in all Churches, and that imposed by necessity of a commandment and prescript out of the Word of God: it is a matter volumes have been compiled of, and therefore cannot receive a brief dismissal. I, for my part, do confess, that in revolving the Scriptures, I could never find any such thing; but that God had left the like liberty to the Church government, as he had done to the civil government; to be varied according to time, and place, and accidents, which nevertheless his high and divine providence doth order and dispose." So also Paley, in a sermon preached in the Castle Chapel, Dublin, at the consecration of Bishop Law, observes, that " whilst the benefits of Christian morality and the fundamental articles of the faith are, for the most part, precise and absolute; are of perpetual, universal, and immutable obligation; the laws which respect the discipline, instruction, and government of the community, are delivered in terms so general and indefinite, as to admit of an application adapted to the mutable condition and varying exigencies of the Christian Church."
—*Works*, vol. v. p. 32.

and law to the Irish districts was expected quickly to accomplish the improvement of the natives. It was followed by some satisfactory results, but by no means to the degree that was anticipated. In truth the change was too abrupt and too complete. Reform, to succeed, must accompany, not outrun, the growth of society. Many Irish reluctantly exchanged the freedom of their old independence for the restraints of civilization.

The effect, however, of his other great measure, the Ulster Plantation, upon both the civil and ecclesiastical interests of the country was extensive. The northern counties were transformed into a high state of cultivation, covered with towns, villages, and the comfortable residences of opulent proprietors and farmers. The Established Church gained increased endowment; the churches and glebes were restored and put in order; the numbers of her members were augmented by the English colonists. But, on the other hand, the Scotch settlers brought with them the dislike to episcopacy which animated their own countrymen: and although such sentiments were discouraged by the Government, they adhered to them. Ultimately they founded a distinct Church upon their own principles. Henceforward the Irish religious system, representing the differing opinions of the three races of which the people were composed, becomes separated into three divisions—Roman Catholic, Protestant with episcopacy, and Protestant without episcopacy.

## CHAPTER VII.

[1625-1660.]

WHEN Charles the First came to the throne he found England divided by religious controversies relating to ecclesiastical government, discipline, and doctrine. These had commenced early in the reign of Queen Elizabeth. They originated with the exiles who, having resided upon the Continent during the persecution of the Reformers by Mary, returned after her death, bringing with them ideas in relation to all these subjects more in consonance with the organization of foreign Protestant Churches, than with the religious system which was being established in England. At first the questions raised were not of importance. Some ceremonies and procedure sanctioned by the Prayer Book were objected to; the apathy of the clergy commented upon; and abuses in the administration of affairs within the Church pointed out. From these topics those who took this side went on adding to and increasing their grounds of censure, until at last many repudiated episcopacy altogether; and a considerable number formed separate and independent sects. The progress of the assailing party was met (reaction being always proportioned to the action which causes it) by corresponding resistance. The defenders of the Church kept pace with its adversaries; the claims put forward on its behalf became higher and more exclusive. At first it was thought enough to prove that the ceremonies and matters of like kind which were condemned were things indifferent; that the State had much authority in such cases, and that certainly the Church could make its own ordinances as to non-essentials: it was even admitted that there were imperfections, and the difficulty of removing what had grown up with so much that was good was pleaded. Afterwards no concession would be allowed; everything that had been done or established was right, and was alone right: episcopacy was not merely the preferable, but the only permitted, form of Church government; and the orders of ministers not ordained by bishops, even though they were of the foreign Churches which had no episcopate, invalid.*

The antagonism between these two parties reached its utmost height in the three first parliaments of Charles. In each of them, so far as the House of Commons, the

---

* Bacon, in his Tract entitled, *An Advertisement touching the Controversies of the Church of England*, remarks that "some indiscreet persons have been bold enough in open preaching to use dishonourable and derogatory speech and censure of the Churches abroad; and that so far as some of our men ordained in foreign parts have been pronounced to be no lawful ministers." In the same he says of the opposing Church parties, " the beginnings were modest, but the extremes are violent ; so as there is almost as great a distance now of either side from itself as was at first from the other." (See the Tract in Spedding's *Life and Letters of Bacon*, vol. i. p. 73).

On the question of episcopacy this growth of opinion—at least as expressed in argument—will be seen by comparing the reasoning of Whitgift answering Cartwright in 1573, that the Church had from very early times determined to be governed by bishops, and of Saravia in 1590, that episcopal government came immediately from God, and men cannot alter it of their own free will. (See Keble's Preface to Hooker, pp. lxiii, lxvi.)

party of change (who for many years had previously, either as a reproach, or from their own choice, been known by the appellation of Puritans) prevailed. In doctrine Calvinistic, they at this time added to their other grounds of dissatisfaction with the administration of ecclesiastical affairs, a complaint that Arminianism (which they termed a covert road to Popery) had for some time been favoured in the patronage of the Crown, had gained ground upon the episcopal bench, and was increasing among the clergy.

Puritanism was in general united with an indisposition to admit the high prerogatives claimed for the Crown by Elizabeth and James, and was therefore by those princes dreaded as a source of dissension in the State. Charles, like them, looked at it from a political aspect, but he added to their objections a disapprobation of it on religious grounds. He was unquestionably attached to episcopacy from a conscientious opinion that it was an institution of divine authority; and his doctrinal opinions were those of Arminius, not of Calvin.

During the four years of his reign, which elapsed before he dissolved his third parliament (for in that short time he had called and dissolved two parliaments), his patronage in the Church was distributed among such of the clergy as were understood to hold in a decided and unqualified manner the ideas with which he sympathised. One of his appointments was the translation to the See of London of Laud, then Bishop of Bath and Wells, the most zealous and uncompromising, if not the ablest of the party, which, from its ideas upon Church government and doctrine, may for distinction (although the name was not given until a much later date) be from this time designated the High Church party.

Neither Charles nor the House of Commons in any of these three parliaments would make the least concession to each other: the differences, more particularly upon ecclesiastical and religious questions, being by each side considered matters of principle, could not be reconciled. When the third parliament was dissolved the King, despairing of obtaining any more support for his policy in a new parliament than he had already found, proceeded to rule, and even to levy taxes, either of his own absolute authority, or with the advice and sanction only of his Privy Council. In this course he persevered for eleven years.

During this time Laud (on whom, in 1633, he conferred the Archbishopric of Canterbury) was his adviser in ecclesiastical affairs. Owing to his counsel, as well as to the King's predilections, the High Church party continued to be favoured in episcopal appointments. Partly from this cause, and partly from the zeal and learning of their leaders and advocates, the principles which they maintained gradually spread among the clergy, and ultimately acquired predominance in the Church.

Both the civil and the ecclesiastical policy of the King displeased the laity. The prerogatives claimed by the former would have left with the Commons little authority or influence; and the latter was supposed to aim at establishing, what was equally unpopular, clerical ascendency. The discontented joined, or if they did not actually join, encouraged the Puritan party, which alone seemed able to resist the progress of arbitrary power. When, in 1640, a fourth parliament met, members in connexion or sympathy with Puritanism formed a majority of the House of Commons, and disagreement between them and the King was at once manifested.

In Ireland the religious dissensions which at this time divided society in England had not as yet arisen. The Church was, however, involved in troubles of a different character. They arose from mismanagement of its property, and from relaxed discipline. The latter subject appears to have attracted Charles's attention about 1631, for in that year he addressed to the four Irish archbishops, and through them to the bishops and clergy, a letter which pointed out, among other matters which are observed upon, the necessity of the clergy being careful in the discharge of their duties; that they should preach and catechise in the parishes committed to their charge, and " live answerable to the doctrine which they preached to the people."*

The condition of the Church in Ireland, and an intention to provide remedies for its abuses, were probably among the considerations which determined Charles to entrust the government of that country to some Minister of pre-eminent ability. Wentworth, on whom he at a later date conferred the title of Earl of Strafford, was selected. It also seems to have been with a view to the conduct of measures of ecclesiastical reform that Bramhall, who afterwards attained the highest station in the Irish Church, and whose capacity for business had then attracted notice, was at the same time induced to resign his preferments in England, and become Strafford's

---

* Cited by Mant, vol. i. p. 438, from Parr's *Life of Usher*, p. 38.

chaplain in Ireland. Certainly, both Strafford and Bramhall proceeded, immediately upon their arrival, in 1633, as if the improvement of the Church was the first, or one of the first, duties with which the former had been charged.

A regal visitation, in which Bramhall assisted, and other investigations made by him, confirmed the truth of the complaints which had come to England respecting the management of the property of the Church and the discipline of its clergy. Except in Ulster, where lands were acquired in the Plantation, its financial state continued to be very much what we have seen that it was at the close of Queen Elizabeth's reign; for although many impropriations that remained vested in the Crown were restored to the parishes by King James, and augmented their resources, upon the other side must be counted losses of Church lands occasioned by improvident grants and leases, and in many instances also from the forcible intrusion of laymen. As yet there would appear to have been few of the clergy educated in Trinity College; generally unlearned, secular in habits, the parochial incumbents were very little respected.*

---

\* A correspondence of this period between Laud on the one hand, and Strafford and Bramhall on the other, has been published, which records the condition of the Irish Church as the latter found it—"An unlearned clergy" (says Strafford), "which have not so much as the outward form of churchmen to cover themselves with, nor their persons anyways reverenced or protected: the churches unbuilt; the parsonage and vicarage houses utterly ruined; the people untaught through the non-residency of the clergy . . . the possessions of the Church to a great proportion in lay hands; the bishops aliening their very principal houses and demesnes to their children, to strangers." (Letter, 31st Jan., 1634; Strafford's *Letters*, vol. i. pp. 186, 187; and see also, to the same effect, a letter of Bedell

The power of the Irish Government, which at this time was almost despotic, was used by Strafford to compel the restitution of much ecclesiastical property. Thus, from the Earl of Cork tithes worth about two thousand pounds a-year, which he had taken possession of, were recovered. Other tithes alienated from the Church, which were beyond the reach of such interference, were purchased back by Bramhall with the proceeds of subscriptions for the purpose in England, and of loans upon the property to be regained. At the same time the King restored impropriations according as the existing leases of them expired.*

The authority of the Deputy was also used to induce the enforcement by the bishops of order and discipline among the clergy: in particular noticing their habitual non-residence in their parishes, and the vain expense in which (he says) they indulged in towns to the disservice of their cures and the great scandal of the Church, he required that they should be compelled "to repair to their churches, and attend that charge whereof they owed an account both to God and man."†

The object, however, connected with ecclesiastical affairs in Ireland which especially engaged the attention

---

to Laud, 1st April, 1630, cited in Burnett's *Life of Bedell*.) Vesey in his *Life of Bramhall* says that there was not one bishopric in the province of Cashel " that had not the marks of the sacrilegious paw upon it."

\* The grants of impropriate tithes and lands by James I. and Charles I. to the Church will be found enumerated in the Report of the Commission to inquire into the revenues and condition of the Established Church (Ireland), 1868. (See Appendix to this Report, No. 29, p. 169.)

† *Strafford's Letters*, vol. ii. p. 7 ; Mant, vol. i. p. 511. Leland (who is not in general favourable to Strafford) says that under him " abler and more respectable teachers were generally provided for the people."— *History*, vol. ii. p. 40.

of Strafford and Bramhall, and was sought by them with most anxiety, was to terminate the difference between the Churches of England and Ireland in respect of the Articles which formed the standards of doctrine in each, and to effect an absolute uniformity between them. It is said that this measure was desired by the King, and was one of the matters which he gave into the charge of Strafford, when he sent him to Ireland.* Nor was this wholly for reasons of a theological character: it was thought that agreement between the two kingdoms in ecclesiastical affairs would promote harmony also in political.

Accordingly, when Convocation met in 1634, occasion was taken to propose that the English Thirty-nine Articles should be adopted in Ireland. The subject was first brought forward in the Upper House by Bramhall, who had shortly before been created Bishop of Derry. Nothing was there said as to the Irish Articles of 1615 being either condemned or approved. Bramhall's observations were directed to urge the expediency of having "the correspondence between the Churches of England and Ireland more entire and accurate." He also pointed out "the convenience of having the Articles of peace and communion in every national Church

---

\* Carte's *Life of Ormond*, vol. i. p. 149. The Irish Articles displeased the High Church party in England. Their estimate of them, it may be assumed, is represented in the language used by Jeremy Taylor when preaching at Bramhall's funeral, in Dublin. In his sermon on this occasion, after alluding to Bramhall having caused the English Articles to be accepted, he says, " that they and we might be *populus unius labii*, of one heart and one life, building up our hopes of heaven on a most holy faith, and taking away that Shibboleth which made this Church lisp too undevoutly, or rather in some little degree to speak the speech of Ashdod, and not the language of Canaan."

worded in that latitude, that dissenting persons in those things that concerned not the Christian faith might subscribe, and the Church not lose the benefit of their labours for an opinion which, it might be, they could not help."\*

In this Convocation Ussher was President of the Upper House—a question of precedence in dispute between the Sees of Armagh and Dublin having been decided in favour of the former by Strafford a short time before. Lesley, Dean of Down, was Prolocutor of the Lower House. The Upper House readily voted for adopting the Thirty-nine Articles.† In the Lower House there was opposition, and the difficulties raised were overcome only by the interference of Strafford, who insisted that the English Articles as they stood should be voted for affirmatively or negatively, without amendment or alteration, and without any accompanying expression of approval of the Irish. He himself drew up the form which was to express the resolution he desired from Convocation, and it was his draft which, being adopted by them, became the First Canon.‡ It was expressed in the following words:—". . . For the manifestation of our agreement with the Church of England

---

\* Cited by Mant (vol. i. p. 489) from Vesey's *Life of Bramhall*.

† There were at this time four archbishops and nineteen suffragan bishops, of whom only Ussher and Martin, Bishop of Meath, were educated in Trinity College, Dublin ; the rest were English or Scotch. (See Note W of Appendix.) Bramhall says he did not remember any except two who spoke in favour of the Irish Articles : " If there were any, they were very few, and did it faintly."—*Works*, Anglo-Cath. Lib., v. 81.

‡ Strafford, when sending his draft of the Canon, conveyed his wishes to Convocation in a communication marked by that despotic imperiousness which marred his great qualities, and was one cause of the enmity which pursued him to his end. . . . " Mr. Prolocutor—I send you here

in the confession of the same Christian faith and the doctrine of the sacraments, we do receive and approve the Book of Articles of religion, agreed upon by the archbishops and bishops, and the whole clergy in the Convocation at London, in the year of our Lord 1562, for the avoiding of diversities of opinions, and for the establishing of consent touching true religion. And, therefore, if any hereafter shall affirm that any of those Articles are in any part superstitious or erroneous, or such as he may not with a good conscience subscribe unto, let him be excommunicated, and not absolved before he make a public recantation of his error."

Strafford succeeded in preventing any declaration by Convocation in affirmance of the Irish Articles of 1615; but neither was there, it is to be noted, any express repeal of them. The consequence was, that by some it was supposed that both sets of Articles were to be in force; and among these seems to have been Ussher, who, when writing to a correspondent in England, says of the Irish: " We let them stand as they did before; but, for manifesting our agreement with the Church of England, we have received and approved your Articles concluded in the year 1562." * Whether Ussher, or any bishops agreeing with Ussher, required both the

---

enclosed the form of a Canon to be passed by the votes of this Lower House of Convocation, which I require you to put to the question for their consents, without admitting any debates or other discourse: for I hold it not fit, nor will suffer, that the Articles of the Church of England be disputed. Therefore I expect you to take only the voices consenting or dissenting, and to give me a particular account how each man gives his vote. The time admits of no delay, so I further require you to perform the contents of this letter forthwith, and so I rest, your good friend, WENTWORTH." This letter, not printed in Stratford's *Letters*, will be found among Laud's *Letters*, Anglo-Cath. Theol., vii. 98.

\* Letter to Dr. Ward, 15 Sept., 1635 ; *Works*, vol. xvi. p. 9.

English and Irish Articles to be subscribed, is not clear; certainly most of the bishops, holding the Irish to be impliedly revoked by the authoritative document of later date, treated the English as alone obligatory upon the clergy at their admission into the Church and institution to benefices. After the Restoration the Irish Articles fell entirely into disuse; and from that time the subscription required from the clergy by all the bishops was to the Canon enacting the Thirty-nine Articles.\*

Bramhall, having succeeded in inducing Convocation to accept the Thirty-nine Articles, endeavoured to obtain their assent also to the English Canons. These, it is said, were in some respects supposed to conflict with the ideas of the Puritan party, to which the clergy leaned in opinion.† Their acceptance was also resisted upon the ground that they related to matters on which each Church should exercise its judgment, accommodating its rules to its own peculiar circumstances—a reason which met Ussher's support. The result was, that distinct Canons were enacted, differing from the English in their arrangement, mode of expression, and in several of their provisions; but not on any points of importance. Agreement with the English Church was affirmed not only by the Canon as to the Thirty-nine Articles already cited, but also by another prohibiting the use in the Churches of any form of liturgy or divine service other than that which was established by law and comprised in the Book of Common Prayer. Some of the Canons make provision for needs occasioned by local circumstances, enjoining that, where the people were Irish, certain portions

---

\* Elrington's *Life of Ussher*, p. 493.
† Carte's *Ormonde*, vol. i. p. 149. See also *Strafford's Letters*, vol. i. p. 381.

of the Service should be read in Irish as well as English, if the Ordinary approved : and that in such cases, if the clergyman were English, a parish clerk able to read them should be chosen : also that there should be an Irish Bible and Prayer Book at the expense of the parish. In lieu of the special directions in the English Canons as to kneeling and gestures, there is substituted a general direction that all persons shall use "such reverent gestures and actions as by the Book of Common Prayer are prescribed in that behalf, and the commendable use of the Church received." In reference to the administration of the Communion, they, like the English, prescribe that "the minister shall deliver both the bread and the wine to every communicant severally."*

Statutes benefiting the interests of the Church were obtained by Strafford, during his rule as viceroy, from Parliament; the most important of which was one intended to prevent the alienation or improvident disposition of the lands belonging to the bishops and other ecclesiastical persons. This regulated the lettings which were thenceforth to be allowed of Church lands, fixed for them limited periods, and defined what rents might be reserved. It rendered any act, by incumbents of sees or benefices, not in conformity with the powers thereby conferred, void against their successors. There was also an Act passed which facilitated the restoration of impropriations to the parishes.†

In 1640, Strafford was finally removed from Ireland.

---

\* The Irish Canons, and their differences from the English, are discussed by Mant, *History*, i. 497, and by Elrington, *Life of Ussher*, p. 180.

† These Acts were 10 & 11 Charles I., ch. 2 (Irish); 10 & 11 Charles I., ch. 3 (Irish).

His departure was followed by a series of events adverse to the welfare of the Church, which render its history for the next twenty years merely a record of depression and suffering: of calamities inflicted by external violence, and neither caused nor increased by its own acts or defaults.

The first in order of these events was the insurrection which, from the magnitude it assumed, is known as the rebellion of 1641. On the night of the 23rd of October in that year, at a large number of places situate in the counties of the Ulster Plantation, the dwellings and settlements of the English were attacked by armed bands of the native Irish; and (as nothing of the kind was expected) with almost unresisted success. It is not improbable that the immediate cause which led to this outbreak was apprehension that proceedings hostile to the Roman Catholic religion in Ireland, and designed to oppress such as adhered to it, would be taken by the Puritan party, who were rapidly becoming predominant in England; but, if so, this was only the proximate, and neither the sole nor the chief, cause. The native population which remained in Ulster after the Plantation were numerous. They were compelled to resign to the colonists the most valuable portions of their lands : they were treated as a subject and inferior race ; and they regarded with indignation the usurpation which deprived them of their property and former social condition. Beside, they resented the loss of the independence which, until the Plantation, they and their chieftains enjoyed. To set these elements of disturbance in motion needed only—what the time and occasion furnished—ambitious leaders. The movement, under their guidance, assumed a character of greater magnitude than the redress of local grievances. A barbarous people, as the insurgents undoubtedly were, without the restraint of military discipline, may be always expected to indulge remorselessly the passions which civil war engenders : and in the present instance, with a large proportion of the assailants, these were heightened to peculiar exasperation, since their incursions were made upon the soil from which they had been evicted, and against those who had dispossessed them. Hence, the insurrection was followed by extreme loss of life. The estimates of this loss by historians* have varied much, and from the nature of the case no calculation can be relied upon as accurate; since to the deaths in battle or other conflict, which might have been counted, are to be added numbers slain by scattered bodies of insurgents who rose tumultuously over the country, of whom there could not be any complete record; numbers more, who, despoiled of everything, and driven from their homes to seek shelter in Dublin and other towns, were swept away by the hardships they endured or the diseases they contracted in their flight, and perished unnoticed. The same causes which occasioned an excessive loss of life led to an unsparing destruction of property. The farm-houses and other buildings of the colonists, their chattels of every kind, were plundered or destroyed. The land became a waste.

The consequences of this rebellion fell principally upon the members of the Church, the Scotch at first not being assailed, and thus having time and opportunity to organize a defence. The clergy fled or were driven

---

* See note X of Appendix.

away along with their congregations; many churches and glebe-houses were reduced to ruin. In much of Ulster the Church ceased to exist.

This insurrection was followed by the extension to Ireland of the great Civil War between Charles and the English Parliament. During its continuance the Church was exposed to the enmity alike of the Irish and of the Parliamentary party, and its interests peculiarly suffered.

While these occurrences were taking place in Ireland, the party hostile to Episcopal Church government was acquiring an ascendency in the English Parliament. In 1643 they obtained the appointment of a body of persons, consisting of eminent divines, of some peers, and some members of the House of Commons, " to confer and treat among themselves of such matters and things concerning the liturgy, discipline, and government of the Church of England, and the vindicating and clearing of the doctrine of the same from all aspersions and misconstructions, as should be proposed by either or both Houses of Parliament and no other." This body, meeting in Henry the Seventh's Chapel, or the Jerusalem Chamber, Westminster Abbey, acquired the name of the Westminster Assembly. The opinions of the majority were Calvinistic and Presbyterian. With these original members were afterwards joined Commissioners from Scotland.

In the same year was framed in Scotland the declaration in reference to ecclesiastical reform, which was termed the Solemn League and Covenant. This bound those who subscribed it to preserve the reformed religion in the Church of Scotland; also to uphold the reformation of religion in England and Ireland according to the Word of God and the example of the best reformed Churches; and to bring the Churches of God in the three kingdoms to the nearest conjunction and uniformity in religion, confession of faith, form of Church government, directory for worship and catechising ; also to endeavour, amongst other things, the extirpation of Popery, Prelacy, " that is " (it explains), " Church-government by Archbishops, Bishops, their Chancellors and Commissioners, Deans, Deans and Chapters, Archdeacons, and all other ecclesiastical officers depending on that hierarchy."

This declaration was approved by the Westminster Assembly, and adopted by the English Parliament, with a title describing it to be for the peace and safety of England, Scotland, and Ireland

Beside approving the Solemn League and Covenant, and thus condemning Episcopacy, the Westminster Assembly issued a Directory for public worship, a Confession of Faith, a longer and a shorter Catechism, intended to supersede the English Prayer Book, Articles of Faith, and Catechism. The Directory was a code of instructions as to public worship, which expressly set aside the former liturgy. The Confession was a standard of doctrine in character decidedly Calvinistic.

When the " Solemn League and Covenant," and these other theological compendiums of the Assembly had attained acceptance in England, the Presbyterian party sought to have them introduced and put in force in Ireland. " The League" was first tried. It was rejected by the army under the command of the Marquis of Ormonde ; but in the North there were Scotch troops, commanded by General Munroe, who had been sent from their own country by the king to aid in putting down the rebellion, and by this officer and his soldiers it was at once accepted. It was also received with favour by numbers of the Ulster Protestants, especially by those of Scottish descent. The Directory was first enforced in 1647, when Ormonde surrendered Dublin to Commissioners of the Parliament, who forthwith prohibited the use of the English Liturgy in the churches in that city, and ordered the regulations of the Directory to be followed.

During the Protectorate the prohibition of the use of the services of the English Prayer Book, which thus commenced in Dublin, was continued and extended to the country generally. External action on the part of the Protestant Episcopal Church ceased. The revenues of the bishoprics were seized for the purposes of the State; vacancies in the office were not filled. Presbyterianism also was at first discouraged. Religion it was proposed to maintain through the agency of persons "of pious life and conversation," who should be found by Commissioners (selected for the purpose) qualified with gifts for the preaching of the Gospel, and by paying these persons stipends from the public revenues.* Afterwards Cromwell relaxed the severity of his rule towards the Presbyterian clergy, and contributed to their support;† but there was no change in his treatment of the Episcopalian clergy, whom he seems to have regarded as

---

\* Reid's *Hist. of Presbyterian Church in Ireland*, vol. ii. p. 160.

† See *Ecclesiastical History of Ireland*, by Dr. Killen, late Moderator of the General Assembly of the Presbyterian Church in Ireland, vol. ii. pp. 104–107.

enemies of his government,* and whose public ministrations were (with only a few exceptions) therefore silenced. His victorious despotism established itself upon the total ruin of the civil and ecclesiastical polity which had been before upheld in Ireland by the English Government.

---

\* Cromwell, when excusing his policy towards the episcopal clergy in England, told Archbishop Ussher that he was advised by his council not to grant any indulgence to men who were restless and implacable enemies to his person and government.—Elrington's *Life of Ussher*, p. 274.

## CHAPTER VIII.

**USSHER AND BEDELL.**

DURING the Protectorate of Cromwell, Ussher, Archbishop of Armagh, died. The part which he took in connexion with some of the most important events affecting the Church of Ireland—especially the preparation of the Articles of 1615, and the enactment of the English Articles in 1635—has been narrated when referring to these periods; but more than an incidental notice of a prelate, whose pre-eminence in learning was in his own day universally admitted, is called for in any history of the Church of Ireland, however brief.

James Ussher was of an English family named Neville, which in the reign of King John settled in Ireland, and from the founder of the Irish branch holding the office of Usher to that prince, he assumed the latter name. He was indebted for his early education to a singular circumstance. James the First, before his accession, sent two Scotchmen, named Fullerton and Hamilton, to Dublin, to promote his interests among the Protestant gentry. To disguise from the jealous observation of Elizabeth their real objects, they assumed the character of teachers, opened a school in Dublin, and gave instruction to many (among whom was Ussher), which, in the condition of the country at that time, they could not otherwise have received.*

In the College which Elizabeth founded, Fullerton and Hamilton were appointed Fellows, in addition to those named in the Charter. Ussher came with them as a student; was then one of the Scholars; afterwards Fellow and Professor of Divinity. From this office he was, as has been already mentioned, promoted to the bishopric of Meath, and thence translated to the archbishopric of Armagh.

When the insurrection of 1641 broke out Ussher was in England. The disturbed state, then, of the North of Ireland, and subsequently of the entire kingdom, the predominance of the Puritan party hostile to episcopacy, and ultimately the measures adopted for its suppression, prevented him from ever again returning to Ireland. He suffered great losses of property in the rebellion. Soon after he, like the other bishops of the Irish Church, ceased to receive any revenues from the lands of his See. Charles gave him the bishopric of Carlisle *in commendam*, but he derived little from it: an intended grant to him from the See-lands of Armagh seems to have failed;† and before his death he was indebted to friends.

Ussher, so long as he was permitted, discharged the duties of the episcopal office with admirable diligence, setting to his clergy an example of personal piety and

---

\* Hamilton was by James, in 1622, created a Peer, with the title of Viscount Claneboye. "Whenever," says Dr. Parr, one of Ussher's biographers, "the Archbishop recounted the providences of God to himself, he would say that he took this for one remarkable instance of it, that he had the opportunity and advantage of his education from those men (*i.e.* Fullerton and Hamilton), who came hither from chance."

† Elrington's *Life of Ussher*, p. 271.

K

active exertion, and publishing admonitions and instruction to guide them. He was least successful as a ruler. "For the governing part of his function (says Burnet) he was not made: he had too gentle a soul for the work of reforming abuses." We ought to take into account, however, when judging him, the difficulties caused by the condition of society in his time and the circumstances with which he had to deal.

When detained in England, in 1641, Ussher joined Charles I. at Oxford, and he appears to have been then and afterwards consulted by the King, and much in his confidence. His counsel on one momentous occasion is recorded. In conjunction with Juxon, Bishop of London, he advised that the royal assent should be refused to the Bill for the attainder of Strafford. When, contrary to his remonstrances, the assent was given, he attended Strafford in the interval until his execution, and accompanied him to the scaffold.

No question was more debated between Charles and the Long Parliament than the continuance of episcopacy in England. The English divines induced Ussher to join them in defending the Order, and two tracts were written by him, having relation to the subject. One was entitled, "The Original of Bishops and Metropolitans briefly laid down," and the other, "A Geographical and Historical Disquisition touching the Asia properly so called." The ground of episcopacy (he asserts) is derived partly from the pattern prescribed by God in the Old Testament, and partly from the imitation thereof brought in by the Apostles, and confirmed by Christ himself in the time of the New. Its history he traces from the appointment of Timothy by St. Paul as bishop at Ephesus. The Seven Churches mentioned in the Apocalypse he holds were metropolitical, and the angels of them, spoken of by St. John, their bishops. For the age next after that time he mentions (to use his own words) a succession of witnesses to episcopacy.

These tracts are only directed to maintain on historical grounds the office of bishop, and do not discuss its nature. On that subject Ussher's views are said to have been extremely moderate. It is reported by his chaplain, Dr. Bernard, that when interrogated by him upon the point, he answered, . . . "I have ever declared my opinion to be that *Episcopus et Presbyter gradu tantum differunt, non ordine*, and consequently, in places where bishops cannot be had, the ordination of presbyters standeth valid." With reference, however, to some ordinations by presbyters in England, and lest from his opinion of the office he might be supposed to sanction them, he added . . . "holding, as I do, that a bishop hath a superiority in degree over a presbyter, you may easily judge that the ordination made by such presbyters as have severed themselves from those bishops unto whom they had sworn canonical obedience cannot possibly by me be excused from being schismatical."*

It is not improbable that it was the moderation of his views in relation to this subject which suggested either to himself, or other advisers of the King, that he should draw up some scheme of episcopal government in connexion with synods, which might be offered as a compromise to the parliamentary party. This he seems

---

* Cited in Elrington's *Life of Ussher*, p. 258, from Bernard *On Ordination*, p. 125.

to have done a short time before the civil war commenced; but his propositions were not debated, with a view to being a subject of treaty, until the King was a prisoner in the Isle of Wight, when the clerical part of the Commissioners sent by the Parliament to the King received them favourably; but the lay rejected them. What they were appears from a tract published by Dr. Bernard after his death, entitled, "The Reduction of Episcopacy unto the form of Synodical Government received in the Ancient Church," which is on the title-page stated to have been drawn up in 1641, "as an expedient for the prevention of those troubles which afterwards arose about Church government."

To state the scheme put forward in this paper shortly—it proposed that the rural deans should be suffragan bishops, such as those sanctioned by an Act of Henry VIII., each with a synod of the rectors within his precinct, and that according to the votes of the majority of the synod matters should be determined. The diocesan bishops were to have higher authority, and also to act with synods, at which these suffragans and a select number of rectors were to attend, and the greater matters to be considered and decided, the majority prevailing: and at the head over all was to be a provincial synod, composed of the diocesan and suffragan bishops, and of clergy elected by the dioceses, at which the Archbishop of the province was to preside.*

---

* In 1670, Archbishop Leighton, who had many opinions in common with Ussher, endeavoured, but without success, to compose the controversies in Scotland respecting Church government, upon the basis of an episcopacy acting with presbyters and synods. (See Burnet's *Own Time*, book ii., and Leighton's tract, entitled, *Defence of a Moderate Episcopacy*.)

During the Protectorate, Ussher was treated with respect by Cromwell, and was on some occasions consulted by him; but, notwithstanding, he was unable to obtain from him permission for the public use of the Church services. Upon the Archbishop's death, Cromwell ordered a public funeral, but his contribution to the expense was of inadequate amount, and left much to be paid by the surviving relatives.

Selden—and no man was more competent to pronounce judgment on the subject—declared\* that the learning of Ussher amounted to a prodigy. Even as early as his collegiate career it was recognized: *acatholicorum doctissimus* were the terms in which even then he was described upon the Continent. Unquestionably in the department of ecclesiastical history he is without a rival either in his own time or since.

The theological opinions of Ussher, at the date of the Articles of 1615, are reflected in them. Upon the subject of predestination he appears to have modified his views in the latter years of his life. " I can testify (says Dr. Brian Walton), that having often discoursed with the late Most Reverend Father in God, James, Lord Primate of Armagh, concerning divers controversies in divinity, and in particular the last time he was in London, which was not long before his death, concerning the controversies of grace and free-will, election and reprobation, and the dependents thereupon: he did declare his utter dislike of the doctrine of reprobation, and that he held the universality of Christ's death, and that

---

\* Jacobus Usserius, vir summâ pietate, judicio singulari, usque ad miraculum doctus, et literis severioribus promovendis natus.—Selden, *Preface to Marmora Arundeliana.*

not only in respect of sufficiency, but also in regard of efficacy, so that all men were thereby salveable: and that the reason why all were not saved was because they did not accept of salvation offered, and that the grace of conversion was not irresistible, but that men might, and often did, reject the same: that in these points he did not approve the doctrine of Geneva, but was wholly of Bishop Overall's opinions."* Hammond, however, who agrees with Walton in stating that Ussher "did for many years acknowledge universal redemption," shows that this was with a qualification, or as he terms it, a distinction, *non ex æquo pro omnibus*—a distinction which, in the form of its expression, is of the more importance, because it is in direct contradiction to words used upon the subject by one of the ancient fathers.†

Ussher has been justly censured for his views in reference to the political treatment of Roman Catholics. A sermon which he preached on the subject drew (as has been already mentioned) reproof from Archbishop Hampton; and afterwards, in 1626, upon the occasion of a proposal to enlist Roman Catholics in the army, he

---

\* Overall (Burnet, in his comment on Article XVII., says) espoused Arminian tenets. He was one of the authors of the Church Catechism, in which one answer affirms of our Lord, " who hath redeemed me and all mankind." The reference to Overall, therefore, had peculiar significance.

† The words of Hammond (as cited by Dr. Elrington, *Life of Ussher*, p. 291) are:—"The Bishop (Ussher) did for many years acknowledge universal redemption, but that with a distinction of *non ex æquo pro omnibus*, which puts me in mind of the words of Holy Maximus that χριστὸς ὑπὲρ πάντων ἐξ ἴσου, which last words (when I read them long since) I could not guess why they were added, till I saw there was somebody that granted the ἀπέθανεν ὑπὲρ πάντων, but denied the ἐξ ἴσου."

joined others of the Irish bishops in a protest against toleration.* But in judging a great man in reference to a question of this character, the ideas of his age must be kept in mind; he cannot be measured by the standard of subsequent enlightenment. At this time no theological writer in England had advocated toleration of dissent from an established religion, and even statesmen and legislation generally proceeded upon a contrary principle.

The biographers of Ussher represent him in every capacity (except that of ruler, in which he was open to the reproach already mentioned) as an almost perfect character. " Passion, pride, self-will (says Burnet), seemed not to be so much as in his nature." The meekness, forbearance, unperturbed temper, and habitual cheerfulness, which he displayed under many trials, are especially remarked.

It is proper to note that he attributed much importance to the effects produced by preaching; that he considered this duty more incumbent upon bishops than was generally supposed; and that in his diocese, and afterwards in England, until prohibited, he was

---

Baxter, who also testifies to Ussher's later views, would seem to have himself held opinions similar to those which Hammond attributes to Ussher. (See Bishop Harold Browne on Article XVII.). They may also be traced in *Paradise Lost* :—

> " Some I have chosen of peculiar grace
> Elect above the rest ; so is my will :
> The rest shall hear me call, and oft be warned
> Their sinful state, and to appease betimes
> Th' incensed Deity, while offered grace
> Invites."

* Mant, *History*, vol. i. p. 423.

frequently in the pulpit; speaking extempore, with fluency, in a plain, unadorned style, easily understood, with much success in reaching the hearts and consciences of his hearers.

Contemporary with Ussher, Bedell presided over the diocese of Kilmore—a prelate of apostolic piety and zeal, deserving to be placed beside Ussher in any record of their times. Of him Father Paul, the great historian of the Council of Trent, with whom he had become intimate, when he resided in Italy as chaplain to Sir Henry Wotton (ambassador from James I. to the Court of Venice), said, "that he had learned from him during their intercourse more of theology and practical religion than from any other person during his whole life."

This exemplary person was English by birth, and came over to Ireland in consequence of an invitation (suggested by Ussher) from the Fellows of Trinity College, Dublin, to become their Provost. Accepting the office, he held it for about two years, during which he effected considerable improvements in the discipline and rules of the institution. Of these James, who thence advanced him to the united See of Kilmore and Ardagh, takes notice in his letter of appointment—" By his care, and good government of the College, there have been (he says) wrought great reformations to our singular contentment."

The dioceses over which Bedell was to preside had been long neglected. He has himself recorded their condition—" The churches unrepaired, and in a manner ruined ": incumbents " holding two, or three, or four, or more vicarages apiece ": some of the best of the clergy English, " who had not the tongue of the people, nor could perform any divine offices, or converse with them," so that they could be understood. To meet these evils he exerted himself with energy, resigning the bishopric of Ardagh in order to exhibit his condemnation of pluralities; examining with great strictness the candidates for Orders; appointing to benefices with judgment; obliging residence, and translating into Irish a catechism, forms of prayer, and selected passages from Scripture. An Irish Version of the Old Testament, which was afterwards in 1685 published, was due to him, he having employed the person by whom it was made, and having himself revised it.

At the commencement of the insurrection of 1641 Bedell was treated by the natives with forbearance and respect, and was even allowed to give shelter to fugitives from the rebels. This indulgence was due very much to the example and precept of the Roman Catholic Bishop of Kilmore, Dr. Swiney, who offered, if it were necessary for the protection of Bedell, to take up his residence with him. After about two months Bedell, refusing to send away those whom he sheltered, was taken away by force, under an allegation that it had been so ordered by the Council of Kilkenny, and was confined in a castle upon an island in Loughouter, where, with his son and chaplain, he was kept until they were exchanged for some leaders of the rebels who had been made prisoners by the loyalist party. Forbidden to proceed to Dublin, he took refuge with a clergyman in the neighbourhood of the castle; but his health and strength were then much impaired, and he did not long survive his removal.

Bedell did not publish any theological works: some

writings of his, it was said, were destroyed or lost during the rebellion; but if so, it is not probable that they were either numerous or important. His life was spent in the practice of piety, and in impressing upon others its necessity. Christianity (he used to say) was not so much a system of opinions, as a divine principle renewing and transforming the heart and life: "with Augustine, I look for fruit, not leaves."

After his death a remarkable testimony to his excellence was given by the conduct of the very people who had been arrayed against him during the rebellion. Numbers of them followed his funeral, and while declaring that he should be the last of the English, expressed in the strongest terms his praise. One bystander, a Roman Catholic ecclesiastic, moved by the remembrance of his many virtues, exclaimed aloud, *sit anima mea cum Bedello.**

---

* Bedell has had several biographers. One of the latest and best sketches of his life will be found in Wills' *Lives of Illustrious Irishmen*, vol. iv. p. 130.

# CHAPTER IX.

[1660-1685.]

WHEN the rule of the Commonwealth was established in Ireland, the entire kingdom was treated as if it had been involved in rebellion, and as if the landed property of its inhabitants was forfeited to the State. Those who could prove their "constant good affection" to the Parliamentary party during the Civil War, as also husbandmen, ploughmen, and persons of like condition, who it was thought would be of use to any new colonists that might be introduced, were alone exempt from proscription.

The consequence of this policy was that immense territories in Ireland were placed at the disposal of the English Parliament. These they proceeded to redistribute, but conducted the redistribution upon principles differing materially from those which guided the arrangements of the Plantation under James. Then a portion of the forfeited lands was reserved for the dispossessed natives; now, in three provinces (Leinster, Munster, and Ulster), the native Irish, and many Roman Catholic Anglo-Irish who were classed with them, were ordered to migrate to Connaught, and to accept in its wild and uncivilized districts whatever settlements might be allotted to them as a substitute for their former interests in landed property.

The effect of the transplantation* (as it was called) thus decreed, although in practice it was carried out with exceptions and dispensations, was extensive. It removed the most formidable of the natives and Roman Catholics to places where they could no longer endanger the English authority. It consequently reduced their party to a condition of extreme weakness.

In the room of proprietors who were deprived of their property new owners were introduced. These were Protestant in religion, but imbued with sympathies differing from those of the old gentry of Anglo-Irish race, who were almost all loyalists, and attached to the Church which had been established in alliance with the Crown. At the Restoration many of these new settlers were as little favourable to Episcopacy as the Scotch colonists in Ulster.

Hence, although there was in Ireland under the Commonwealth a considerable increase in the number, strength, and influence of the Protestant part of the

---

* The most complete account of the transplantation of the Irish to Connaught will be found in Mr. Prendergast's *Cromwellian Settlement in Ireland*. He seems to think that this oppressive measure was adopted in order to protect the colonists; but there is some reason to think there was also a vindictive motive, originating in resentment caused by the sufferings of the Protestants during the insurrection of 1641. Certainly Cromwell assigned this reason for his own cruelty in the war. When answering a remonstrance of the Roman Catholic bishops and clergy (1649) he says : . . . "You, unprovoked, put the English to the most unheard-of and barbarous massacre (without respect of age or sex) that the sun ever beheld." . . . "We are come to ask an account of the innocent blood that hath been shed."—Carlyle's *Letters and Speeches of Cromwell*, vol. ii. pp. 210–223, ed. 1871.

population, this by no means brought a proportionate increase of adherents to the Protestant Episcopal Church. It was depressed, not merely by the ordinances of the Parliament directed against the public ministration of its clergy, but by the absence of support from a most active, and then, owing to the success of the Parliament, most powerful class. Many of the parish churches, not merely in Ulster, but also elsewhere, came into the possession of ministers who had not received episcopal ordination; also on them often devolved the spiritual care of the parishioners.

Not only, therefore, was the constant opposition of the Roman Catholics to the Church, which, however, was at this time of less political weight than at any former period, to be considered by the King and his ministers when determining whether, in Ireland, the establishment was to be reinstated in its previous pre-eminence and endowments: they had also to take into account an increased Protestant dissent from its system. This, as might be expected, manifested itself, under the guidance of the ministers not episcopally ordained, in objection to the government of bishops and to the use of the services of the Prayer Book.

A similar question arising as to the English Church was at once decided in its favour. The ecclesiastical policy pursued in England had always from the Reformation been repeated in Ireland. That the same course should be now followed was urged by the Marquis (afterwards Duke) of Ormonde, the King's principal adviser in reference to Irish affairs. Warmly attached to the Protestant Episcopal Churches in both countries, he now urged that their restoration followed as a necessary consequence from the restoration of the monarchy: succeeding in his advocacy of these views, he then pressed that as this principle had been acknowledged in England it should be also in Ireland, without waiting for a Parliament, of which the constitution could not be foreseen with certainty.

The result was, that a few months after his return the King announced his recognition of the restored position of the Irish Church; acknowledged that it had resumed its former rights and privileges, unaffected by the intervening usurpation; and declared that he would, therefore, proceed to fill the bishoprics, which, with the exception of eight, were all vacant.

A little later he addressed to the clergy, in answer to a petition from them seeking his protection, a letter* in which, further indicating his future ecclesiastical policy, he stated that he would by all the ways and means in his power preserve their rights and those of the Church of Ireland, so far as by law and justice he might; and that nothing could give him more content than, when occasion should be offered, to add to the revenues thereof (which, he observed, had been too much diminished by rapacious or improvident hands), and to restore it to its ancient patrimony; in proof of which he referred to letters he had sent granting the impropriate, and forfeited tithes in his gift to the incumbents of the parishes liable to pay them.

One of the vacant bishoprics was Armagh. To this, the highest office in the Irish Church, Bramhall, one of the eight surviving bishops, was translated. The See of

---

\* 24th December, 1660.  Carte's *Ormonde*, iv. p. 22.

Derry, thus rendered vacant, and all the other vacant bishoprics were subsequently filled.

On the 27th January, 1661, two Archbishops and ten Bishops were consecrated at St. Patrick's Cathedral, Dublin, by Bramhall and four assisting Bishops. The ceremony was attended by the Lords Justices, by the Mayor and Aldermen of Dublin, and by the general Convention, which had been assembled before Parliament was regularly summoned, at whose head was their speaker, Sir William Domvile.*

Among the Bishops who were upon this occasion consecrated was Jeremy Taylor, then justly reputed the most eloquent of English divines.† He had held during the Commonwealth a Lectureship in Ireland at Lisburn, which appears to have escaped interference. He came thither from England, having suffered much during the Civil War, in which he ardently espoused the King's cause. The reputation of his writings was about this time at the highest: under the disadvantage of circumstances most adverse to study, he had sent forth from the remote retreats, in which he took shelter from the persecution inflicted by the dominant party upon the Church of England, not merely sermons and addresses of extraordinary eloquence, but elaborate treatises upon pro-

---

* Mason, in his *History of St. Patrick's Cathedral* (p. 192), has compiled a minute account of this remarkable ceremony, from a MS. of Dudley Loftus, then Judge of the Prerogative Court, preserved in Marsh's Library, Dublin, and from a newspaper called *The Kingdom's Intelligencer* of 11th February, 1661.

† Hallam, speaking of Taylor as an orator, says: "We have no reason to believe, or rather much reason to disbelieve, that he had any competitor in other languages."—*Literature of Europe*, vol. ii. p. 360. 3rd edition.

found theological subjects, characterized by much learning and research.

The popularity of Taylor's practical writings has survived the vicissitudes of literary taste. He had not the precision of expression requisite to treat theological questions of difficulty, or to conduct controversy successfully, but in the expression of devotional feeling, occasionally of elevated thought and pathetic reflection, he rises to a height which, except it be by some relics of primitive Christianity, has never been surpassed.*

Among Taylor's merits not the least must be reckoned that he was the first English author who issued an elaborate argumentative pleading for toleration upon questions of a theological nature. His celebrated treatise, "The Liberty of Prophesying," written with that object, was published in 1647. It is characterized by the same eloquence and learning as mark his other writings, and by, perhaps, more ingenuity of argument and reasoning. It produced, at the time, great effect upon public opinion, and thus prepared the way for the more accurate and comprehensive views of later times upon the subject.

The qualities which recommended Taylor for one of the bishoprics now filled suggested his selection to preach upon the occasion of the Consecration. His sermon

---

* Taylor's biographers, Bishop Heber and Archdeacon Bonney, both cite the characteristic sentence, in which Dr. Parr, placing him in a pre-eminence shared only by Hooker and Barrow, pronounces Hooker the object of our reverence, Barrow of our admiration, and Taylor of our love. Ὄκηρον μὲν σέβω, θαυμάζω δὲ Βάρρουον, καὶ φιλῶ Ταίλωρον. Heber, probably justly, places Taylor first of this triumvirate, "in imagination, in interest, in that which properly and exclusively deserves the name of genius."

remains. It discusses the questions connected with the episcopal office, and contends for the views respecting them then entertained by the High Church party. The apostles, he holds, were the first rulers of Christ's followers; their office was not to die with them: it was as necessary for perpetuating as for founding the Church. The eminence of power which they enjoyed must therefore be transmitted; hence the order of bishops was requisite; it was to take the place of the Apostles as to government, and to possess similar authority. Accordingly, to bishops he attributes the foundation and preservation of the Church—the foundation, not only because the apostles, who were (he says) bishops, had been the first preachers of the Gospel and planters of churches, but because the apostolical men whom the apostles used in planting and disseminating religion were by all antiquity affirmed to have been diocesan bishops: the preservation, because they have the power of ordaining the clergy—a power which (as he confines to those so ordained the right to administer the sacraments) becomes, in his estimate, of momentous importance.

Not long after the consecration of the Bishops, a Parliament, which had been convened, met. In its depressed condition the Roman Catholic interest was unable to return representatives to the House of Commons. The members of that assembly were Protestants, generally either of the Episcopalian party, or persons who, if not of the Episcopalian party, were yet of moderate ideas, indisposed to thwart the policy of the Government. The general enthusiasm for the Restoration had at the elections swept before it all opposition, and rejected those from whom hostility was to be apprehended either by the Monarchy or by the Church in alliance with the Monarchy.

Taylor, now Bishop of Down, was appointed to preach before Parliament. Selecting for his text, "To obey is better than sacrifice," he urged the obligation of obedience to superior authority, both in Church and State: but accompanied his observations with admonitions to his hearers who, as constituting the Parliament, were part of this authority, that they on their side should exhibit justice and mercy: duties which the questions about to arise before them in respect of the forfeited estates rendered especially fitting to be inculcated.

The House of Commons, composed, as it was, either of active friends of episcopacy, or of persons who would not oppose its friends, proceeded at once to pronounce in favour of the Church formerly established. It directed that a resolution should be drawn up requiring all subjects of the kingdom to conform to the episcopal model of Church government and to the liturgy as enjoined by law. This was followed by a declaration that the Solemn League and Covenant imposed by the parliamentary party in the reign of Charles I. was against the laws of God and the fundamental constitution of the kingdom; and that any person going about to defend or justify the same should be accounted an enemy to his Majesty and to the peace and tranquillity of the nation. Proceeding yet farther in the same spirit, the House also ordered that the entries in its journals in the same reign, which appeared to censure Lord Strafford, Bramhall, and other eminent persons, should be expunged.

In a declaration which Charles, before returning from

exile, had issued from Breda, he, among other matters, promised that no man should be disquieted or called in question for differences in matters of religion, which did not disturb the peace of the kingdom; and that he would be ready to consent to such an Act of Parliament as, upon mature deliberation, should be offered to him for the full granting of such indulgence. This declaration, it was alleged by the ministers without episcopal orders, who were at the time in possession of parish churches, contemplated that such of them as had come in upon vacancies were not to be dispossessed, and were to be relieved from question as to the validity of their orders, and from obligation to use the services in the Prayer Book.

Whether the declaration from Breda did or did not reach to the extent alleged by the Presbyterian party, there seems little doubt that it would have been wiser to have yielded the claims which they founded upon its language. If this course had been adopted, it would probably have then retained, in connexion with the parish Churches of the Establishment in both countries, all the Protestants; their children and descendants would have grown up in habits of attendance upon the Churches; then, as the occupying incumbents died off, successors of episcopalian principles would have taken their place; and time and usage might have been trusted to gain over whatever in the end remained of dissent among the congregations.

At the same time it must be admitted that the engagements which, by taking the Solemn League and Covenant, almost all the ministers not episcopally ordained had taken against prelacy, raised difficulties in the way of concession. It was thought uncertain whether, if protected in their titles, they would not use their position to create an anti-episcopal feeling within the Church itself, and thus not improbably a schism upon a point of vital importance.

But whatever might now be our decision in reference to the rights of those ministers, or as to the expediency of yielding to their claims, neither the English nor Irish Parliament of that age exhibited any sympathy with a policy of conciliation. On the contrary, first in the English, and afterwards in the Irish Parliament, a stringent Uniformity Act was passed, and in each country it was enacted that all ministers in possession of benefices who then had not obtained, and before a certain prescribed day should not have obtained, episcopal ordination, were to be, *ipso facto*, deprived.

When the Irish Uniformity Act was passed, there could be no question as to the necessity of episcopal orders to qualify for a benefice; but the previous law, it seems to have been then assumed, equally required such orders; and in the interval from the Restoration the bishops had acted upon this supposition. When the clergy at their Visitations presented their letters of orders, if they appeared to be from a non-episcopal authority, they were held not to show a valid title. Bramhall in his diocese, where numbers of the incumbents in possession had received only Presbyterian orders, being desirous to retain them, offered to re-ordain such, and accompanied the proposal by a declaration that he did not thereby dispute the value of their previous ordination, nor those acts they had exercised by virtue of it, but that he did not see how they could recover their tithes, if any were to refuse to pay them, unless they were episcopally ordained.* This proposal met some acceptance in his own diocese; but in the other Ulster dioceses the clergy who had not received episcopal ordination united in rejecting any overtures from the bishops for their reordination, and were deprived.

In England, besides pressing for indulgence to the ministers not episcopally ordained, the Protestant Dissenters sought to have the Prayer Book revised. A controversy arose upon the subject, and ultimately there were numerous alterations; but, with the exception of a few of no importance, they were not at all in agreement with the suggestions of the Non-conformists. In Ireland, also, the English Prayer Book, as then revised, was adopted.

The following were the principal changes introduced into the Prayer Book at this time: — The version of the Bible of 1611 was substituted in the prefatory Sentences, in the Epistles and Gospels, and (with the exception of the Psalter, the Ten Commandments, and some portion of the Communion Service) in all the other extracts from the Bible. The word "priest" was substituted for "minister," in the description of the person who was to read the Absolution. To the occasional prayers were added

---

* It will be observed that Bramhall put the case upon legal, not theological, grounds. He accordingly introduced into the letters of orders issued to those whom he reordained the words, " non annihilantes priores ordines (si quos habuit) nec validitatem aut invaliditatem eorum determinantes, multo minos omnes ordines sacros ecclesiarum forensicarum condemnantes, quos proprio judici relinquimus: sed solummodo supplentes quicquid prius defuit per canones ecclesiæ Anglicanæ requisitum" (Vesey's *Life*). See further, as to the position of ministers with Presbyterian ordination at this time in possession of benefices, Note Y of Appendix.

a second prayer "in the time of dearth and famine"; two prayers for Ember week: prayers for Parliament, and "for all sorts and conditions of men"; a Thanksgiving for restoring public peace at home; and the General Thanksgiving. In the prayer for the Church Militant, the present clause respecting saints departed was inserted. The direction to kneel in the Communion Service, which had been in Edward's Prayer Book, and was omitted in Queen Elizabeth's, was restored; in the explanatory note at the end of this service, the words "corporal presence of Christ's natural flesh and blood" were substituted for "any real or essential presence therein being of Christ's natural flesh and blood." Services for the 30th January and 29th May (the anniversaries of the execution of Charles I. and the accession of Charles II.) were added; and also forms of prayer to be used at sea, and a service for the baptism of those of riper years.

In the Irish Prayer Book there was inserted a service for the 23rd of October, the anniversary of the commencement of the Rebellion of 1641. This day had by a previous Act been ordered to be observed in the churches, by saying morning prayer, and giving thanks for deliverance and preservation from the rebellion.* The Irish Prayer Book also contained a prayer for the chief governor or governors of Ireland.

Of the Bishops of this reign Bramhall most influenced the course of ecclesiastical policy. He held the highest office in the Church, and brought to the discharge of its duties pre-eminent abilities. His writings are of

---

* 14 & 15 Charles II., sess. 4, ch. 23 (Ireland), A.D. 1662.

great excellence, characterised by original thought and much power of reasoning. He was reputed to belong to the High Church school of theology; hence, and from his zeal for the King's interests, he was unpopular with the Puritan and Parliamentary party, and was by them classed with Laud: Cromwell applying to him the appellation of the Irish Canterbury. But, if he was of Laud's opinions, he advocated and acted upon them with very different judgment and discretion. His history and character have been illuminated by Taylor, who preached his funeral sermon, with the utmost splendour of eloquence. An impartial judgment may demand some abatement from the language of this brilliant panegyric; but, after it has been made, we must still concur in ranking this prelate among the greatest of his Order either in England or Ireland.

The only political measures passed under Charles II. which affected the interests of the Church were those relating to the estates confiscated by Cromwell. His redistribution of them was complained of by the loyalists: by such Roman Catholics as, having abstained from hostilities, claimed to be regarded as innocent: and by the Church. By the Acts of Settlement and Explanation, a compromise was effected between these various claimants and the proprietors who had been placed in possession, and new arrangements were made. The Church not only received back property of which it had been deprived, but had additional grants bestowed for its benefit.

## CHAPTER X.

[1685-1702.]

IN Ireland, from the time when the authority of the Crown of England had been first acknowledged, until the death of Charles II., the uniform policy pursued by successive English Governments, even when, as in the reign of James I., it was desired to conciliate the native Irish, was to maintain the ascendency of the colonists over the rest of the people. During the portion of this period which elapsed subsequent to the Supremacy Act (excepting only while Queen Mary and the Commonwealth ruled), there was united with this object—and indeed regarded as essential to it—the determination to uphold the superiority of the Church, as reformed under Henry and Elizabeth, over other religious systems.

This policy was interrupted by James the Second. He had, for some years before coming to the throne, avowed his conversion to the Roman Catholic faith. He had taken this course from such deep-rooted conviction as outweighed all considerations of personal advantage, and impelled him to disregard the danger to his succession which might arise from the disapprobation of the English people, then influenced by decidedly

Protestant sentiments and opinions. Acting from similar motives, he, when he became King, proceeded to direct his conduct and measures to advance the interests of the Church which he had joined, and, if possible, to ensure its predominance.

In England these 'designs were successfully resisted. James, flying from the kingdom, was held to have abdicated, and the Crown was transferred to his daughter Mary, wife of the Prince of Orange, and her husband. In Ireland for some time he succeeded: and it was not without civil war, nor until he had been defeated in two great battles, that he was dethroned.

The difference in the course of events in the two kingdoms was the natural consequence of differences in the condition of society in each. The English people, although descended from several distinct races, were at this time one nation, which was in its religious profession Protestant. In Ireland the larger number of the people were of native descent, and of these almost all were Roman Catholics. Some of the colonists, descended from the first settlers in the Pale, or from followers of the Anglo-Norman lords who, in other parts of the country, had been substituted for the native chieftains, were also Roman Catholics. Only a minority of the people was Protestant. James, therefore, had in Ireland what he had not in England, a majority of his subjects predisposed by religious sympathy to view his measures with approbation.

The policy of James produced important changes in Ireland; and had its operation and further progress not been prevented by William's victories, it would have effected a revolution. Before his abdication the chief departments of the State, the army, the magistracy, the Judicial Bench, had been remodelled by Tyrconnell, his Lord Lieutenant. As before this time all offices and employments under the Crown were filled with Protestants, so they were now with Roman Catholics. One form of ascendency was substituted for another. After his abdication, it was sought by legislation to effect still more extensive alterations. A parliament, convened in the spring of 1689, when James himself was in Ireland, composed, with merely a few exceptions, of members of his party and religion,* proceeded to undo the distribution of landed property made by the Act of Settlement of Charles II. One of its statutes enacted that, where subsequent to the 22nd October, 1641 (the day before the rebellion of that time began), lands had come into the possession of new owners, the original proprietors, or their heirs, might enter in and regain possession of them. In cases where the new owners, who would thus be dispossessed, derived directly under the grants of the State, they were to receive no compensation; in cases where they were purchasers from such grantees, for pecuniary considerations, they were to be reprized (so it was expressed) out of the forfeitures which were expected to accrue when William's adherents should be overcome. Along with this Act was passed another which, if it had taken effect, would

---

\* Six of the bishops attended in the House of Lords. One of these, Dopping, Bishop of Meath, spoke with courage and ability against the Bills passed in this parliament (King's *State of the Protestants of Ireland under James II.*). Dopping was a prelate whose excellence was generally acknowledged. Archbishop King calls him " a most useful and eminent pillar of the Church." (Cited by Mant, *History*, vol. ii. p. 91.)

probably have placed at the disposal of James for the benefit of his friends a very large additional extent of land. By it more than two thousand Protestants were by name attainted: one class (who were supposed to be actively engaged on the side of William), unless by a prescribed day they came in and submitted themselves to a trial; another class (who had left the country, and who were charged with not giving James the assistance which, by a proclamation, he had required from his subjects), unless within a defined time they returned, and established their innocence before an Irish judge.*

With James's defeat passed away the predominance of the Roman Catholic interest. The offices of the State were again filled by Protestants; the legislation, dealing with landed property, and attainting the supporters of the Revolution, being that of an assembly not convened by the authority of William and Mary as a Parliament, was treated as absolutely null and void. This was declared by express enactments of both the English and Irish Parliaments: of the former in 1690, and of the latter in 1695. The Irish, in addition to these declarations against the validity of the proceedings of James's Parliament, directed that for the better guiding and assuring the minds of his Majesty's good subjects, and that no memorial might remain, all the pretended Acts, and the rolls on which they were engrossed, and all proceedings by the persons pretending to be such

---

* The proceedings of Tyrconnell, and subsequently of James's Parliament, are very fully narrated by Macaulay (*History*, vol. iii. chap. xii.). With him, as regards the latter, should be compared Lecky (*History*, vol. ii. chap. vi. pp. 184-194). In one respect James's Parliament set a good example; they passed a Toleration Act.

Parliament, and also all writs issued for calling the said pretended Parliament, and all its journals, should be brought before the Chief Governor at the Council-chamber, and there be publicly and openly cancelled, and utterly destroyed.*

The Established Church shared in the vicissitudes of civil policy in the reigns of James and of William and Mary. Under James it was depressed. An Act of the Parliament of 1689 withdrew from the clergy the tithes payable by Roman Catholics, that is, the greater part of their emoluments in three provinces, without compensation to the existing incumbents. Under William and Mary the Church was reinstated in its old position, and restored to its former pre-eminence and endowments, with some addition to the latter from a grant for its benefit of impropriations forfeited to the Crown.

During the reign of James several Irish bishoprics had fallen vacant, and were by him left unfilled. To these William and Mary, when order had been in some degree restored, appointed; the first exercise of their patronage being in the month of December, 1690, by the translation of Narcissus Marsh from the See of Leighlin and Ferns to the Archbishopric of Cashel. This promotion was well-merited by the zeal and fidelity with which, until compelled to abandon his diocese and take refuge in England, this prelate had discharged the duties of his office.†

Although the Church henceforward enjoyed its

---

\* 7 William III., ch. 3 (Irish).

† The Church was indebted to Marsh for an excellent library in Dublin, intended chiefly for the clergy, and an endowment for it, by which it is still maintained.

ancient privileges, it is remarkable that neither by William and Mary, nor by William when he reigned alone, was Convocation ever summoned. The right to tax the clergy, which this assembly had in Ireland exercised under James I. and Charles I. and II., was now assumed by Parliament: very probably in imitation of what had taken place in England, where, in 1664, authority to tax the clergy had been conceded to Parliament under an arrangement between Archbishop Sheldon and Lord Chancellor Hyde, the clergy in return receiving or assuming the privilege of voting for members of Parliament.* Taxation of the clergy by Parliament was opposed by the Irish bishops in the House of Lords, and their protest claiming this power for Convocation was recorded in the journals of that assembly.†

It is probable that the refusal to summon Convocation arose from the supposed attachment of the Irish clergy to the House of Stuart. Like their English brethren, many of them inclined to the doctrine of divine right and indefeasible authority in the King claiming by descent. They were not, however, equally ready to become martyrs for the theory; and, while in England, some Bishops, and about four hundred of the clergy, refusing to take the oath of allegiance to William and Mary, were deprived of their preferments, and seceding, formed the sect of the Non-Jurors, in Ireland very few refused to comply with the law. Among those were, however, two of note, Sheridan, Bishop of

---

* Carwithen's *History of the Church of England*, vol. iii. pp. 106-112.

† See letter of Archbishop King to the Bishop of Worcester, 9th February, 1699, cited by Mant, *History*, vol. ii. p. 100.

Kilmore, and Charles Leslie, Chancellor of the diocese of Connor.*

Leslie was a theological writer of great ability. He was noted for the acuteness and logical power of his arguments. "Charles Leslie," said Dr. Johnson, emphatically, "is a reasoner, and a reasoner not to be reasoned against"†—a panegyric well deserved, if by no other of his writings, by his treatise entitled, "A Short Method with a Deist." In this, laying down certain tests to distinguish a true history of events, he applies them to the accounts of the institution of the Mosaic and Christian religions. These tests were—(1) that the matters of fact alleged be such as could be judged of by the senses, seen and heard; (2) that they shall have occurred publicly in the face of the world; (3) that monuments, acts, and observances, in memory of them shall have existence and continue; (4) that these shall have their commencement and institution from the time that the matters are said to have occurred.‡

Convocation not being summoned, there was not,

---

* Another Non-Juror of celebrity, Henry Dodwell, was an Irishman. He was a layman, and then Camden Professor of History in the University of Oxford; but previously he had been a Fellow of Trinity College, Dublin. He was noted for his erudition, a chronological work of his being still cited. His theological opinions went beyond those of any other of the High Church party. According to him the immortality of the soul is conveyed in baptism, and its efficacy comes from the bishops through the clergy ordained by them; sacerdotal absolution is necessary for the remission of sins (see his *Epistolary Discourse*). An Irish Bishop, Mills of Waterford, and Dr. Clarke, published replies to his writings.

† Boswell's *Life of Johnson* (Croker's edition), vol. v. p. 186, *note*.

‡ Leslie was son of Bishop John Leslie (Clogher): he went to the Continent and joined there the Court of the Pretender; was allowed to return home again, and died at his own house, Glasslough, in the county of Monaghan, where his descendant, Sir John Leslie, now resides.

except in Parliament, where the Bishops represented the interest of the Church, any public discussion or debate in respect of Irish ecclesiastical affairs. Under William, however, several measures relating to them became law. Thus statutes were passed for abolishing the writ *de haeretico comburendo* (which as yet continued to be legal in Ireland); suppressing profane cursing and swearing; regulating the days to be observed as holy days, and enforcing the observance of Sunday. The erection of glebe-houses was encouraged by obliging the incumbent who succeeded the builder to repay a portion of the expense of construction, and by enabling him to obtain contribution again from his own successor.*

The Primate from the accession of William and Mary, until the death of William, was Michael Boyle, previously Bishop of the united diocese of Cork, Cloyne, and Ross. This prelate was also Lord Chancellor; the last ecclesiastic who in Ireland ever filled the office. The Court of Chancery was indebted to him for some of the rules which long regulated its procedure. It is characteristic of the mode in which the government of the Church of Ireland was conducted in the seventeenth century, that when Bishop of Cork, Boyle held with the office six parochial benefices; until his own kinsman, Lord Orrery, when President of Munster, compelled him to resign them.

Another instance of the open violation of the laws of the Church is furnished by the case of Hacket, Bishop of Down and Connor, deprived in 1694, by a visitatorial

---

\* The Acts of the Irish Parliament referred to in this paragraph are : 7 Wm. III., ch. 2; 7 Wm. III., ch. 9; 7 Wm. III., ch. 14; 7 Wm. III., ch. 17; 10 Wm. III., ch. 6.

commission, for non-residence, simony, and other offences. He had, during twenty years previously, been tolerated in almost total absence from his diocese without excuse.

From the time when the sovereignty of William and Mary had been established, the political policy pursued was devoted to the aggrandizement of the Protestant party. The Parliament which then (1692) was convened met under influences not favourable to a calm and statesmanlike review of affairs. It was composed exclusively of Protestants, of whom many had been excluded from office by Tyrconnell, and more had seen the title to their lands endangered by the legislation of James's Parliament. Animated by resentment, and the pride of victory, they sought only how to assert and keep for themselves the ascendency which the defeat of James had secured for them, and, that they might the better accomplish that purpose, to render their adversaries incapable of making any resistance. The same spirit continued in the succeeding Parliaments. At the death of William there were upon the statute-book several Acts directed against persons professing the Roman Catholic religion, and particularly against the clergy of that faith. These formed the commencement of the laws which, from their extraordinary severity, are known as emphatically "The Penal Code," and which, completed in the next reign, will more properly come to be considered in connexion with its events.

Beside the Act annulling the proceedings of James's Parliament, the English Parliament passed other statutes professing to bind Ireland. Some of these related to the Church: one of them imposed new oaths, and abrogated the oath of supremacy which was then prescribed in Ireland.* This appears to have been unpopular with the clergy, and being added to the refusal to summon Convocation, and to the taxation of ecclesiastical persons by Parliament, to have created extreme dissatisfaction. Referring to these causes of complaint, and to others which affected the laity more than the clergy, Bishop King, who had been appointed to the See of Derry by William and Mary, states the opinions of the time in the following terms: . . . "These considerations are very afflictive and uneasy to the people of Ireland, and make them sensible that they are not like to be so happy a people as they promised themselves on the Revolution."†

If the legislation of the English Parliament, in relation to Ireland, had been confined to the Acts which were passed concerning the Church, it is not probable that the exercise of the power which was thus assumed would have excited much attention from any except those whose interests were directly affected. But civil affairs were also included within its scope, and it was proposed to deal with Irish trade. The woollen manufacture had prospered in Ireland; and its success was prejudicial to the interest of persons engaged in the same business in England. By them it was proposed that English legislation should be used to put down this manufacture in Ireland; and one of the measures suggested was, that the export of Irish wool to the Continent should be prohibited, lest it might be worked up by foreign industry to compete with English cloth. When it was seen that the power assumed by the English

---

\* See 3 William and Mary, ch. 2 (English).
† See letter to Bishop of Worcester, already referred to, p. 157, *note*.

Parliament might be used for purposes in the highest degree injurious to the trade of Ireland, discontent arose, and led to an examination of the precedents and reasons which were alleged in support of this assumption.

In 1698 appeared an elaborate discussion of the subject in a treatise entitled, "The Case of Ireland being bound by Acts of Parliament in England stated," written by Molyneux, Member for the University of Dublin in the Irish Parliament, who was then much esteemed both in England and Ireland for his scientific attainments.* In this the right of the English Parliament to legislate for Ireland is controverted upon constitutional and historical grounds, with much force and ingenuity of reasoning.

The appearance of Molyneux's work was followed by considerable excitement in England. The House of Commons voted an unanimous resolution that "the book published by Mr. Molyneux was of dangerous tendency to the Crown and people of England, by denying the authority of the King and people of England to bind the kingdom and people of Ireland, and the subordination and dependence that Ireland ought to have upon England, as being united and annexed to the imperial Crown of that realm." Not content with this resolution, they ordered the book to be burned by the common hangman; and they presented to King William an address urging that such of their laws as related to Ireland should be enforced.

---

* Locke terms Molyneux "that very ingenious and studious promoter of real knowledge, the learned and worthy Mr. Molyneux"; and mentions a problem proposed by him to illustrate the degree in which ideas attributed to the sight are acquired from experience.—*Essay on the Human Understanding*, book ii., ch. 9, s. 8.

William, deeming it inexpedient to come into conflict on this question with the English Parliament, promised compliance with the address. The Irish Parliament remained passive. The consequence was, that the opposition to the proceedings of the former, which was begun by Molyneux,* died away, and the claim of England to supreme legislative power was in practice acknowledged.

In this manner, for the time, terminated the controversy between the English and Irish Parliaments: not, however, without consequences of the utmost importance. To the discussions connected with it was due the commencement among the Anglo-Irish of an Irish interest separate from an English; of distinct parties to maintain each, which included the clergy as well as the laity, and differed as to the policy proper to be pursued in reference both to ecclesiastical and civil affairs.

---

* See Note Z of Appendix.

# CHAPTER XI.

[1702–1714.]

THE reign of Anne in Ireland is associated with the Penal Code, which, as there has been occasion to mention in the preceding chapter, beginning with some statutes passed before William's death, had, under this Queen, its provisions very considerably extended, and its operation enforced with increased efficiency and stringency.

It would not be consistent either with the plan of the present treatise, or with the space which it allows for consideration of political events, to enter into the provisions of the various statutes which constituted this code. Also, the examination they have received in civil histories and in essays renders anything beyond a summary of their effect not needed. It suffices, therefore, now to say that the code (which, however, had some additions later in date than Anne's reign) reduced the Roman Catholic part of the people to the lowest point of depression that can be conceived capable of coexisting with their being recognized as a portion of the community. Under its enactments they were neither eligible to be members of Parliament or of the municipal corporations: nor could they vote at elections to return

such members; in no official capacity under the Crown
were they employed; no profession, except the medical,
was open to them; they were not permitted to acquire
landed property for more than limited interests; and
upon its descent, if the heir or devisee did not conform to Protestantism, the inheritance was subdivided.
Neither clergy, nor schoolmasters of their religion, were
even tolerated.

Laws of this character were not peculiar to Ireland:
similar enactments proceeded at this time from the Parliament of England; and with less excuse, since whatever might be said respecting the danger to the Protestant Constitution as established at the Revolution,
which might result from giving Roman Catholics political power in the former country, where they were numerous, no such reason could be assigned in the latter,
where they were few. For the same reason, however,
the English penal legislation, while more unjustifiable,
was less oppressive than the Irish—the former affected
a sect, the latter four-fifths of the people.*

The injustice, and not less the impolicy, of the
Penal Code, the obstacles it interposed in the way of
social improvement, the interruption to the internal
peace of the community, and consequent peril of the
State caused by its intolerant distinctions of classes,

---

\* This was Archbishop Boulter's calculation of the proportion of Roman Catholics in 1731 (see his *Letters*, vol. ii. p. 57). Others, however, at that time thought the estimate should be higher, and there are authorities for a lower. Until a denominational census was taken in Ireland, statements as to the statistics of religious profession cannot be held to rest on a secure basis. The evidence bearing on the question, so far as the first half of the eighteenth century, is referred to by Lecky, *History*, vol. ii. p. 255.

are now universally admitted. It has not been with equal clearness perceived that in Ireland no interest, no institution, suffered more from its effects than Protestantism. So long as the provisions of its statutes continued in force, Roman Catholics were divided from the rest of their fellow-countrymen by a legislative barrier: it was intended that they should be as distinct as the Helots from the Spartans. In practice the intention was imperfectly fulfilled, but this was due not to the law, but to the instincts of human nature overcoming the law. Was it to be expected that those who suffered under such legislation should distinguish between its authors and their creed, or fail to regard both with distrust and resentment?

As the progress of Protestantism among the people was at this time obstructed by injudicious enactments, so also was the progress of the Church among Protestants by a similar cause. Its members were placed in a position of invidious elevation over Protestant Dissenters. One provision of the laws passed by the Irish Parliament under Anne imposed as a qualification for office or trust under the Crown the obligation of receiving on some Sunday the Sacrament of the Lord's Supper, according to the usage of the Church of Ireland. Thus, a Presbyterian, or other Protestant Nonconformist, whom conscientious scruples might hinder from participating in this rite, was excluded from official position.

The clause which introduced this obligation is said to have been inserted in England by the Council, when the Bill in which it appeared was, in conformity with a provision of the laws then in force, sent over for approval.* Whatever may have been its origin, subsequent efforts to repeal it failed, and it continued in operation until the next century.†

The completion of the Penal Code, and the Sacramental Test, were the measures of Anne's Irish Parliament which call for notice in connexion with ecclesiastical history. The Peers and Commoners who passed them were almost all of the Established Church; but it was not so much to advance its interest as to secure the ascendency of themselves and their descendants that their policy was designed. Nothing really for the advantage of the Church was done. The impropriations, the consequent poverty of many benefices, the frequent unions and pluralities, were left without any attempt to provide a remedy.

One benefit, not large in amount, but, from the use made of the revenue thus acquired, of much service to the Church, was conferred by the Queen herself. Under the existing law, the Crown continued to receive from the clergy the First Fruits and Twentieths, which, as has been mentioned, Henry VIII. and Elizabeth appropriated. ‡ Anne remitted the latter tax altogether, and granted the other to a Board of Trustees, to be applied by them in providing glebes for the incumbents of parishes, and in purchasing impropriations.§

The case of the Irish Church for relief in respect of these imposts was placed before the Queen and her ministers by Swift, who had some time before been

---

* Burnet, *Own Time*, vol. iv. p. 23.

† The Sacramental Test was not by law abolished for either England or Ireland until 1828.

‡ See as to Henry, p. 29, *supra*, as to Elizabeth, p. 58.

§ Anne's grant was confirmed by an Act of George the First.

promoted to a small benefice in Ireland in the patronage of the Crown. He represented the scarcity of glebes, and the number of impropriations which impoverished the parochial incumbents.... "Hardly one parish," he says, "has any glebes, and the rest very small and scattered, except a very few, which seldom have any houses. There are, in proportion, more impropriations in Ireland than in England; which, added to the poverty of the country, makes the livings of very small and uncertain value, so that five or six are often joined to make a revenue of £50 per annum; and these have seldom above one church in repair, the rest being destroyed by frequent wars and other causes. For want of glebes, the clergy are forced to take farms in their own or the neighbouring parishes, and to live at rack rents."*

A statement made on such an occasion must be regarded as an official communication, and may be taken to represent not inaccurately the state of the Irish Church at its date. The same cause which, before the Reformation, impoverished the clergy still existed—that from numerous parishes their revenues were withdrawn: as then for the monks, so now for the laymen who had been substituted as owners. Parliament left the distribution of Church revenues without change; and the law not being effective to oblige impropriators to make adequate provision for the parishes of which they were the lay rectors, several had to be united in one incumbent to make up a moderate income.†

---

* Memorial presented to Harley, Oct. 17th, 1710; Swift's *Works*, vol. x. p. 126.

† Swift, in the memorial to Harley, says the impropriations were more numerous in Ireland than in England; but the poverty of the

The same desire to serve the Established Church that led to the grant of the First Fruits and Twentieths induced the Queen and her ministers to revive the practice of summoning the Irish Convocation, which had, from the reign of Charles II., been discontinued. It met along with Parliament in 1703, 1705, 1709, 1711, and 1713.*

In 1703 the principal business transacted by Convocation related to the suggestion of means to be used for converting the natives. Notwithstanding that more than five centuries had elapsed since the English first acquired dominion over the Irish race, and although they had planted in the country numerous English-speaking colonies, the use of the Irish language among the portion of the people who were of Irish descent continued.† The Lower House of Convocation, considering that, except through the medium of written and oral communication with them in their own language, the conversion of the natives could not be accomplished, sent to

---

clergy seems to have been there just as great. Burnet says that "hundreds of cures have not of certain provision £20 a-year, and some thousands have not £50."—*Own Time*, vol. iv. p. 33.

\* Mant does not mention any meeting of Convocation in 1713; but see Dr. Reeves's Paper on Convocation in Ireland, referred to at p. 20 *supra*.

† The use of the Irish language is now confined to a few districts along the West Coast of Ireland. Its discontinuance elsewhere is, however, of comparatively recent date. The tenacity with which it was retained by the natives finds parallels in Wales and the Highlands, where also the people were Celts. It has an equally remarkable parallel in the case of the Galatians, to whom St. Paul addressed his Epistle. Originally a colony from Gaul to Asia Minor, the Galatians are found in the time of Jerome, six centuries after their emigration, to retain in the middle of a Greek population the Celtic language. (See Bishop Lightfoot's Introduction to his *Commentary on Galatians*, p. 12.)

the Upper House a resolution asserting the expediency of employing preachers in the Irish tongue, and requesting the bishops to take into consideration what number of preachers would be required, and how they were to be supported.* But the resolution was not then followed by any active measures.

In 1705 the Lower House was occupied with canons for the reformation and restoration of discipline; the subject, however, received no attention from the Bishops, and the proceedings of the Lower House became inoperative. " There has been a session," says Archbishop King, " without one clause for the good of the Church."†

In 1709 and 1711 the question of converting the natives was again before Convocation. On the former occasion the Upper House initiated the consideration of the subject, as a matter of concern to all Protestants and particularly to the clergy; and the Lower House passed resolutions directing the printing of Irish versions of the Bible, and of the English liturgy, and the use of services and the employment of preachers in the Irish tongue.†

In 1711, besides entering on the subject of the conversion of the natives, Convocation, having received the royal licence, framed some canons; also it approved of forms of prayer for prisoners and debtors, which were afterwards printed in Irish editions of the Prayer Book.

In 1705 an attempt was made by the Lower House of Convocation to regain the power of taxing the clergy,

---

\* See Archbishop King's letter to the Bishop of Cloyne, 26th June, 1705; and also his letter to the Archbishop of Tuam, 17th April, 1705, cited by Mant, *History*, vol. ii. pp. 177 and 178.

† See Richardson's *History of Attempts to Convert the Natives of Ireland*, published in London, 1712; and Mant's *History*, vol. ii. p. 217.

and an address to the House of Commons in relation to the subject was prepared; but their proceedings were treated by that House as a contempt, and their actuary committed to the custody of the sergeant-at-arms.* In the end the claim seems to have been relinquished. No subsidy was voted by any Convocation in Anne's reign.

From the death of Anne until the disestablishment of the Irish Church (1869) the Irish Convocation was never convened by the Crown; and, not being summoned or licensed to meet, it could not during this period legally assemble. Its discontinuance was said to have been at first owing to fear of the Jacobite tendencies of the clergy; afterwards, from other political motives.†

It appears to have been thought at this time that, although Convocation was engaged at its meetings in considering the question of converting the natives, there was much less zeal for the requisite proceedings than was professed. "I do not find," writes Archbishop King, "that it is desired by all that the natives should be converted." ‡ It was thought by some that if they were they would be too powerful; by others, that any attempts towards their conversion might be followed by social disturbances. Also it was still considered impolitic to disseminate publications in the Irish language, as tending

---

* See Dr. Reeves's Paper on Convocation, already cited.

† After 1717 the English Convocation, although it continued to be summoned, did not receive a licence to proceed to business. Hence Pope's line, "The Convocation gaped, but could not speak." It now receives, and for some years previously has received, the requisite licence, and is permitted to debate the most important questions.

‡ In his letter to Swift, cited by Mant, *History*, vol. ii. p. 230; also another to Swift, dated Sept. 1, 1711, published in Swift's *Works*.

to encourage its use, and thus to keep alive a marked distinction between the natives and other portions of the people.*

Notwithstanding that at this period, and on these various grounds, a powerful opposition existed among persons of influence to any organized plan for effecting the conversion of the natives to Protestantism, considerable exertions were made to spread its principles among them. Irish versions which had been completed of the New Testament in 1603, and of the Old Testament in 1685,† were reprinted and circulated—also the English Prayer Book, with the Church Catechism and an Exposition of it, all in Irish, as recommended by Convocation, were published. To meet the necessary expenses, subscriptions in Ireland, and aid from the English "Society for Promoting Christian Knowledge" were obtained. In various districts where Irish was spoken, some of the clergy preached in that language. And, with a view to train up candidates for the ministry to speak the Irish tongue, its study was encouraged in Trinity College.

---

\* In 1767, objections were made to the publication of the Bible in Erse or Gaelic, similar to those urged against its publication in Irish. These were answered at that time in a very able letter from Dr. Johnson. "I did not," he says, " expect to hear that it could be, in an assembly convened for the propagation of Christian knowledge, a question whether any nation, uninstructed in religion, should receive instruction; or whether that instruction should be imparted to them by a translation of the holy books into their own language. If obedience to the will of God be necessary to happiness, and knowledge of His will be necessary to obedience, I know not how he that withholds this knowledge or delays it can be said to love his neighbour as himself."—Croker's *Boswell*, vol. ii. p. 29.

† See Appendix, Note T.

The success, however, resulting from these proceedings was small.*

Between the Revolution and the death of Anne there were many vacancies in bishoprics. The greater number of these occurred before her accession, and were filled by William and Mary, or by William. In 1702, the Primacy became vacant by the death of Boyle, of whom mention has been made in the preceding chapter. It was conferred upon Narcissus Marsh, Archbishop of Dublin. On his death in 1713, Thomas Lindsay was translated from the See of Raphoe to Armagh. Upon the promotion of Marsh, Bishop King, then of Derry, was promoted to Dublin.

Both at Dublin and Armagh Marsh was deservedly esteemed. Of Lindsay there is little to be said. His promotion is reported to have been advocated by Swift, who had, in the last years of Queen Anne's reign, much influence with her then ministers, Harley and Bolingbroke, and was their guide as to Irish affairs. Lindsay was reputed to be of weak character, and not suited to be placed at the head of affairs. He has, however, the merit of munificence to the Church. To him the choir at Armagh Cathedral was indebted for a liberal endowment.

Archbishop King had in his own day no superior in the Irish Church, either as a Bishop or as a theological author. His writings will be subsequently considered. His conduct in the dioceses which were successively

---

* See, as to exertions to convert the natives, Richardson's *History* already referred to, and Mant, *History*, vol. ii. p. 218–230.

† See as to Lindsay, Mant, *History*, vol. ii. p. 408.

under his rule may be now referred to. When he went to Derry, he found the country in great disorder. It had suffered much during the civil war. Tillage had been then neglected, the live-stock destroyed, the buildings dilapidated. Hence, the farmers and peasants were impoverished. Along with the social, the ecclesiastical condition of the diocese decayed; many of the clergy fled; those who remained were poor; most of the churches and glebe-houses (the latter at that time few in number) were out of repair. These evils were met by corresponding exertions on the part of the Bishop —with such success that, upon his translation to Dublin, he transmitted to his successor a diocese, which might favourably compare with any other in Ireland.

As Archbishop of Dublin, King displayed similar energy and zeal. Swift, a severe judge of character, describes him, a few years after his translation to the office, as spending his time in acts of hospitality and charity, in building churches, repairing his palace, and in introducing and preferring the most worthy persons he could find, without other regards: "in short, in the practice of all virtues that could become a public or private life."*

It was in Anne's reign that Swift received the office with which his name is principally associated. In 1713 he was nominated Dean of St. Patrick's Ca-

---

\* This character of Archbishop King appeared in the first edition (1708), of Swift's *Letter from a Member of the House of Commons of Ireland*. In Faulkner's edition of his works (Dublin, 1739), the letter is published without this portion relating to King: the preface says, "some passages are omitted, which relate to certain persons, and are of no consequence to the argument."

thedral, Dublin. After his installation he returned to London. On the Queen's death in the next year he came back to Dublin, and, with some occasional absence, resided in Ireland during the remainder of his life, devoting himself with extraordinary energy to advance the interest of the country in which his lot was cast.

The vacancy which enabled the appointment of Swift was caused by the promotion of Stearne, the previous Dean, to a bishopric. This prelate is described as diligent in the discharge of his duties, personally pious, and singularly generous and charitable: if only the qualities of character suited to his office be considered, none of his contemporaries deserved more esteem.

While, however, Marsh, King, Stearne, and some other of the episcopal bench would have reflected honour upon any period of ecclesiastical history, many of their brethren exhibit an unfavourable contrast. They were reproached with habitual neglect of duty, and said to be constantly absent from their dioceses. In 1714, in the province of Armagh, which then comprised more than a third of the Irish bishoprics, and these, from the number of Protestants in them, perhaps the most important, there were, according to Archbishop King, but two bishops resident, and for several years previously there had been but one.* In some degree this absence of the bishops from their dioceses was caused by attendance upon the House of Lords whenever Parliament sat. It existed most among the bishops transferred from the English Church, who, leaving a higher degree of civilization,

---

\* King to Annesley: *Letter*, July 3, 1714. Cited by Mant, *History*, vol. ii. p. 156.

were seldom reconciled to the state of society with which they came in contact in such parts of the country as were remote from Dublin.

Before the close of this reign the Penal Code had begun to operate upon the social condition of the people.* At the same time, from another cause, there occurred a great change in the ownership of landed property, which completed the depression of the Roman Catholic portion. The estates of the proprietors who followed James had been confiscated by William, and conferred upon the Generals of his army and his personal friends. But the English Parliament annulled his grants, assumed the right to dispose of the forfeited lands, and vested them in trustees, in order that they might be sold. Roman Catholics were disabled from purchasing, and thus all this vast extent of territory came to be assigned exclusively to Protestants.

The result of the policy of this period was the establishment in every department of a Protestant ascendency. The Roman Catholics were as numerous as ever, but they were dispirited and without leaders. Deprived of the power to acquire landed property, and not allowed to rise in the service of the State, they turned to the pursuits of trade and commerce. Many in this manner became rich; the rest, especially those concerned with land, did not, until about sixty years later, regain social power or influence.

---

* As early as 1708 Swift looked upon the Roman Catholic interest as inconsiderable. "Their lands (he says) are almost entirely taken from them, and they are rendered incapable of purchasing any more; and for the little that remains, provision is made by the late Act that it will daily crumble away."—*Works*, vol. iii. p. 146.

# CHAPTER XII.

[1714–1760.]

DURING the reigns of the first two kings of the House of Hanover there was not any relaxation of the penal laws. The social system in Ireland retained without alteration the form which it had assumed under William and Anne. None of the legislation of that time can be said to have operated upon the course of ecclesiastical affairs. Protestantism made few converts; and the relative numerical proportions between its denominations continued much as they had previously been. There is, therefore, for a considerable period little in the external history of the Church to detain attention, and its internal state, the sentiments and ideas which influenced its members, and the general condition of society as regards religion, may now properly be brought under examination.

At the commencement of the eighteenth century, both in England and Ireland, the effects of the reaction from Puritanism which accompanied the Restoration were still felt. The licentiousness of manners which prevailed under Charles II. had indeed in some degree passed away, and virtue and morality, then the subject of ridicule, began to be again treated with respect.

But still a sceptical spirit, which had arisen about that time, continued prevalent; and literature and the conversation of the educated classes were largely imbued with irreverence for sacred subjects, and with loose and unsettled notions as to the authority of revealed religion, which took the name of free thinking.

With not a few persons, opinions of this character reached to a profession of even absolute infidelity. So late as 1736, the great author of the "Analogy" stated that many took for granted that Christianity was at length discovered to be fictitious, and assumed this to be an agreed point among people of discernment.* These were, however, the smaller part of those who sympathised with Scepticism. In the case of most of those who did so the authority of Christianity was impaired, but not wholly annulled: they did not altogether deny, but they ceased to be impressed with, the sanctions claimed for its precepts; and the influence of religion over them was weakened, not destroyed.

Under such circumstances there was, as might be expected, little external demonstration of respect for the Church among the laity, either in England or Ireland, and small attendance upon its observances and services. In no neighbouring state or country, according to Addison,† was there less appearance of religion than in the former kingdom. In the latter, the genera-

---

* Advertisement prefixed to the first edition of the "Analogy" (1736). Compare Berkeley's *Discourse addressed to Magistrates and Men in Authority, occasioned by the enormous Licence and Irreligion of the Times*: published in Dublin, 1735. In this he mentions a society in Dublin for the purpose of " studied, deliberate indignities against the Divine Majesty."

† *Freeholder*, No. 37, A. D. 1715.

lity of men (it was said) cast an ill aspect upon the Church and upon Churchmen.*

If we regard society, irrespective of its religious character, and merely with reference to its general standard of opinion, a judgment equally unfavourable must be pronounced. An age of Unbelief is always an age of low aims and objects. The attraction upwards, derived from looking to the divine superintendence and a future state of reward and punishment, is withdrawn: the faith which exalts human nature above human frailty ceases to operate.† Motives of interest, the calculations of selfishness, take the place of higher impulses. Accordingly, the history of the period records nothing dignified or ennobling. Manners were unrefined; mental cultivation was restricted to a few; conversation was coarse and indelicate.‡ External decorum, not virtue, was the utmost that the most rigid censor required. In every class excessive indulgence in drink prevailed. In Ireland the habits of the gentry were convivial to an excess, and were attended very frequently by expense out of proportion to their means of supporting it.

---

\* So Archbishop King says in a letter to Bishop Foy. In the same letter he adds :—" The faith of religion is very weak amongst all, and the sense of it almost lost," and complains " how diligent some persons of great quality are to propagate irreligion."—Mant. *History*, vol. ii. p. 95.

† Bacon supports this line of observation by an illustration from animal nature: . . . " Take (he says) an example of a dog, and mark what a generosity and courage he will put on when he finds himself maintained by a man, who to him is instead of a God, or *melior natura*— which courage is manifestly such as that creature, without that confidence of a better nature than his own, could never attain."—*Essay on Atheism*.

‡ Swift, about 1720, speaks of the corruption of morals among the English people.—*Letter to a Young Clergyman*. *Works*, vol. ii. p. 308.

Although the clergy of the English and Irish Established Churches must be exonerated from the allegation of having adopted sceptical opinions, and from charges of vice or positive misconduct, it cannot be said that they were exempt from the influences of the time. They were superior, but generally little superior, to the laity. The greater number had an inadequate appreciation of the charge entrusted to them; they were negligent in the discharge of professional duties, and without zeal or fervour. They compared, it was then thought, unfavourably in these respects with the clergy of other countries: were more remiss in their labours, and less severe in their lives.\* Their sermons seldom rose above commonplaces upon morals.

In the case of the Irish clergy, some circumstances peculiar to their position operated injuriously. Much the larger proportion of them lived surrounded by a population that rejected their ministry; they had consequently no spiritual work to perform beyond reading prayers and preaching to the few Protestants who attended church upon Sunday. The discipline of character, which is supplied by visiting, instructing the young, consoling sickness and suffering, was wholly wanting. The incumbents of the parishes where, as was generally the case, the inhabitants were almost all Roman Catholics, were simply country gentlemen of moderate or humble fortune.

A judicious exercise of patronage might have done

---

\* This is the judgment of Burnet as to the English (*Own Time*, vol. iv. p. 344). He also says: "The main body of our clergy has always appeared dead and lifeless to me; and instead of animating one another, they seem rather to lay one another asleep."—p. 342.

something to counteract these disadvantages; it might, at least, have supplied a stimulus to study and mental cultivation. But the patronage of the day was administered from very different motives. The bishops (all appointed by the Crown) were chosen, in most instances, with a view to political services already rendered by themselves or those who recommended them, and with the expectation that they should attend in the House of Lords and vote for the measures of the King's ministers, whoever they might be. The general character of prelates so chosen could not be other than secular, and from them a secularism of ideas and habits spread to those who looked up to their example, and depended upon them for promotion.

While, however, for most of the Irish clergy, the standard of duty and intellectual attainment was low, noble examples to the contrary were to be found among them—men blameless in their lives, and diligent in their calling. There were also some of high distinction in literature, whose works deserve to be classed among the ablest contributions to the theological and philosophical controversies of the period.

These controversies, so far as they related to religion, referred to subjects different from those which previously engaged attention. Doctrinal tenets or modes of Church government were no longer debated; it was the existence of Christianity that was in peril. And, accordingly, with this as the paramount question, the discussions of the period were concerned, either directly: as, for instance, when the truth and authority of the Scriptures were examined: or indirectly, as when the relations which they reveal between the Supreme Being and His creatures were considered, and the moral government of the world was vindicated.

Among the Irish writers who took part in these discussions, Archbishop King (whose administrative ability and excellence of character there has been already occasion to mention) is entitled to a pre-eminent place. His treatise *On the Origin of Evil*, and his *Discourse on Predestination*, are characterized by thought and reasoning of a high order. They are still always referred to when the topics of which they treat come under examination.

The treatise *On the Origin of Evil* was the first of these publications. It was composed in Latin, and translated into English by Edmund Law, afterwards Bishop of Carlisle. The explanations offered in this work of the difficulties it proposes to solve have been censured, upon the ground that they contain speculative propositions not sufficiently restrained by a sense of our finite capacity and limited knowledge. But of what other attempts to reconcile the mystery of the existence of evil with the omnipotence of a Supreme Being of infinite goodness may not the same be said? Here, if anywhere (to use an expression of Hooker), our safest eloquence is our silence.

The sermon on Predestination is wholly free from the faults attributed to the essay. Indeed, so admirable is its moderation of idea and expression, and so judicious are its observations upon the limits of our powers, that, as has been remarked by the very distinguished prelate* who in our own time republished and edited the sermon,

---

* Archbishop Whately. The sermon, with comments upon it, is now published along with Whately's other works.

it might justly have borne the title of a "Rule for interpreting rightly the Scripture accounts of God." Accordingly, there is no attempt to explain the foreknowledge of contingent events, or by reasoning to reconcile free-will with prescience; the argument aims merely at demonstrating that what seems to us contradictory may have that appearance, not because of anything in its own nature, but because of the imperfection of our faculties and our consequent ignorance.*

Contemporary with King was Peter Browne, Bishop of Cork (1710-1735). He had been Provost of Trinity College, and to him it was due that the pursuit of mental philosophy was especially encouraged in this institution, and that the writings of Locke, although then condemned at Oxford, were recommended for study. Browne's merits as a writer on metaphysical subjects have been always recognized;† he was also a mathematician, and learned in theological studies. He appears to have been extremely effective in the pulpit. It is recorded that having preached before Queen Anne upon the text, "Never man spake like this man," he received

---

* It is perhaps right to note that another Irish prelate (Bramhall), in a work of earlier date than King's, had sought to explain these difficulties. "The readiest way (he says) to reconcile contingence and liberty with the decrees and prescience of God is to subject future contingents to the aspect of God, according to that presentiality which they have in eternity.... The knowledge of God comprehends all times in a point"— a view not improbably suggested by the great mediæval theologian, Aquinas, who terms eternity *Nunc Stans*, "an ever-abiding now." See Works of Bramhall in *Lib. Anglo-Cath. Theol.* vol. iv. pp. 153-190.

† Professor Webb terms Browne "the most original and independent of the followers of Locke" (*Isis*, p. 3). Dugald Stewart (*Works*, iii. 38, 9), shows that Browne, on some important points, anticipated Hume and Reid.

from her the praise that the text might justly be applied to himself.* There are preserved pamphlets and a sermon published by Browne in condemnation of drinking to the memory of the dead. These were suggested by a practice then commencing, and not yet altogether discontinued, of giving as a toast, "the glorious, pious, and immortal memory of King William III." Such toasts he considers profane, and not free from disrespect to the sacrament of the Lord's Supper.

The writings of Bishop Browne of most importance are entitled, *The Procedure, Extent, and Limits of the Human Understanding*, published in 1728, and *Things Divine and Supernatural conceived by Analogy with Things Natural and Human*, published in 1733.† In the first he builds on the foundation laid by Locke. Of all our knowledge, both human and divine, he holds that the senses furnish the groundwork. The mind is at first a *tabula rasa;* according to the dogma of the schoolmen, *nihil est in intellectu quod non prius in sensu.* The second aims at establishing that when we proceed from the faculties, properties, and operations of our own spirit to the divine and supernatural, we must use merely analogies and resemblances.

Another contemporary of King was Berkeley, Bishop of Cloyne (1734–1753), than whom there was no one

---

\* Campbell's *Philosophical Survey*, p. 421. After Browne's death two volumes of his sermons were published. (London, 1749.) When Bishop, he diligently promoted the welfare of his diocese. Mant, *Hist.*, vol. ii. p. 194.

† Butler's *Analogy of Religion, Natural and Revealed, to the Constitution and Course of Nature* was of later date than Browne's treatise. But except in the use of the word "Analogy" on the title-page, there is no resemblance between them.

in his own age the object of more affectionate admiration. This popularity was due partly to the brilliant theories suggested by a genius singularly subtle and original, and partly to the charm of a character shadowed by few imperfections. His excellence has been described by Atterbury—an acute observer, little disposed to unmerited panegyric—in a few pregnant words that need no addition : . . . "So much understanding, so much innocence, such humility, I did not think had been the portion of any but angels, until I saw this gentleman."

Berkeley had been a Fellow of Trinity College, Dublin, and was thence promoted to the Deanery of Derry. This office, which was the most lucrative Church preferment (not episcopal) in Ireland, he proposed to resign, and with three of the Fellows of Trinity College, whom he induced to join him, to proceed to Bermuda, and there to found an educational establishment, which should form a centre of civilization for the American savage tribes. He allotted to himself as its President an income of £100 a-year, and to each of the disinterested persons who were to accompany him £40 a-year. The resignation was not accepted by the Crown, but the project was entered upon, and for some years was in operation. It was then abandoned in consequence of the persistent refusal of Walpole to support it. Justly did Swift say of Berkeley, "he is an absolute philosopher with regard to titles, wealth, and power"; * still more justly might he have described him as something higher and better ; for when did philosophy ever prompt to such sacrifices ?

Berkeley ranks at the head of metaphysical writers in

---

* Letter of Swift to Lord Carteret, Sept. 4, 1724. *Works*, xi. 249.

the interval between Locke and the Scotch School. In 1709 he published his *Essay towards a new Theory of Vision*, in which he put forward the doctrine—until lately generally accepted, and still maintained by high authority—that the eye conveys only sensations of colour, and that the perceptions of distance, magnitude, form, are acquired as the result of experience, by substituting impressions really derived from the touch.*

The *Theory of Vision* was followed by the *Principles of Human Knowledge*, unfolding his ideal theory. The world, which seems to be external, exists only in mind; in his own words, "all the choir of heaven and furniture of earth, all those bodies which compose the mighty frame of the world, have not any substance without a mind." There is nothing actual but spirit: the Divine Spirit, and the finite spirits created by the Divine. Of these speculations it is no exaggeration to say, that without themselves producing conviction, they have exercised a profound influence over the course of modern thought, not only in Great Britain, but in Germany and France.†

In 1732, Berkeley published an elaborate answer to the then popular objections to revealed religion. It was

---

* A treatise entitled *Sight and Touch* (London, 1864), by Mr. Abbott, one of the Fellows of Trinity College, Dublin, contains an elaborate argument against Berkeley's theory. At the same time he admits that it was generally accepted. Professor Webb, in his *Isis*, and Mr. Mahaffy, in his introduction to a *Translation of Kuno Fischer's Kant*, take the same side. Mill, Hamilton, Professor Fraser (the recent editor of Berkeley's works), support Berkeley.

† The Idealism of Berkeley has been recently discussed, and the various modifying or opposing theories enunciated in reference to the subject traced in a series of Essays by Professor Webb, with an acuteness not unworthy of Berkeley himself.—*Isis*, Dublin, 1885.

entitled *Alciphron, or the Minute Philosopher*,* and consists of seven dialogues, in which a debate is maintained between two advocates of Free Thinking (one representing the notions of intellectual sceptics, and the other those current in fashionable society), and two defenders of the truth of Christianity. In the discussion thus conducted, the whole domain of thought and knowledge, such as it was at that day, and so far as it bore upon the subjects treated, is traversed with extraordinary ingenuity and learning.

In zeal to promote Irish interests, Berkeley ranks with Swift; but his patriotism extended farther. Swift thought only of the Anglo-Irish; Berkeley of the whole people. So far as appears, he is the first who asked the question, whether a scheme for the welfare of the nation should not take in the whole inhabitants.† Nor is this the only matter as to which he was before his age. In the remarkable publication, where he suggested the ideas as to Ireland which have been mentioned, he, through the medium of questions—a mode of instruction probably suggested by what he had read in his favourite Plato concerning Socrates—developed his views on other subjects also, and made many admirable suggestions, then novel, and little encouraged, designed to promote social and political reforms.

---

\* The name "Minute Philosopher" seems to be derived from a passage in the *de Senectute*, which Berkeley prefixed as a motto. In this, Cicero, having expressed how, if to believe in the immortality of the soul were an error, he preferred to err, adds, sin mortuus (ut quidam *minuti* philosophi censent) nihil sentiam : non vereor, ne hunc errorem meum mortui philosophi irrideant.

† See *Querist* (published by Berkeley in 1735), query No. 255. There are several other interrogatories to a like effect.

Prior to Berkeley's *Alciphron* had appeared a defence of Christianity against the Free Thinkers by Abbadie, Dean of Killaloe (1699–1727). As Berkeley is in some respects the forerunner of Butler and the *Analogy*, so is Abbadie of Paley and the *Evidences*. Unfortunately for his fame in this country, Abbadie's work is in the French language. In a compressed form it touches upon most of the evidential proofs, more fully expanded by subsequent writers—the need of a revelation, exhibited in the corruption of natural religion by Paganism; the superiority of the Judaic views of the Supreme Being over all before known; the succession and relation of Christianity to Judaism; the testimony to its divine origin afforded by prophecy, by the miracles, life, death, and resurrection of its Founder, and by the majestic purity and self-denial of its teaching. He anticipates later writers in observing that the first missionaries of Christianity were martyrs for the assertion, not of opinions, respecting which they might be mistaken, but of facts.\*

William III. desired to confer upon Abbadie the Deanery of the Cathedral of St. Patrick, Dublin, but his defective knowledge of English prevented the King's wishes being carried out. The objection was waived as to Killaloe, a remote place, where there were few

---

\* The title of Abbadie's work is *Traité de la Verité de la Religion Chretienne*. It first appeared at Rotterdam, in 1684. It obtained from Mr. Pitt the praise of being the best book upon the subject that he had read. (See Lord Stanhope's *Life of Pitt*, vol iv. p. 84.) It is interesting to note Pitt's opinion, now that evidential proof has fallen into disesteem; and to compare with it another declaration made by him to Wilberforce, in which he stated that (as often happens with apologetical defences) Butler's *Analogy* had raised more doubts in his mind than it answered.—*Life of Wilberforce*, by his Sons, vol. i. p. 95.

Protestants. Abbadie was Swiss by birth, and had been minister in a French Church in the Savoy, before he became connected with the Irish Church.

A controversy, which cannot be considered to have yet terminated,* arose out of some statements in the writings of King, Browne, and Berkeley, which we have been considering. In the sermon on Predestination of the first were observations to the effect that we cannot draw inferences as to moral attributes—such as justice, mercy, love—in a Supreme Being from what we know of them in ourselves, any more than we can of his power from what we can do: and that as regards their nature, what he termed an analogical knowledge is all that we are capable of in our present state. Berkeley in his *Alciphron* expresses the opinion that such qualities may, by the finite nature, be attributed proportionally to the infinite; and that we may affirm that all sorts of perfection which we can conceive in a finite spirit are in God, without any of the alloy which is to be found in his creatures.† Browne, in his treatise *On Things Divine and Supernatural conceived by Analogy with Things Natural and Human*, answered Berkeley, and maintained that the divine moral attributes differ from human, not merely in degree, but in kind,‡ and that there is only a similitude or correspondency between natural or human knowledge and moral qualities, and a divine supernatural knowledge and attributes.

---

\* See the note on the "right of the moral faculty to judge of the Divine attributes," appended to the *Sermons on the Efficacy of Prayer*, by Dr. Jellett, the present Provost of Trinity College, Dublin.

† *Alciphron*, Dial. iv. s. 21.

‡ See page 263 of Browne's book, ed. 1733. Browne's comments

An examination of the state of the Irish Church, during the period which we are now considering, would be imperfect without reference to the division of both clergy and laity into parties representing, one the English, and the other the Irish interest, which, commencing some years before, had now widened and increased. During the reigns of William and Anne, if these interests were opposed, the English triumphed; in particular, the trading and commercial regulations between the two countries were then based upon the supposition that only England was to be regarded. For the great offices of Church and State, until the next century, Englishmen were preferred, not merely before the Irish, but before the English colonists in Ireland. General discontent prevailed, and with none more than the clergy, who saw the great prizes of their profession taken from them, and numbers of parochial benefices, even when in Episcopal patronage, conferred upon such relatives and friends of the Englishmen who obtained Irish bishoprics as accompanied or followed them from their own country.

This peculiar conjunction of affairs called into action the commanding abilities of Swift. His motives may not have been free from a mixture of disappointed ambition

---

on Berkeley exhibit little of the calmness to be expected from a philosopher. Their contemporary, Skelton, author of *Deism Revealed*, addressed a *Letter to the authors of the Minute Philosopher and of the Divine Analogy*, in which he sought to reconcile them, and to which he prefixed the motto:—

"Ne tanta animis assuescite bella,
Neu patriæ validas in viscera vertite vires."

Skelton was Rector of Templecarne, in the diocese of Clogher, and added to his attainments as a theologian the merit of being a most admirable parish clergyman.

and animosity towards the political party, then in the
ascendant; but, unquestionably, his paramount object was
to advance the measures which he thought would serve his
native country. To promote its interests he dedicated
his whole time and energy, a capacity for command,
and a sagacity to discern, which have never been rivalled. No man without official station has exercised
equal political authority. Until his mind decayed he
maintained an undisputed ascendency over the Irish
people. After his death the influence of his policy still
survived; and it can be distinctly traced in the tone
of public opinion during the rest of the eighteenth century, and in the legislative measures then passed.

Swift's great powers were developed least in his profession. Neither by study nor inclination was he suited to
it; and he is said to have observed, that when he desired
to prepare a sermon he produced a pamphlet. Such
of his writings as were connected with the Church or
religious subjects are, however, not without interest,
and deserve notice.

Of these writings, one of the most remarkable is a tract
designed to mediate between the extreme parties which
divided the Church of England, entitled "The Sentiments of a Church-of-England-Man with respect to Religion and Government." In this Swift expressed opinions
upon the question of Episcopacy which may properly be
added to those of other eminent persons who have been
cited in the course of the present treatise in connexion
with the subject.* . . . "A Church-of-England-Man (he
observes) hath a true veneration for the scheme estab-

---

* *Supra*, pp. 108, 111, 131, 145.

lished among us of ecclesiastical government; and although he will not determine whether Episcopacy be of divine right, he is sure it is most agreeable to primitive institution: fittest of all others for preserving order and purity, and under its present regulation best calculated for our civil state. He should, therefore, think the abolishment of that order among us would prove a mighty scandal, a corruption to our faith, and manifestly dangerous to our monarchy: nay, he would defend it by arms against all the powers on earth, except our own legislature: in which case he would submit as to a general calamity, a dearth, or a pestilence."

Swift's sermons—as from his character we may anticipate—do not rise above good sense and practical observations. One preached upon the Doctrine of "the Trinity," and another "On the Difficulty of Knowing One's Self," well merit attention. The opening of a discourse against sleeping in church will illustrate the sarcastic spirit which accompanied him even into the pulpit. Having read the passage in the Acts of the Apostles which records how Eutychus, while listening to St. Paul preaching, fell from the window, he proceeds:—"I have chosen these words with desire, if possible, to disturb some part in this audience of half an hour's sleep, for the convenience and exercise whereof this place (St. Patrick's Cathedral) at this season of the day is very much celebrated.... The accident which happened to the young man in the text hath not been sufficient to discourage his successors; but because the preachers now in the world, however they may exceed St. Paul in the art of setting men to sleep, do extremely fall short of him in the working of miracles; therefore, men are become so cautious as to choose more safe and convenient stations and postures for taking their repose without hazard of their persons: and, upon the whole matter, choose rather to trust their destruction to a miracle than their safety."

When engaged in his celebrated controversy respecting Wood's copper coinage, Swift did not hesitate to preach a sermon upon the subject. Anticipating objections to such an use of the pulpit, he refers to the mischievous effects which he anticipates from the project, and observes that "it is time for the pastor to cry out that the wolf is getting into his flock, to warn them to stand together, and all to consult the common safety." The sermon accumulates the motives which ought to induce patriotism, or the love of one's country; alludes to the condition of affairs which at that juncture rendered the practice of this virtue highly necessary, and points out that every man's exertions may be of advantage; "for there are few people (he observes) so weak or mean who have not sometimes in their power to be useful to the public."

## CHAPTER XIII.

[1760–1800.]

THE reign of George III. began in 1760, and ended in 1820. When about forty years had elapsed, the Act of Union between Great Britain and Ireland was passed. This measure brought with it changes of great magnitude in the relations between the two countries, operating as well upon ecclesiastical as civil affairs. Its date will, therefore, form a convenient division in the narrative to be now entered upon, and attention may for the present be confined to the events which preceded it.

Some time before the death of George II. a religious spirit had begun to revive within the Church both in England and Ireland. Necessarily its progress was gradual; for at first it found a clergy to whom zeal and fervour were distasteful, and a laity apathetic and difficult to move. In both countries its development was principally among the humbler classes of society.

This revival of religious sentiment is now generally acknowledged to have been due principally to John Wesley, and a small number who associated themselves with him. They were all members of the Church of

England. Wesley himself was an episcopally ordained clergyman. His teaching was at first directed solely against irreligion; he sought to arouse the people from their almost universal neglect of sacred duties, and by the discipline of observances to confirm habits of personal piety. He made no objection to the doctrines or formularies of the Church of England; had no design of separating from it; and to the end of his life he adhered to this policy. In 1773, observing among his followers in Ulster a tendency to abandon their connexion with the Established Church, he preached against the project at Omagh, and, as he records in his *Journal*, " warned them of the madness which was spreading among them of leaving the Church."* And two years later, at Bath, he said: ... " I believe one reason why God is pleased to spare my life so long is to confirm them (the Methodists) in their present purpose not to separate from the Church."†

It is obvious that this course ensured for Methodism, (by which name Wesley's system was generally known), an acceptance and influence it could never otherwise have gained. Numbers who would have shrunk from the notion of following a Sect, and who, if Methodism had been announced as one, would never have inquired what it had to offer either as to doctrine or practice, were

---

\* Wesley's *Journal: Works*, vol. xvi. p. 106.

† Sermon cxv. *Works*, vol. xvi. p. 267. Shortly before his death, Wesley wrote in his *Journal*:—" I never had any design of separating from the Church. ... I live and die a member of the Church of England." (See as to Wesley's position towards the Church, and as to Wesleyanism generally, a lecture on the Wesleyans in Canon Curteis's *Bampton Lectures on Dissent in its relations to the Church*.)

brought in contact with its teaching. They were also, by the presence of its followers among themselves, compelled to observe that the rule of life and conduct prescribed by its discipline was more strict than had been usual. Thus attention to both the example and precept of its founders was forced upon the clergy and laity of the Established Churches.

Methodism had many preachers and adherents in England before it was introduced into Ireland. At first its missionaries, when they appeared there, excited surprise rather than hostility, and were listened to by the lower orders of all religious denominations. In a short time opposition arose. The Roman Catholic clergy withdrew their flocks. To the Presbyterians the Wesleyan form of Methodism, which was that presented to them, could not be acceptable, for it was entirely opposed to the standard of faith adopted by their Church upon the questions of Predestination and Election;* as it also was upon the subjects of Episcopacy and Episcopal Orders. Wesley's disciples in Ireland were therefore recruited from members of the Established Church, and as its clergy in general disapproved of his system, almost altogether from the laity. With them its progress was constant and steady; and at the time of the Union it was computed that Methodism numbered about 90,000 in connexion with its discipline, beside grown-up children and hearers of its preachers.†

---

\* A portion of the Methodists under Whitefield, held Calvinistic opinions. Wesley always opposed them. His sermon of Free Grace was expressed so strongly that it led to a breach with Whitefield. (See Southey's *Life of Wesley*, ch. xxv.)

† This is the calculation of Alexander Knox, who had been Lord

But the indirect effect of a religious movement very often exceeds the direct. While the clergy of every Church in Ireland rejected Methodism, they nevertheless felt its influence. It stimulated an emulative zeal. All awoke to the necessity of competing with their rivals at least by a diligent discharge of their professional duties.

Later than Methodism arose another party within the English Church. The name "Evangelical"* was subsequently given to its adherents. The first leaders of this party generally adopted Calvinistic tenets. In consequence of their ability in preaching and of their personal piety, they, after some time, acquired influence; much less extensive, however, than Wesley possessed. Their opinions after some time spread to Ireland, but until the next century they did not obtain more than a small number of converts.

Contemporaneously with these religious impulses, there was going forward a general improvement in the modes of thought, and in the manners prevailing in society. The standard of opinion at the end of the eighteenth century, both in England and Ireland, was

---

Castlereagh's secretary before the Union, and who being in great intimacy with Wesley, and after his death with his followers in Ireland, had peculiar opportunities for investigating the subject. (See letter of Knox to Lord Castlereagh, Feb. 19, 1801, in the *Castlereagh Correspondence*, vol. iv. p. 55.)

* The names "Methodist," "Evangelical," were given by the adversaries of the systems they denominate, and derisively. So "Quaker," and many other designations applied to sects, had a similar origin. Nay, the word "Christian," seems, according to the better opinion, to have come first at Antioch not from disciples, but enemies of the religion it described.

higher than it had been at the beginning. The means of education were, at least for the middle class, more adequate, and it was more widely diffused. Increased refinement of sentiment, respect for virtue, and decorum of conduct, were generally to be found.

In the English and Irish Established Churches, as the clergy were taken from the middle class, and for the most part received their education in the same schools and colleges as laymen, they shared with them in the vicissitudes of social progress. Hence, the advance of society co-operated with the other influences which, as has been pointed out, beneficially affected the clerical order at this time. A decided improvement in their ideas and habits took place.

In the instance of the Irish clergy, this improvement was more in the younger than the older; in the parochial incumbents rather than the higher dignitaries. Upon the latter, especially the Bench of Bishops, the mode in which the patronage of the Crown was exercised operated detrimentally. From the accession of George III. (1760) until the Union (1800), just as had been the case under the two preceding kings,* political motives guided the selection for ecclesiastical appointments. The ministers, on whose recommendations from time to time they were made, seem seldom to have looked beyond support already received, or to be secured for the future.

Two Prelates of the eighteenth century strikingly illustrate the effect of such a system of promotion. One of these, George Stone, held the Archbishopric of

---

* See p. 181, *supra*.

Armagh, the highest office in the Irish Church, for eighteen years (1747–1765); the other, Frederick Augustus Hervey, Earl of Bristol, Bishop of Derry, was in possession of the most richly endowed bishopric in Ireland for thirty-five years (1768–1803).

Stone, when appointed to the Primacy, was about forty years of age; yet he had already filled three bishoprics in succession—Ferns and Leighlin, Kildare, and Derry. Of a handsome person, agreeable manners, considerable conversational powers, with industry and ability for business, he was chosen in order that he might assist the Government in the House of Lords, and generally in the conduct of affairs. How he first became connected with the Irish Church (for by birth and education he was an Englishman) does not appear; nor is it certain to what interest he owed his appointment, in 1732, to the Deanery of Ferns, the first valuable preferment which he received. His brother, Andrew Stone, was in favour with Frederick Prince of Wales, and it has been suggested that by his influence the Primate's advancement was aided. But whatever support he may have obtained in this way, there is no doubt that it would have availed little without the qualities which enabled him to take advantage of any opportunity that opened. Ambitious, energetic, devoting his whole attention to public affairs, he was precisely the person of whom the Irish Government stood in need, and whom, therefore, they preferred to every competitor. Nor, when he gained power, did he disappoint the expectations of those who selected him. In the counsels of successive Irish administrations, in Parliament, with the Protestant public, he soon won, and afterwards during his life retained, an ascendency which only one man (Boyle, at first Speaker of the House of Commons, and afterwards Earl of Shannon) attempted to rival. Professional merit he neither had nor desired to be supposed to have. "Look on me," he is reported to have said to the English physicians whom he consulted when his health gave way, "not as an ordinary clergyman, or as subject to the diseases of the clerical profession, but as a man who has injured his constitution by sitting up late and rising early to do the business of Government."*

The Earl of Bristol was as ill-qualified for his office as Stone. His manners, his ideas, his pursuits, were wholly foreign from the clerical profession. The family of which he was the head was noted for eccentricity; and it used to be said that all the eccentricity of the race was concentrated in him. Possessing, in addition to the large revenues of his bishopric, an ample private fortune, of high rank as a spiritual, and higher as a lay Peer, he was discontented unless he could also acquire popularity and political power. Accordingly, he resolved to convert all the advantages of his station and wealth into means toward this end. When the Convention of Volunteers assembled with the object of assisting the national party in Parliament—then demanding reform in the parliamentary representation—the Bishop caused

---

* Stone and Lord Shannon died within nine days of each other. They were both at the time Lords Justices. (See Hardy's *Life of Charlemont*, vol. i. p. 201.) Not denying that Stone had in some respects far juster views than his contemporaries, Hardy says, "his own aggrandizement predominated over every other consideration." The anecdote of his conversation with his physicians is told in Campbell's *Survey of the South of Ireland* (London: 1778), p. 55.

himself to be returned from Derry as a delegate to attend it; and, surrounded by a troop of light cavalry, raised at his own expense by his nephew, the unfortunate George Robert Fitzgerald,* proceeded to Dublin. Thus surrounded, this singular representative of Irish prelacy was received along the road everywhere with military honours. Upon his arrival he was met by a troop of Volunteers, with whom, in addition to his own escort, he went in state through the city, until he reached the place where the Convention was assembled. In that body he then took his seat, and was for some time among its most prominent leaders. He afterwards went abroad, and spent the last years of his life in Italy.†

If the character of other Irish bishops selected, like Stone and Lord Bristol, from inducements of a political nature, is examined, it will be found that worldliness altogether predominated. Their ideas and habits were not such as became ecclesiastics. Of some in Swift's time, if his representations were to be followed implicitly, still stronger censure ought to be expressed; but descriptions of his contemporaries, whether lay or clerical, by this great satirist, must be read with caution; he is seldom fair in speaking of his political opponents, or of those patronised by them.‡ The

---

\* George Robert Fitzgerald, a noted duellist, was executed for murder at Castlebar in 1786.

† See as to Lord Bristol, Hardy's *Life of Charlemont*, vol. ii. p. 102; Sir Jonah Barrington's *Rise and Fall of the Irish Nation*; Mant, *History*, vol. ii. pp. 688–696. A writer in the *Quarterly Review* (vol. lxxxii. p. 514), in a review of Mr. Croker's edition of Lord Hervey's *Memoirs*, alludes to the bishop as "the celebrated 'Comte-Evêque' of the Continent"—*notus nimis omnibus*, eccentric there as well as at home.

‡ The sarcasm attributed to Swift on the English portion of the

bishops whom he condemned owed their appointments to the Whig party, against whom, from the time he joined Harley and St. John until his death, he maintained a perpetual and bitter controversy. They had, also, many of them been English clergymen; and Swift, at the head of the Irish interest and Irish party, made the preference of Englishmen for the great offices in Church and State the object of his most severe censure.*

One of the complaints most frequently made as to both bishops and clergy in Ireland in the eighteenth century was non-residence. To this several causes contributed. Many parishes had no glebe-houses, and houses suitable for the incumbents were not to be procured. Another cause was, that from the poverty of the separate parishes several were often united together, and of course there could be a resident rector only in one of them. Englishmen, whether bishops, or in possession of benefices conferred upon them either by the Crown or by the Englishmen who were bishops, seldom were content to reside in remote districts, and sought excuses for absence.

The proceedings of the Irish Parliament for about

---

Episcopal Bench in Ireland (I do not know on what authority originally) is too often cited, as if it were serious. The persons selected were (he said) good and excellent; but "as the worthy divines crossed Hounslow Heath, on their way to Ireland, they have been regularly robbed and murdered by the highwaymen frequenting that Common, who seized their robes and patents, came over to Ireland, and are consecrated bishops in their stead."

\* There is an excellent letter (July 3, 1725), from Swift to Lord Carteret, the Lord Lieutenant, pressing the claims of the Irish clergy to be considered in the exercise of Church patronage by the Government. "The misfortune (he says) of having bishops perpetually from England, as it must quench the spirit of emulation among us to excel in learning and the

thirty years before the Union were of extreme importance. Much of the Penal Code was repealed, or relaxed. A policy of justice towards the Roman Catholic portion of the people was favoured. So far, indirect benefit accrued to the Church from its legislation, but direct consideration of its interests there was none. Yet never was reform more needed. Redistribution of the revenues, long requisite in order to compensate for the poverty inflicted upon many parishes by the impropriations, was now required to provide for others pauperised by the loss of the tithe of agistment, which, condemned by a resolution of the House of Commons in 1735, was no longer collected. Indeed the whole tithe system required amendment. It was levied in kind, a mode of collection by which the owner was defrauded, and the payer oppressed.* The consequent abuses were a subject of declamation, but the remedy attainable by substituting the composition of an annual money payment, fairly adjusted, was not even suggested.

Reserving a further account of the civil history and legislation of this period for the next chapter, it remains now to advert to such of the more remarkable

---

study of divinity, so it produces another great discouragement, that those prelates usually draw after them colonies of sons, nephews, cousins, or old college companions, to whom they bestow the best preferments in their gift; and thus the young men, sent into the Church from the University here, have no better prospect than to be curates or small country vicars for life."—*Works*, vol. xi. p. 272.

* Tithes in kind were collected by the agency of tithe-proctors. The clergy were generally glad to compound with them for less than the rightful amount: the proctors made as much more as they could. "There are not (says Swift) ten clergymen reputed to possess a parish of £100 a-year, who for some years past have received £60, and that with the utmost difficulty and vexation."—Swift's *Works*, vol. viii. p. 419.

ecclesiastical persons as then or previously in the eighteenth century held office in the Irish Church, and have been as yet unnoticed.

Of the Englishmen sent to Ireland during that period, Stone and Lord Bristol have been mentioned; both had been chosen because they were Englishmen, and in order to forward political objects. Another, of very different character, but selected for similar reasons, was Boulter, Archbishop of Armagh (1724–1742). This very eminent prelate at once on his arrival became the head of the English interest and party, and obtained paramount influence in civil as well as ecclesiastical affairs. In advising as to patronage, his policy never rose above conferring every office in Church and State upon an Englishman. His correspondence with the English Ministers was, after his death, published, and exhibits the pertinacity with which, whenever a vacancy either upon the judicial or the episcopal Bench occurred, he presses that an Englishman should be chosen to fill it. He seems to have thought that there was no safety for the English dominion if Irishmen were trusted.* This prejudice detracts from Boulter's fame; in other respects his government of his diocese, and his measures for the Church, were admitted, even by those who disliked his politics, to be entitled to approbation. He

---

* See in the published correspondence of Boulter letters to the Duke of Newcastle, dated 19th January, 1724, 1st May, 1725, 3rd December, 1st January, 16th January, 9th February, 18th February, 1726 (O. S.); also letter to Duke of Dorset, 17th August, 1730. In one to the Duke of Newcastle, 4th March, 1724, he says—"If I be not allowed to form proper dependencies here to balance all the present Dublin faction on the Bench (of Bishops), it will be impossible for me to serve His Majesty in my present capacity."

was, during his life, most liberal in gifts for charitable purposes; and at his death he bequeathed his fortune to provide glebes where they were wanted, or to endow poor parishes.

Robinson, created in 1777 Lord Rokeby, Archbishop of Armagh (1765–1794), is another Englishman whose merits deserve acknowledgment. To great administrative capacity he added a noble munificence, and unwearied zeal for the interests of the Church. He found the diocese of Armagh (as might be expected, since Stone was his predecessor) in disorder. Before his death, churches built and repaired, numerous glebe-houses provided, a house and demesne constructed for the see, manifested the energy of his rule. Extensive improvements in the city of Armagh, the erection of an infirmary, a public library, an astronomical observatory (the two latter maintained by endowments which were his gift), still attest that his desire for the public good was not confined to ecclesiastical affairs.

Boulter and Robinson have both been censured for not rising above the political ideas of their age. The censure forgets their profession. They, and the other ecclesiastics of the time, may be excused, until it is shown that the statesmen, their contemporaries, exhibited any superior degree of enlightenment. When the march of political opinion did bring into effect an improved policy it met little opposition* from the Irish bishops, and was not without at least one of its ablest advocates among them.

---

* This is observed by Mr. Croker in an Article upon Irish affairs in the *Quarterly Review*, vol. lxxvi. p. 259.

The prelate referred to is John Law, Bishop of Clonfert (1782–1787), subsequently of Killala (1787–1795), and of Elphin (1795–1810), who zealously supported the measures for relief of the Roman Catholic part of the people, which were promoted in the later years of the eighteenth century.

Law was son of the Bishop of Carlisle, who translated and edited King's *Origin of Evil.*\* He had been a Fellow of one of the Cambridge Colleges, and had obtained previously high academic distinction. He was there the friend of Paley, and shared many of the opinions of this admirable writer. The chapter in Paley's *Moral and Political Philosophy* upon reverencing the Deity, certainly not inferior to the rest, has been attributed to Law. Before he was moved to Ireland he had been Archdeacon of Carlisle, and while in that office he obtained the character " of great variety of knowledge, uncommon genius, and sincere religion."†

Law seems to have had many ideas in common with his great contemporary Edmund Burke‡ respecting the relations of the State and of the Church to Roman Catholics in Ireland. At Killala he found that almost all the people were members of that Church. Considering their conversion to Protestantism hopeless, he sought, as he expressed himself, to make them good Catholics; and with a view to their instruction caused the works

---

\* See p. 182, *supra*.

† See in reference to Law, Mant, *History*, vol. ii. pp. 685–6, and Croker's *Boswell*, vol. iv. p. 294.

‡ Burke's *Letter to a Peer of Ireland* against the Penal Laws is dated in 1782; his letter to Sir Hercules Langrishe on the question of admitting them to the franchise, in 1792.

of Gother, a Roman Catholic divine, inculcating piety and morality, to be at his own expense printed and distributed.*

In a like spirit in 1793, when the Bill for relieving the Roman Catholics from disabilities and restrictions under which they suffered, and for admitting them to the parliamentary franchise, was before the House of Lords, he expressed himself in the following words: ... "I look upon my Roman Catholic brethren as fellow-subjects and fellow-Christians, as believers in the same God, and partners in the same redemption.† Speculative differences in some points of faith with me are of no account. They and I have but one religion—the religion of Christianity. Therefore, as children of the same Father, as travellers in the same road, and seekers of the same salvation, why not love each other as brethren? It is no part of Protestantism to persecute Catholics; and without justice to the Catholics there can be no security for the Protestant Establishment: as a friend, therefore, to the permanency of the Establishment, to the prosperity of the country, and to the justice due to my Catholic brethren, I shall cheerfully give my vote that the Bill be committed."‡

---

* Mant, *ut supra*, citing Nichols.

† Compare Berkeley in his *Word to the Wise*. Addressing the Roman Catholic clergy, he says: ... "I consider you as my countrymen, as my fellow-subjects, as professing belief in the same Christ. And I do most sincerely wish there was no other contest between us but who shall most completely practice the precepts of Him by whose name we are called, and whose disciples we all profess to be."

‡ *Debates in the Parliament of Ireland for the Session* 1793: Dublin, 1793. Bishop Dickson (Down) also advocated a policy favourable to the Roman Catholic claims. See Froude, *English in Ireland*, vol. iii. p. 294; Mant, *History*, vol. ii. p. 760.

Another of the bishops sent from England obtained considerable celebrity in his own time—Rundle, Bishop of Derry (1735–1743). He was unquestionably a person of ability and attainments. He is said to have excelled in conversation, but with such "vivacity of wit," as carried him into indiscreet expressions. He was intended for an English bishopric, but put aside on account of objections raised to his orthodoxy. Under such circumstances his appointment was at first unpopular in Ireland; but in a short time the dissatisfaction was overcome by his manners and conduct; and, according to Swift's description, he was "esteemed as a person of learning, conversation, and humanity, and beloved by all people."*

Percy, Bishop of Dromore (1782–1811), had, when Dean of Carlisle, been one of the brilliant circle which gathered round Johnson. His collection of ancient English poetry had much influence upon the character of poetical literature in the nineteenth century. Percy, when a bishop, is said to have been revered for his piety and benevolence.

Not many bishops of this time, who were Irish by

---

* Letter to Pope, Feb. 27, 1736; see also *Life of Archbishop Secker*, cited by Mant, *History*, vol. ii. p. 538. "What do you say," writes Pulteney to Swift, "to the bustle made here to prevent the man (Rundle) from being an English bishop, and afterwards allowing him to be good Christian enough for an Irish one?"—Swift's *Works*, vol. xiii. p. 160.

Swift and Pope were both on Rundle's side. The former contrasted Rundle with the other Irish bishops, of whom he wrote with bitter sarcasm (*Works*, vol. xvii. p. 178):—

"Rundle a bishop! well he may,
He's still a Christian, more than they.
We know the subject of their quarrels;
The man has learning, sense, and morals."

birth were eminent. The most distinguished seems to have been O'Beirne, appointed to the See of Ossory in 1795, and promoted to Meath in 1798. This prelate was originally a Roman Catholic, and it is related that while he rose to eminence in the Protestant Church his brother was about the same time promoted in the Roman Catholic. He was noted for attention to the discipline of his clergy, and especially for his efforts to repress the evil of non-residence. In one of his charges, having pointed out the example of the Roman Catholic clergy, who (he says) all lived among their flocks, and were in familiar intercourse with them, he urges, that "if we hope to succeed in our good cause we must come down to an emulation of their exertions: an emulation not of envy and strife; not of angry controversy or disputation; not of any intemperance of proselytism, where the idle contest is merely to swell the number of nominal votaries, without making better Christians or better subjects, and with the continual breach of Christian charity and benevolence, but an emulation in the discharge of such pastoral duties as are most calculated to secure us the respect and the attachment of our flocks."

Hamilton, at first Bishop of Clonfert (1796–1798), and afterwards of Ossory (1798–1806), and Matthew

---

Pope selected four bishops for panegyric, and Rundle was one of them:—

"Even in a bishop I can spy desert:
Secker is decent, Rundle has a heart.
Manners, with candour, are to Benson given,
To Berkeley every virtue under heaven."

It will be observed that of the four bishops two were on the Irish Bench.

Young, Bishop of Clonfert (1798–1800), had been Fellows of Trinity College, and were distinguished for mathematical attainments. They were both esteemed for conscientious attention to their official duties. Young has received in every capacity no ordinary praise, being described as combining with his scientific powers other intellectual endowments, and a character irresistibly engaging.*

With the close of the century a change in the style of preaching began to be perceptible. Sermons had been essays on morality, or explanations of doctrinal questions. Kirwan (exclaimed Grattan) came to interrupt the repose of the pulpit;† and from the time of his appearance a tendency to appeal to the emotions as well as the reason may be dated. His eloquence, if judged by its effects, its power to touch the heart, and impel to acts of generosity and benevolence, has not been since equalled; but as is also the case with Whitefield, a preacher of extraordinary persuasiveness, no record of it which has been preserved is worthy of his contemporary reputation. His manner was modelled upon the examples of Massillon and the other great French preachers. To the study of their oratory he was probably directed by the circumstance that his education was at a Jesuit College at St. Omer, which he entered with a view to becoming

---

* See as to Young, Mant's *History*, vol. ii. pp. 743–5.

† Speech in the House of Commons, January 17, 1792. It was in speaking of Kirwan, and the inadequate preferment conferred upon him, that Grattan used the expression so often since applied with little appropriateness: ... "The curse of Swift was upon him to have been an Irishman and a man of genius, and to have used it for the good of his country."

a member of the Roman Catholic priesthood. Controversial discussion he entirely avoided. The highest dignity to which this brilliant ornament of the Irish Church rose was the poor Deanery of Killala. More sense of his merits was shown after his death, when his widow received from the King a liberal pension.

From 1795 to 1800 Newcome was Primate. He was translated from the bishopric of Waterford and Lismore. It is said that in his appointment public utility alone was considered, and that it was "his unassuming virtue, conduct, principles, and erudition, which recommended him for the office."*

---

* Letter of Lord Charlemont. Hardy's *Life*, vol. ii. p. 224.

# CHAPTER XIV.

### THE UNION.

IN the year 1800, the Union of the Kingdoms and Churches of Great Britain and Ireland was enacted by the Parliaments of the two countries. The supreme importance of a measure of this character justifies a slight digression to notice not merely its provisions but the events which led to its adoption.

In 1707, Scotland was united with England; and from that time the Parliament of Great Britain asserted the same predominance over the Parliament of Ireland, and the same right to legislate for the latter country, which the English Parliament maintained in the reign of William III.* In order to place its claims beyond dispute, about five years after the accession of George I. (1719), a statute was passed, which declared that Ireland hath been, is, and of right ought to be, subordinate unto, and dependent upon, the Imperial Crown of Great Britain, as being inseparably united and annexed thereto; and that the King's Majesty, by and with the advice and consent of the Lords and Commons

---

\* See page 162.

of Great Britain in Parliament, had, and of right ought to have, full power and authority to make laws and statutes of sufficient force and validity to bind the kingdom and people of Ireland.

This enactment of the Parliament in England was in form declaratory. If the proposition which it asserted, namely, that the Parliament of Great Britain was entitled to make laws for Ireland, was true, the statute was unnecessary; if it was not true, it had no validity or effect. Nevertheless, it was of supreme importance, for it exhibited the determination of the British Parliament to persist in its assumption of legislative authority over Ireland, and its language offered a distinct challenge to the Irish Parliament; and if this were permitted to pass without notice, acquiescence in the claim thereby made might fairly be inferred.

The Act of George I. operated as an external check upon the movements of the Irish Parliament. The power which it asserted for the English Parliament was a restraining force in reserve, liable to be called into action. Another law more directly and more constantly controlled the proceedings of the Irish Parliament. By a statute passed in Ireland in the reign of Henry VII., known as Poynings' law from the Deputy under whose rule it was enacted, it was provided that before a Parliament should be held in Ireland the Chief Governor and Council were to notify to the King the causes and considerations for it, and all such Acts as it seemed to them should pass; that such causes, considerations, and Acts, should be affirmed by the King and his Council in England to be good and expedient; and that the King's licence thereupon, as well in affirmation of the said causes and Acts as to summon the said Parliament, should be obtained under the Great Seal of England. An amending Act of Philip and Mary empowered the Chief Governor and Council in Ireland, in case events necessary to be provided for should happen during a session of Parliament, to certify to the King such other causes and provisions as they should think good: which, if returned approved by the English Council, might then be enacted. This statute expressly provided that no other Acts, except those transmitted back from England, either before or during the Session of Parliament, could become law. From the time of Charles I. it was held, that without violating these statutes Parliament might consider, not a Bill, but "heads for a Bill," although no previous approval had been obtained either from the Lord Lieutenant and Irish Council or from the King and English Council; and at the time with which we are now concerned this was the practice. When "the heads" were adopted by Parliament, they were laid before the Lord Lieutenant and Irish Council, in order that they might be transmitted by them to the King, and be brought before the English Council, without whose consent there was to be no further progress. A Bill returned by the English Council, whether this occurred before or during the Session of Parliament, might be accepted or negatived by the Irish Parliament, but could not be altered or amended.

It cannot be denied that under the restrictions imposed by Poynings' law, and so long as the claim to legislate for Ireland was maintained by the Parliament of Great Britain, the Irish Parliament was reduced to a position of subordination and dependence. Nevertheless there was no appearance before 1780 of any move on the part of either Lords or Commons in Ireland to obtain an alteration of the relations between the two kingdoms created by these laws.

This acquiescence was, however, confined to Parliament. About five years after the Act of George I. was passed, Swift, in his letters respecting Wood's coinage, renewed the protest which Molyneux, as has been stated, made in the time of William against legislation by the English Parliament, and, like him, repudiated its authority. Molyneux, he said, had opposed the assumed authority, "as far as truth, reason, and justice were capable of opposing;" but against his opposition "the love and torrent of power had prevailed." "I have," he adds, "looked over all the English and Irish statutes, without finding any law that maketh Ireland depend upon England, any more than England does upon Ireland. We have, indeed, obliged ourselves to have the same King with them; and consequently they are obliged to have the same King with us."

For a time Swift aroused a spirit of nationality; but before his death it had become dormant; nor was it until about the middle of the century that it again revived. Then it appeared in the speeches of Lucas, a member of the Corporation of Dublin, who became prominent in political affairs. With Lucas many of the gentry combined; and, at a later period, a large number of them expressed their discontent, and complained that the Irish Parliament was subject to so much control. They regarded the English Parliamentary system as a model, and thought themselves injured in the instances wherein the Irish differed.*

Upon the accession of George III. (1760) a new Parliament was necessarily summoned in Ireland. It reflected public opinion in a much greater degree than did its predecessor, which had sat during the entire reign of George II.—a period of thirty-three years. After some time a party, professing to be animated by patriotic sentiments, zealous for Irish, not English, interests, grew up in the House of Commons. At its head appeared leaders of remarkable eloquence and political knowledge.

At the same time the power and influence of the English House of Commons were increasing. Great questions arose for its consideration, and were debated with conspicuous ability. Thus the form and the proceedings of a perfect representative assembly, engaged upon subjects of supreme importance, free and unrestrained in its treatment of them, were constantly before the eyes of the Irish Parliament, and presented a contrast to their own depressed condition. A desire to attain similar independence began to be felt, if not by a majority, certainly by a large minority, of the Commons.

The year 1778 brought to the Parliamentary patriotic party a great accession of strength. They acquired allies, with whose aid they could no longer be resisted. Volunteers for the defence of the kingdom were then embodied. Enlisted from all classes and all parts of the country, the Volunteers were imbued

---

* See Lecky, *History*, vol. iv. p. 353; and see also Note A A of Appendix.

with the ideas then popular, and quickly manifested their sympathy with the friends of national interests in the House of Commons.

The immediate result of this alliance was seen in concessions by the Government upon commercial questions. Regulations oppressing Irish trade, and in the highest degree injurious to its prosperity, were abandoned; and it was enacted that there should be free export and import to and from Ireland with the West Indies and with the British settlements and colonies in America and Africa—subject only to such duties being levied in Irish ports as were or might be levied in British.

When this success had been attained, it was seen that no further reforms were to be expected, unless the barriers interposed by Poynings' law and the Act of George I. should be removed out of the way. Nor was this the only reason alleged for condemning these statutes. They not only (it was said), protected wrong, but were a wrong themselves. Ireland was a kingdom, and their provisions reduced it to a province.

On the 19th of April, 1780, the first proceeding was taken towards obtaining Irish independence. On that day Grattan moved in the House of Commons a resolution that the King's most excellent Majesty and the Lords and Commons of Ireland were the only power competent to make laws to bind Ireland. "If (he said) I had lived when the Act of William took away the woollen manufacture from Ireland, or when the Act of George I. declared the country to be dependent and subject to laws to be enacted by the Parliament of England, I should have made a covenant with my own conscience to seize the first moment of recovering my country from the ignominy of such acts of power; or if I had a son I should have administered to him an oath that he would consider himself as a person separate, and set apart for the discharge of so important a duty."

The motion did not then succeed; but it initiated a movement, the result of which was that about two years later all that Grattan demanded was granted. By one statute the Act of George I. was repealed,* and by another it was declared that the right claimed by the people of Ireland to be bound only by laws enacted by the King, and by the Parliament of that kingdom, was established and ascertained;† also the restrictions of Poynings' law were abolished: the previous assent of the King and Council for the bills to be proposed ceased to be necessary: they could be proposed and debated without it.‡ For the final validity of statutes the royal assent was required; and as it was thought advisable that this assent should be given upon the advice, not of the Irish, but of the English Ministers of the Crown, it was provided that it should be expressed under the Great Seal of England.

The independence of the Irish Parliament was conceded without either limiting its range of action, or providing for the case of its disagreeing with the English Parliament upon subjects of imperial interest, which there might be occasion to submit to both. There was no reason why the Irish Parliament could not have a separate foreign policy, a separate com-

---

\* 22 George III., ch. 51 (English).
† 23 George III., ch. 28 (English).
‡ 21 & 22 George III., ch. 47 (Irish).

mercial policy; why it could not impose protective duties, or decide for itself upon such constitutional questions as might at any time arise.

If two independent ruling authorities dealing with the same subjects have the same interests, they may be trusted to work harmoniously together; but England and Ireland had not, or at least were supposed not to have, the same interests in reference to political questions. Accordingly, in no long time, disagreements arose between their Parliaments. The first of these occurred about three years after the repeal of the Act of George I. Resolutions which were designed to regulate the commercial relations between England and Ireland, and which were intended in many respects to serve Ireland, were adopted by the House of Commons and the House of Lords in England. In the Irish House of Commons these resolutions, opposed fiercely and supported feebly, although of the utmost importance, had to be abandoned.

Four years later a subject of even more importance, affecting the very foundation of the executive government, again provoked controversy. George III. became disabled by mental infirmity from discharging the duties of a Sovereign. Did the Prince of Wales by right succeed to his authority, or did the succession and the terms of it depend upon the decision of Parliament? The Irish Parliament took the former view; the British the latter. As the King recovered his health the cause of dissension ceased; but, if it had been otherwise, the Prince would have been in England a Regent with limited powers—in Ireland a King in all but name.

When a spirit of disagreement had manifested itself in reference to domestic affairs, English Statesmen became apprehensive, lest it might extend to relations with foreign countries also, and weaken the means of carrying on the war then waged by Great Britain with France. Moreover, it began to be perceived that, even as to affairs exclusively Irish, there were disadvantages attending separation of the Legislatures. The views of a local Parliament were necessarily bounded by local sentiments and local prejudices.*

These considerations induced a conviction that some change was required. What direction, then, was the change to take? Subordination of the Irish Parliament had been tried and failed. It was condemned by the universal voice of the Irish people, and its injustice had been acknowledged by English statesmen.† It could not be revived. A third course lay open. The Legislatures of the two kingdoms might be fused together; and one united Parliament would then take the place of a Parliament for England and a Parliament for Ireland.

---

* Jan. 23, 1799, Pitt first stated his reasons for advising the Union. He referred to the advantage of "an impartial legislature, standing aloof from local party connexion, sufficiently removed from contending factions, to be advocate or champion of neither"; to the disagreement which had already occurred between the two Parliaments, and to the possibility of further disagreement upon "subjects involving the safety of both kingdoms: as, for instance, upon alliance with a foreign power—upon the army, the navy, any branch of the public service, upon trade or commerce."—*Speeches*, vol. iii. pp. 354, 358.

† See the speech delivered in the English House of Commons by Fox, as Secretary of State, when bringing forward the repeal of the Act of George I.; see also Pitt's speech (1799), in which he declared his disapprobation of the system terminated in 1782, as unworthy the liberality of Great Britain, and injurious to the interests of Ireland.— *Speeches*, vol. iii. p. 363.

An union of the two kingdoms and of the Parliaments of the two kingdoms was the measure determined upon. If it was to be effected, then it became necessary to consider what course was to be pursued as to the Churches established in England and Ireland. They were then separate and distinct; and the mere fact that the kingdoms and Parliaments were united did not of itself prevent the Churches continuing separate. But analogy and example avail much in politics. If there was union of the kingdoms, why not of the Churches? Besides, it was thought that by becoming connected with the English Church the position of the Irish Church would be strengthened. It then stood alone, surrounded by many enemies and supported by few friends. If it were made part of an united Church, whose numbers would form a majority of the aggregate population of England and Ireland, it might be expected to rest upon a more secure foundation.

Accordingly, union of the churches of England and Ireland met the general support of the Irish Episcopal Bench. One of the ablest prelates, Bishop O'Beirne, seems, however, to have thought that mere union would not ensure safety for the Irish Church; that there ought to be but one Church, and that both in England and in Ireland this should be the Church of England, with the Archbishop of Canterbury as Primate.* On the question of this proposed primacy he cited precedents† from Irish ecclesiastical history.

---

\* See Memorandum by the Bishop of Meath (O'Beirne).—*Castlereagh Correspondence*, vol. iii. p. 2.

† Immediately before the English invasion, and for some time previously, the Bishops of Dublin, Waterford, and Limerick, cities of which

The Union of Great Britain and Ireland, and of their Parliaments and Churches, was carried into effect by two statutes—one of the English, and another of the Irish Parliament—which embodied certain articles of agreement between the two Legislatures. So far as these articles relate to civil affairs, it is not requisite to state more than the following: "... The kingdoms of Great Britain and Ireland were, on and after the 1st of January, 1801, to be for ever united into one kingdom by the name of the United Kingdom of Great Britain and Ireland; for this United Kingdom there was to be one and the same Parliament; four Lords Spiritual, entitled according to a prescribed rotation, and twenty-eight other Lords elected by the Temporal Peers, were to represent Ireland in the House of Lords of the United Parliament, and a hundred members were to be returned to the House of Commons.

As there was to be one United Kingdom, so there was to be one United Church, whose doctrine, worship, discipline, and government should be, and should remain, in full force for ever, as the same were then by law established for the Church of England. It was also declared that "the continuance and preservation of the said United Church, as the Established Church of England and Ireland was to be deemed, and taken to be, an essential and fundamental part of the Union."

There was originally in the draft of the Bill a clause

---

the Danes, or to speak more accurately, a Livonian colony claiming alliance with the Normans, had been possessed, were consecrated by, and swore canonical obedience to, the Archbishop of Canterbury (see Ussher's *Religion of the Ancient Irish: Works*, vol. iv. p. 326, and Ware's *Bishops*).

referring to Convocation, and making provision for the summoning of the Archbishops, Bishops, Priests, and Clergy of the several provinces in England and Ireland, whenever His Majesty should summon a Convocation of the Clergy; but the clause, being thought unnecessary and likely to raise objections, was ultimately omitted, and no mention whatever was made of Convocation.*

Neither in England nor Ireland was any Synod or Convocation summoned to consider the union of the English and Irish Churches, or the provisions connected with the subject. They rested solely on the authority of the Parliaments of the two Kingdoms.

---

* See letter of Lord Auckland to Lord Castlereagh in the *Castlereagh Correspondence*, vol. iii. 294-5.

## CHAPTER XVI.

[1800–1871.]

FROM the Union, as the Church of Ireland and the Church of England were united together, the relations of the State to each was necessarily the same. But this had been the case equally before this event; for the two Churches were from the time of the Reformation established with similar rights, privileges, and incidents. In both the supremacy of the Crown was recognised: in both the power to appoint their archbishops and bishops was vested in the sovereign: in both the express legislation of Parliament came in aid of their formularies and discipline. The most important part of their endowments—tithes—had been possessed by both before the Reformation. Their title to this property may not have owed its origin to the State; but its confirmation, and such a proprietorship in it as was capable of legal enforcement, were due to it.

Except in one particular, no change was made in the rights of either Church by the Union. That was in the case of the Church of Ireland, which previously might have had its own independent formularies, of which the articles of 1616 and the canons of 1634 were examples, but which thenceforward was to have "the same doctrine and worship" as the English Church.

For seventy years the union of the Church of England with the Church of Ireland continued, and the connexion of both with the State, as it existed immediately after the Act of Union was passed, remained unimpaired. On the 1st of January, 1871, the union of the Churches was severed, and the relations then existing between them were terminated. The Church of Ireland was at the same time disestablished and disendowed.

The question of the maintenance of a religious establishment in Ireland, which found its solution in this result, did not assume any prominence until about thirty years after the Union. During the intervening period a controversy in relation to a matter of paramount importance, and requiring more immediate decision, engrossed the attention of the Irish people, and so prevented discussion of other political subjects.

The controversy arose out of the relations which then by law subsisted between the State and such of its subjects as professed the Roman Catholic religion. Many oppressive provisions of the penal code directed against the latter had, before the Union, been repealed by the Irish Parliament, but some disabilities of grave importance still continued to affect their social position. They could not sit in Parliament, and they were excluded from any office of place or trust under the Crown. In the Act of Union no relief was afforded from these grievances. The consideration of them was reserved for the united Parliament by Mr. Pitt and Lord Castlereagh, the ministers who were at that time principally concerned with Irish affairs; and it was their design, that whenever this assembly met, measures should be brought before it which would admit Roman Catholics to the same constitutional rights and privileges as were enjoyed by Protestants.*

Unfortunately the intentions of these statesmen could not take effect, owing to the opposition of George III., in whose judgment to confer political power on members of the Church of Rome was a violation of the principles asserted by the settlement of the Crown upon his family in preference to the Stuarts, and who considered himself disabled from agreeing to any enactment having that operation, however expedient it might be, by the oath he had taken at his coronation.

The policy, which was at this time defeated, did not triumph until 1829. It failed when it would have been attended only by beneficial results. It succeeded when untoward circumstances impaired the good to arise from its adoption. The "Emancipation Act," by which it was carried into effect, had been preceded in Ireland by an organized agitation. It had, therefore, the appearance of being passed, not in acknowledgment of a debt due to justice, but as a concession extorted by pressure.

Under these circumstances the leaders of the popular party, claiming to have won the measures of relief now granted, did not rest content with gaining the objects at first sought: inspirited by success, and perceiving the means which led to it, they turned to other projects, and directed their energies to attain them. The Estab-

---

* It was intended that one of these measures should make a provision for the Roman Catholic clergy. After the Union a proposition to this effect was, upon one occasion, submitted to the House of Commons and was successful. In 1825 a resolution was in that House passed, "That it was expedient provision should be made by law towards the mainte-

lished Church in Ireland at once attracted their attention. Its privileged position, when compared with the magnitude of the dissent from its system, provoked jealousy, and supplied those who refused to conform to it with reasonable grounds for hostility.

The chief source, however, of discontent at the time in relation to ecclesiastical affairs was in connexion with tithe. This mode of raising a revenue is, under any circumstances, attended with objectionable incidents. Being, where there is tillage, a proportion of the produce, the demand increases as the crop increases; consequently improved cultivation is discouraged. In Ireland, where subdivision of the soil was carried to excess, tithe, being paid by the occupier, not the owner, fell largely upon an humble class. From its nature this charge could not well be collected by clergymen; and they therefore were obliged to employ such agents as would undertake a very unpopular office. The conduct of these agents at all times gave rise to much complaint. There had been an Act enabling composition of tithe, but, its application not being made compulsory, its operation was very limited, and the dissatisfaction prevalent before it was passed, had, therefore, been little diminished by its provisions. At no time in Ireland, not even when the Church which owned the tithes was accepted by the people, and all who paid them belonged to it, had they been collected without difficulty.* Now

---

nance of the secular Roman Catholic clergy exercising religious functions in Ireland." There was a majority of 43 in its favour : 205 voting for, and 162 against.

\* The payment of tithes of cattle, corn, and other produce, was enjoined at the Synod of Cashel, convened by Henry II. Whether before

they were levied from farmers, of whom, in three provinces, Leinster, Munster, and Connaught, the great majority were Roman Catholics; and in the fourth (Ulster) many were Roman Catholics, and many Presbyterians. It is, therefore, not surprising that the adversaries of the Church were able to arouse a violent agitation against the payment of tithe. As the incomes of the clergy were thence derived, the tax could not be remitted, and assistance was given by the Government to aid its collection. But the demand was almost everywhere met by determined resistance: combinations were formed to obstruct and terrify the persons engaged to enforce it; violence was without scruple resorted to, and in many places outrages of great enormity were perpetrated. Finally over a large part of the country tithes practically ceased to be levied.

The condition of society forced upon the Government, and subsequently upon Parliament, a consideration of the position of the Established Church in Ireland, and led to measures of importance. In 1832 an Act making composition for tithes permanent and compulsory was passed. In the same year a Royal Commission for inquiring into the revenues and state of the Church was issued, and from its reports subsequently the most

---

that Synod it was legally obligatory does not seem clear. Dr. Carew, Professor of Divinity in Maynooth College, says that until the English invasion the people of Ireland, at least generally, were unacquainted with the tithe system.—*History*, p. 149. The Rev. Mr. Brenan (a Franciscan), in his *History* says, that, notwithstanding the decree of the Synod of Cashel, tithes were not paid in Ireland, except within the Pale, or that mere fractional portion in which the English influence predominated (p. 317). The same view seems to be taken by Protestant writers. (See *Essays on the Irish Church*, 1866, pp. 131, 132, 159).

full and complete information was obtained. Another Commission was also issued in 1834, which was directed to ascertain the number of persons in communion with the Church in each parish.

In 1833 a statute known as the Church Temporalities Act became law, which was amended and supplemented by another in the next year.* These Acts aimed at removing some not unjust grounds of complaint. The expenses of building and repairing the fabrics of churches, and of providing the requisites for divine service in them, were defrayed by assessments imposed at the vestries. These assessments, like the tithes, were paid by Roman Catholics and Protestant Dissenters. In lieu of them a fund applicable for the same purpose was provided from the property of the Church. To supply it, the number of archbishoprics and bishoprics was reduced, the former to two, and the latter to ten; and the revenues of such bishoprics as were no longer to be filled (ten in number) were appropriated for the purpose. The reduction of the number of bishoprics was effected by union and consolidation of Sees. It was to take effect, as vacancies in the Bench of Bishops occurred. A Board of Commissioners was appointed to administer the fund thus created. If there should be an excess of income poor benefices might be augmented. The fund was to be also assisted by a percentage charged upon all benefices and dignities which were above £300 a-year in value; and by the emoluments of sinecures which, under a power given for the purpose, might be suspended by the Privy Council

---

* Church Temporalities Acts (Ireland) 3 & 4 Wm. IV., ch. 37, A.D. 1833, and 4 & 5 Wm. IV., ch. 90, A.D. 1834.

upon the application of the Commissioners. Beside these provisions there was enacted an elaborate scheme for perpetuating the interests of persons holding under terminable leases from the bishops and dignitaries. These had been customarily renewable in consideration of fines for such limited periods as were permitted by previous statutes. The tenant was now enabled, by paying to the Commissioners a certain sum ascertained by them in the manner directed, to convert his tenure into a perpetuity, subject to a fee-farm rent, which represented the former rent and the average annual fine, and was liable to vary at intervals according as the price of grain rose or fell.

The Tithe Composition Act of 1832 not producing much result, the law in relation to this property was again altered in 1838. Then the Tithe Rent-charge Act was passed. This enactment transferred the liability for tithe from the occupiers to the owners of land. In place of a proportion of production, and of the composition which represented it, was substituted a perpetual rent-charge, issuing out of the land, and payable by the owners of the fee or of some long derivative tenure under the fee. The rent-charge was to be equivalent to three-fourths of the composition, and to be recoverable by proceedings similar to those for enforcing payment of other rent-charges, with some additional remedies.*

In 1854, "Ministers' Money," a tax for the maintenance of the clergy in towns, was abolished, and an equivalent made payable by the Commissioners.

There is no doubt that all these measures, as they

---

* 1 & 2 Vict., ch. 109 (Ireland), A. D. 1838.

came into operation, tended to strengthen the Established Church in Ireland. Much the greater proportion of the land was owned by its members, and tithe rent-charge fell upon the proprietor, not the occupier, of the soil. The clergy were therefore in only a small degree supported by those who rejected their ministry. Also, henceforward the expenses of the buildings and of providing requisites for divine service, and after 1854 the provision for incumbents in towns, were defrayed from ecclesiastical property, and, not as before, from taxation affecting Roman Catholics and Protestant Dissenters.

It is, however, also obvious that none of these measures answered, or were designed to answer, a different class of objections to the Irish Establishment. No internal improvement, no amendment of its external relations, could possibly appease the hostility either of those who condemned any alliance between Church and State as wrong in principle, or of those who considered such an alliance, however advisable in other countries, to be unsuited to the actual condition of society in Ireland. The effect of such reforms was, therefore, merely to change the ground occupied in the controversy, and to introduce for discussion a different range of topics and arguments.

The objections of those, who were adverse to Establishments generally, applied equally to the English and to the Irish Church. According to them, any connexion between Church and State was objectionable. Each had its own duties to discharge: those of the State being confined to secular affairs, the ordering and government of the community, the preservation of peace and order;

those of the Church relating to spiritual affairs, the promotion of man's moral improvement and welfare. Their spheres of action, it was said, were therefore distinct, and ought to be kept so. If they were intermingled, the influence of the State, supported by immediate and visible advantages, would preponderate over that of the Church; religion itself would be affected by it; and a secularity of spirit could not fail to pervade the ideas and practice of its ministers.

In reply, it was urged that the State can no more divest itself of obligations in connexion with religion than its subjects can. It is capable of resolving and acting; can receive benefits or injuries; has thus, it may be said, a personality. As each person is indebted for existence and well-being to a Divine Providence, so is each State: as the former, in his individual capacity, is in return bound to manifest gratitude, so also is the latter in its corporate character. An Established Church expresses the national homage to the great Author and Founder of society.

Then, if there is to be an Establishment, could there, it was asked, be a more perfect example than, from the nature of its system, the United Church of England and Ireland presented? By its constitution, the Crown, which was necessarily supreme in the State, was declared to be also supreme in the Church: thus, civil and ecclesiastical authority were united together, and each lent the other support. The former gained for its acts a higher sanction than force could supply; and the latter, while engaged in its divine mission, received protection. No injury ought to accrue to either from these relations: the object was to make the State religious, and there was nothing in the means used for this end which need make the Church secular. There might, indeed, be some ascendency conferred upon Episcopalian Protestantism over other denominations of religion; but it was an ascendency which elevated them also, since it involved an admission by the Civil Power that those principles of faith and practice, which they all alike desired to uphold, were, in importance, before all others.

But was it only as an Establishment that the Church and its maintenance had to be considered? It was endowed as well as established. An Establishment is accompanied by an Endowment; but Endowment may exist without Establishment. Thus, the Presbyterian Church in Ireland was not established, but it received an annual grant from the State. The endowments of the United Church had been consecrated to sacred uses for centuries. Were they now to be confiscated, and when confiscated cast into the common mass, thence to be appropriated for some want of the community unconnected with religion, or, it might be, granted to private owners? Impulses and convictions beyond the calculations of expediency caused their dedication: the same should secure their preservation.\*

The effect of Establishment and Endowment ought,

---

\* These views were forcibly expressed by Sir James Graham in the House of Commons, 30th March, 1835: . . . "The property set apart by the piety of our ancestors to maintain and propagate the Protestant religion is sacred, and must be applied for these purposes. Those who minister at the altar should live by the altar. This decree is high as heaven, and you cannot reach to take it away; it is strong as the Almighty, and you cannot overthrow it; it is lasting as the Eternal, and you cannot unfix it. It now binds you as a legislature of Christian men, acting on Christian principles."

it was contended, to be judged from some example where they had succeeded, not from cases where adverse circumstances hindered or weakened their efficiency. Take the instance of England. There the Church everywhere interpenetrates society. The parochial system brings home its influence to every district, and places in the centre of each, not a self-constituted missionary, but an authorized representative of civilization and religion. To all ranks and classes it sends its representatives. None are superior to their teaching, and none below their care.* The guides and comforters of the poor; the friends and equals of the more wealthy; while descending to instruct the unlearned, they meet the expanding capacities of an age of intellectual activity with mental cultivation and intelligence equal to its own.

If Establishment and Endowment are rejected, there can remain, it was urged, only the alternative—that religious teaching shall be furnished by voluntary agents, supported by voluntary contributions. But will the supply of instruction from such sources be sufficient? Will it have the requisite permanence, universality, and authority? Is it not precisely when and where its aid is most demanded that it will fail? The more man needs, the less he seeks the religious teacher. In periods, therefore, of scepticism and irreligion, at the very time when the ministers of Christianity are most required, how are they to be maintained? The volun-

---

* Goethe, in a criticism on the *Vicar of Wakefield*, makes some observations upon the position of an English country clergyman which deserve to be noted. After observing that the hero of the tale is a husbandman, the father of a family, not separate from the community, he continues:—
" On this pure, beautiful foundation rests his higher calling ; he guides his

tary system is effective with congregations predisposed to welcome it; but its exertions soon languish and grow faint under the discouragement of general apathy and neglect. And as for its authority—when not invited it is an intruder; when invited, a dependent, resting upon the favour and the fancy of those it teaches, coerced to reduce the quality of its preaching to their level, and never venturing to controvert or rise above the ideas which they approve.

In Ireland, however, the objections made to the Church were not founded upon abstract principles applicable to Establishments or Endowments generally. These would have had there little weight. The Roman Catholic Church formerly possessed most of the emoluments which were now owned by a Protestant clergy, and in the enjoyment of them it was then protected and supported by the State. The same Church in many European kingdoms still enjoyed similar property and similar protection. It could not lay down doctrines antagonistic to its own practice. Not Establishment and Endowment were condemned, but Establishment and Endowment of a Church, which was so little in harmony with the religious sentiments of the people among whom it was placed. The Irish Established Church, it was said, was the Church of the few, not of the many; of the rich, not of the poor; for the few who adhered to it were the most wealthy persons in the

---

parishioners through life; he blesses them at all epochs of their existence; he consoles them in all trials; and if other sources of consolation fail, calls up and guarantees the hope of a happier future. It may be a narrow circle in which he lives, but it comes in contact with the highest."—*Warheit und Dichtung*, Book 10.

community. Nor was it merely that its members were few, and therefore not entitled to have privileges for themselves; rich, and therefore not in need of them; but that they were Irish only by birth, descendants from conquerors or colonists of a foreign race, who had during their possession been placed in an invidious predominance. Of this ascendency the Establishment, it was alleged, must be regarded as the representative.

But while these considerations weighed against the Establishment, others of gravity and importance were cast into the opposite scale. The question was not respecting the foundation of an institution of this character in Ireland, but whether having been founded, and having subsisted in its existing form for three hundred years, it was to be removed? Its fall might endanger more than itself. If long possession were in one instance deemed of no account, there were other instances in which it might also be disregarded: if one act of the State were utterly reversed and undone, so might other acts. Would rights connected with secular property continue to be respected if those connected with ecclesiastical were invaded? Then the Reformed Church had not only ancient title and actual possession[*] to plead, but its preservation had been guaranteed by a most solemn compact between two nations. It was by the Act of Union united with the Church of England, and this union of the two Churches had been by the

---

[*] Dr. Lee, in *Essays on the Irish Church* (1868), states that Dr. Slevin, Professor of Canon Law at Maynooth, in evidence which he gave before the Commissioners of Education in 1826, admitted the possession to be beyond the utmost period of prescription laid down by the Court of Rome. This would seem to be a hundred years.

same Act declared to be an essential and fundamental part of the Union of the Kingdoms. What, then, would be the result of severing it? What the effect upon the Union of the Kingdoms?*

Nor, it was by many contended, could only political reasons be regarded in dealing with the Church Establishment in Ireland; others of a different character were also to find a place. The State had deliberately fixed there a system which it believed to represent the most pure form of Christianity; it had maintained it not only for the sake of those who came within its fold, but also of those who refused to come, and who but for the provision thus made for their instruction, could know nothing beyond such notions as they inherited. An Establishment, by the security and independence which it affords its ministers, by the rewards for diligence and eminence which it offers to them, and in some degree also by the social station to which it elevates them, presents peculiar advantages towards the formation in its clergy of a high standard of acquirements and manners. It affects its own followers by direct influence, others by example. The State had, therefore, introduced into Ireland powerful agencies to serve the interests of religion and truth, and the mere fact that their effect had as yet been limited did not justify their withdrawal.†

---

\* Some observations of the Right Hon. Richard A. Blake, a Roman Catholic barrister of eminence, to the effect that the Establishment should be preserved as "a main link in the connexion between Great Britain and Ireland," are cited in Note BB of Appendix.

† Gladstone's *The State in its Relations to the Church*, is the most able of the writings of this period which advocate the maintenance of the Establishment on the grounds of its teaching the truth. See also his speech in the House of Commons, June 1, 1836.—*Hansard*, vol. xxxiii. p. 1317.

Too much stress also, it was argued, had been laid upon the fact that the Church did not make progress among the people generally. Its exertions were obstructed by hindrances over which it had no control. Its friends had been its worst enemies. They had associated it with civil war, with relentless confiscations, with an offensive penal code. Until the legislation which commenced in 1829 it was weighted with these disadvantages. Now these were at an end: Roman Catholic and Protestant met upon an equality as to civil rights: the prejudices which oppression fostered against the reformed religion must fall along with their cause: pride would no longer present an obstacle to conformity. Time should be given for the consequences of these altered circumstances to develop themselves, and for the Church, under the protection of the State, to take advantage of them.\*

Lastly, some social benefits which the organization of the Church conferred could not be overlooked. In a country of absentee proprietors it provided a resident gentry: it had introduced or retained in Ireland, in connexion with itself, learning and ability, much virtue, and excellence. If it was not a missionary of religion, it was unquestionably a missionary of civilization.

In the end the statesmen of highest eminence became disinclined to agitate the question of the Irish Establishment, and the opposition to it for more than twenty years made little progress. Then it was again revived, owing to circumstances which will be afterwards noticed.

---

\* These topics were powerfully used in a speech of Sir Robert Peel in the House of Commons, April 2, 1835.

## CHAPTER XVII.

[1800–1871.]

THE last chapter traces, from the Union until disestablishment, the external history of the Church of Ireland, the legislation affecting it, and the political controversy to which it gave rise. Its internal condition during the same period is now to be examined—what progress, as an institution to teach and promote religion, did it then make?

The religious impulses which before the commencement of the nineteenth century had, as we have seen, appeared within the Church continued to operate afterwards. They received assistance from the general tendency of the age. In the French Revolution the experiment had been tried of a nation without Christianity; of infidelity, under the sanction of authority, reduced to practice. Warned by the results, European opinion now everywhere cherished faith and morals as the only basis of social order.*

Improvement in religious feeling on the part of both the clergy and laity of the Church in Ireland for some

---

\* See reflections to this effect in a Sermon preached in Dublin, in 1796, by Archbishop Magee, then a Fellow of Trinity College.—*Works*, vol. ii. p. 326.

time manifested itself principally in outward acts—in more frequent attendance on divine worship; conversation free from the improprieties of a former time; the formation of societies to discountenance vice, and to disseminate the Scriptures and the writings of such lay and clerical authors as most effectually inculcated piety. But conduct founds itself upon belief, and practice cannot be dissociated from doctrine. Sentiments which urge to action induce investigation of the principles proper to guide it.

When a spirit of inquiry respecting theological subjects arises, there will generally be found, in the Church where it exists, a disposition to recur to the opinions prevailing during its early history, and to the great names that traditional veneration associates with them. Accordingly, now, the doctrines, which in Ireland had been embodied in the Articles of 1615,[*] again came into notice. They had been in abeyance from the time of the Restoration.

At first the supporters of these doctrines were few: influential only in consequence of their virtues. By degrees new converts were added; and at length the number of those who openly professed adherence to them was so considerable that they were estimated as a distinct religious party. In energy and zeal they resembled the first Methodists; but they had not, like the Methodists, either an elaborate organization, a peculiar discipline, or a central authority. They were bound together simply by harmony of sentiments. As a party, they received the designation (given also in

---

[*] See pp. 100-104, *supra*.

England to persons of similar sentiments), Evangelical.*

In a party constituted in this manner absolute uniformity of ideas could not be expected to exist. The right of private judgment, and reference to the Scriptures as the sole test of truth, were encouraged; any authority less than divine was in but a small degree respected. In general, the Evangelical clergy in Ireland entertained (but not without considerable variations in the expression of them) moderate views in respect to episcopacy, clerical orders, the nature of the sacraments, and the degree of importance to be attached to rites and ceremonies. In their teaching, no doctrine had more prominence than the doctrine of justification by faith only.† Some of them connected this doctrine with the Calvinistic tenets as to predestination; but the others, and probably the larger number, held it not in association with these opinions, and it was in very many instances accompanied by even decided opposition to them. In both the clergy and laity of the party there was a tendency to strictness and severity of conduct. They

---

* See p. 197. In Bishop Ryle's *Christian Leaders of the last Century* will be found an account of the clerical founders of the Evangelical party in England.

† Dr. Mahaffy, in his remarkable *Essay on the Decay of Modern Preaching*, comments upon the comparative neglect of other important doctrines by some Evangelical clergymen. "'There is," he remarks, " even a school of pious men who think all Christianity centres round one cardinal doctrine—justification by faith in Christ's atonement; and I have often heard them say that they should feel unable to give an account of their stewardship if a stranger had chanced to attend for once their ministry, and, being ignorant of the truth, had not heard it from their lips."—Page 120.

R

were indisposed to take part in mere amusements, or in any pursuits which were not of a grave character.

In all these respects Evangelicalism (if it may be so called) was a revival of Puritanism; and this circumstance was the cause of and excuse for much resistance to its progress. Both systems (it was contended) deserved the same reproach: they enforced asceticism of manners, and exaggerated the importance of dogma. Such observations were not without effect for some time; but when it was seen that no secession from the Church followed among Evangelicals; that, unlike the Puritans, they appealed to the standards of faith adopted by the Church; that their doctrines were accompanied by active exertions to repress irreligion, to inculcate practical goodness, and to encourage works of benevolence and charity;* the hostility which in the beginning met them, was gradually overcome, and their opinions, at first only tolerated, afterwards received approval, and ultimately became in a high degree popular, especially among the laity.†

Differences of opinion upon doctrinal subjects were

---

* Mr. Froude has borne testimony to his experience of Evangelicalism in Ireland, such as it came under his observation in the family of a clergyman with whom he resided there. He says he "had been brought up to regard Evangelicals as unreal and affected": he found "in this household quiet good sense, intellectual breadth of feeling." . . . "Christianity was part of the atmosphere which we breathed; it was the great fact of our existence, to which everything else was subordinated." . . . "The problem was to arrange all our thoughts and acquirements in harmony with the Christian revelation, and to act it out consistently in all that we said and did."—*Short Studies on Great Subjects*, vol. iv. p. 295 (ed. 1883).

† In the historical work of an eminent Presbyterian Divine, which has been before referred to, will be found an interesting account of the pro-

followed in the Church of Ireland by differences of opinion in reference to education. For some years before 1831, primary education in Ireland was conducted principally by a voluntary Association, which was aided with liberal grants from Parliament. This Association, from the place in Dublin where its offices were situate, was known as the Kildare-place Society. Its rules prohibited proselytism, and so far were calculated to recommend it to the various religious denominations in Ireland; but one of its regulations, requiring the Bible to be read in the schools without note or comment, was disapproved by the heads of the Roman Catholic Church. In 1831, a system of education, which it was hoped would be free from the objections made to that adopted by the Kildare-place Society, was established by the authority of the Government which was then in power, and was placed under the administration of a Board of Commissioners nominated by the Lord Lieutenant. The principle of the new system of National Education may be shortly stated as that of united secular, and separate religious, instruction.*

---

gress of the Evangelical movement among the clergy and laity of the Established Church in Ireland, and of those clergymen whose preaching principally contributed to advance it. (See Killen's *Ecclesiastical History of Ireland*, vol. ii. pp. 383–388.)

* Earl Russell, in his *Reflections and Suggestions* (1875), expresses the principle of the system administered by the National Board of Education in Ireland in words slightly different. . . . "The object of the system (he says) is to afford combined literary and moral, and separate religious, instruction to children of all persuasions, and as far as possible in the same school, upon the fundamental principle that no attempt shall be made to interfere with the peculiar religious tenets of any description of Christian pupils."

Selections from the Scriptures were, however, prepared by, or under the sanction of, the Board, and used in the schools. The separation of religious from secular instruction, the separation of the children from each other when religious instruction was given, and the substitution of selections from the Bible for the Bible in its completeness, were condemned by many of the Protestant clergy and laity.*

That either upon theological or educational questions, or indeed upon any matters of opinion, there will not be, even in the same church or association, disagreements, is a vain expectation: differences in character and intelligence, if there were no other cause, render them inevitable. Nor is it certain that if this were otherwise the interests of truth would be served; since where unanimity exists there is little research or inquiry. But if it be true that disagreements cannot be averted, it is also true that experience and reflection mitigate the asperities of controversy, and abate the sharpness of the distinctions between opposing systems and parties. Long before the period of disestablishment, the divisions within the Church which have been adverted to were growing faint and indistinct; the causes of them were thought to be of diminished importance, and discussion in connexion with them was conducted with increased moderation. Party spirit, although not extinguished, was inactive.

---

* The growth of the system of the National Board of Education will be seen from the following figures (see *Thom's Directory*, 1886):—

|          | Schools. | Number of Pupils. | Parliamentary Grant. |
|----------|----------|-------------------|----------------------|
| In 1834, | 1106     | 145,521           | £20,000              |
| In 1884, | 7832     | 1,089,079         | £756,027             |

The tendency of the Church in this direction had been promoted by the high standard of education in the Divinity School of the University of Dublin. A succession of eminent professors presided over it, and required from the candidates for orders an extensive course of study. Necessarily the result was that enlarged and comprehensive ideas in connexion with theological questions were diffused among them.

No circumstance had, prior to the Union, more injuriously affected the interests of the Church than the mode in which the patronage of the Crown was exercised; nowhere was a more beneficial change perceived subsequently. The small number of bishops entitled to sit in the House of Lords rendered their support of less consequence to parliamentary parties: and hence, though political motives cannot be said to have been overlooked, they were less regarded by Ministers in advising appointments, and, if taken into account, were considered along with professional merit. The great majority of the prelates, during the interval between the Union and Disestablishment, were deserving of their position. Many added to their excellence, as theologians or clergymen, high attainments in other studies.*

---

* To mention only such of the Bishops distinguished for literary or scientific pursuits as were connected with Trinity College, Dublin:—Kearney (Ossory, 1805), Hall (Dromore, 1811) had both been Provosts; Magee (Raphoe, 1819; Dublin, 1822) had been a Fellow; Elrington (Ferns, 1822) had been Provost; Brinkley (Cloyne, 1826) had been Professor of Astronomy; Kyle (Cork, 1835) had been Provost; Sandes (Cashel, 1839) had been a Fellow; O'Brien (Ossory, 1842) had been a Fellow, and a Professor of Divinity; Singer (Meath, 1852) had been a Fellow; Griffin (Limerick, 1854) had been a Fellow; Butcher (Meath, 1866) had been a Fellow, and Regius Professor of Divinity; Graves (Limerick, 1866)

Generally, at the time of disestablishment, the clerical order in Ireland was deservedly held in high estimation : its members were for the most part educated, refined in manners, courteous and conciliatory: where they had parishioners of their own religion, they discharged with diligence the duties of their office; where they had none to attend their ministry, they were at least agents to spread social improvement.*

An examination of the merits of individuals eminent during the period which we are now considering would detain too long, for at no period did a greater number justly claim to be specially noticed. Also it is not probable that such an examination, if undertaken, would prove satisfactory. We are as yet subject to the influences which affected those on whom we should have to pronounce judgment, and are imbued with like prepossessions and sympathies. A contemporary—at least a contemporary who has lived in intimacy with many whose acts must come under review—cannot hope to bring to the task the requisite impartiality. No more, therefore, will be attempted than to notice the most

---

had been a Fellow, and Professor of Mathematics. Dickinson (Meath, 1840), Wilson (Cork, 1848), and Fitzgerald (Cork, 1857; Killaloe, 1862), although not Fellows, were highly distinguished in connexion with academic studies.

* A testimony to the merits of the clergy of the Established Church was, in 1867, given by Dr. Moriarty, the Roman Catholic Bishop of Kerry, equally honourable to himself and them. In a letter to his clergy (Dublin, 1867), advocating disestablishment, he says, . . . " but it must be said, and we say it with pleasure, for we rejoice in all that is good, that in every relation of life the Protestant clergy who reside amongst us are not only blameless, but estimable and edifying. They are peaceful with all, and to their neighbours they are kind when they can; and we know that on many occasions they would be more active in beneficence, but that

important of the writings which, in connexion with the theological controversies of the first sixty years of the nineteenth century, guided the direction of opinion within the Church.

Of these, as being the earliest in date, and as being also of pre-eminent excellence, the well-known work of Magee, afterwards Archbishop of Dublin, upon *The Atonement*, occasioned by the progress of Unitarianism, may be properly first referred to. It presents one of the instances where an author seizes possession of a subject not yet occupied, and, by the skill and ability with which he treats it, appropriates it for ever. In the discourses and dissertations, of which the book consists, great learning is at the command of equally great intellectual power. The matters discussed in them are the general objections to a mediatorial scheme: they do not examine the various theories which have been advocated by those who, concurring in admitting the doctrine of the atonement, disagree respecting questions necessarily growing out of, or connected with it.*

Among these questions, unquestionably the most

---

they do not wish to appear meddling, or incur the suspicion of tampering with poor Catholics. In bearing, in manners, and in dress, they become their state. If they are not learned theologians, they are accomplished scholars and polished gentlemen. There is little intercourse between them and us; but they cannot escape our observation; and sometimes when we noticed that quiet, and decorous, and moderate course of life, we feel ourselves giving expression to the wish: *talis cum sis utinam noster esses."*

* A life of Archbishop Magee, evidently founded upon authoritative information, will be found in Wills' *Lives of Illustrious Irishmen*, vol. vi. p. 353. Magee's reputation for eloquence as a preacher rivalled Kirwan's; but, unlike Kirwan, he has left specimens which perfectly justify the reputation he attained with his contemporaries.

important relate to "Justification"—What are the conditions under which the benefits of the atonement reach to, or are received by, fallen man? By what means is "justification" attained? At the time of Ussher the clergy of the Church of Ireland would have answered that "justification" was "by faith only": at the time of the Restoration, that it was by "faith and works" together, that is, by the obedience of faith. The former, as is well known, was the doctrine of Luther, who pronounced its acceptance or rejection the test of a Church—*articulus stantis vel cadentis ecclesiæ*. The latter tenet, or opinions resembling it, began to find favour with influential Protestant divines about the time of the Synod of Dort.

Among the writings of the older Irish divines who are to be classed of the Lutheran school in relation to the question of Justification, it is sufficient to refer to an elaborate *Treatise of Justification*, written by Downham, Bishop of Derry \* (1616-1634). This very able work treats of justification, the relation of faith to justification, the nature of justifying faith, and the effects of such faith in regenerating those who have it. Justification is defined as "a most gracious and righteous action of God, whereby He, imputing the righteousness of Christ to a believing sinner, absolveth him from his sins, and accepteth him as righteous in Christ, and as an heir of eternal life to the praise and glory of His own mercy and justice." †

The opposing theory is (perhaps more strongly than

---

\* See p. 107, *supra*.

† The *Treatise of Justification* appears to have been written as an answer to Cardinal Bellarmine.

by any other Protestant divine) stated by Jeremy Taylor in a sermon which, when Bishop of Down, he preached in the cathedral of Christ Church, Dublin, and which he entitled *Fides Formata:* or, Faith working by Love. It was on the text in St. James, "by works a man is justified, and not by faith only." This text, he says, "does not assert that we are not justified by faith, for that had been irreconcilable with St. Paul; but that we are so justified by works, that it is not by faith alone: it is faith and works together; that is, by the obedience of faith, by the works of faith, by the law of faith, by righteousness evangelical, by the conditions of the Gospel, and the measures of Christ." . . . "Faith and good works are no part of a distinction, but members of one entire body."\*

The Evangelical school of theology, as has been mentioned, reverted to the ideas of an earlier period in Ireland; and among these to what was then held in relation to justification. In opposition to them, their adversaries either advocated the opinions enunciated by Taylor in the sermon which has been cited, or others intermediate between the views of Taylor and those of Downham.

Among the discussions of the subject which were occasioned by the revival of controversy at this time, none deserve to be rated higher than, on the one side, an examination of the question by Dr. O'Brien, a Fellow of Trinity College, who successively became Professor of Divinity in the University of Dublin, and Bishop of Ossory in the Established Church of Ireland; and on

---

\* See vol. iii., page 321, of Hughes's edition of Taylor's Sermons.

the other side some essays and papers of Alexander Knox, a layman of the same Church, whose philosophical reflections and persuasive eloquence gave, at the time, to his writings, and, perhaps, even more to his conversation,* great influence.

The work of Dr. O'Brien, now alluded to, was published in 1834. It professes for its object to explain and establish the doctrine of justification by faith only, in *Ten Sermons upon the Nature and Effects of Faith*. The sermons had been preached in the chapel of Trinity College in 1829 and 1831.† These sermons follow Luther and the Continental Divines contemporaries of Luther in their exposition of the subject, perhaps even more closely than Downham had done;‡ but with so much that is new of argument and illustration, especially in connexion with an exposition of the moral effects of

---

* The superiority of Knox's conversation over his writings is asserted in a review of his correspondence in the *Dublin University Magazine*, vol. iv., page 242, evidently written by one who knew him intimately. To the affluence of ideas in his conversation Bishop Jebb has borne a striking testimony. . . . "Scarce a day passes in which some energetic truth, some pregnant principle, some happy illustration (and those illustrations powerful arguments), does not present itself, for which I was primarily indebted to the ever-salient mind of Alexander Knox." (Introduction to Jebb's edition of *Burnet's Lives*.) Knox had been Secretary to Lord Castlereagh before the Union; but although urged by him to pursue a political career, and offered a seat in Parliament, he, after that event, withdrew from public affairs to a life of study and religious contemplation.

† *Dublin University Calendar*, 1886, page 411.

‡ In the preface, Dr. O'Brien says: . . . "If I have proved that the doctrine of justification which I have found in the Bible was found there by the Reformers of the Continent and of Britain, I have traced my views of the doctrine to the only human parentage which I feel very solicitous to establish for them."

faith contained in them, that they may fairly receive the praise of originality. Faith is defined in these discourses to be not merely or properly a belief of the truth of the Scripture narrative concerning our Lord, or an assent of the understanding to certain propositions derived from that narrative; but to be trust in Christ or in God through Christ, founded upon such a belief or assent; an entire and unreserved confidence in the efficacy of what Christ has done and suffered for us; a full reliance upon Him and upon His works. Justification is regarded as a judicial acquittal from the consequences of having violated the divine law, and acceptance as if it had been fulfilled. Righteousness of life is the consequence of faith, and receives from that principle the most effective motives and impulses.\*

Knox's opinions in reference to this subject are contained in a collection of essays, memoranda, and letters, that under the title of his *Remains* were published after his death, which occurred in 1831. According to Knox, justification is rather internal than external; a provision not merely to effect acquittal from legal condemnation, but to deliver from the thraldom of sin, and to purify from moral pollution. "Our reputative justification," he holds to be, "the result of previous moral justification." It is, he observes, a departure from the simplicity of Scripture to suppose that to save from sin is no more than to save from its penal consequences—to cleanse from all our sins, the same as to cleanse from the punishment or imputation of them. To forgive is, he

---

\* See pp. 14, 68, 69, 255, of second edition of the Sermons.

admits, to remove the penalty; but then the worst penalty of sin is the reigning power of sin.\*

Knox, while opposing the Evangelical party upon these and other topics, bore testimony to their practical virtues†. Without condemning them, he asserted that there might be, and was, "a more excellent way." Religion, according to him, is a life: its end and object to exercise a transmutative influence over the heart; that it also presents a creed for acceptance, and appeals to the intelligence as well as the affections, he did not deny; but in his estimate the *amanda* ranked before the *credenda*.

Jebb, Bishop of Limerick (1823–1834), was a disciple of Knox. After their deaths a correspondence, which had been carried on between them for thirty years, was published—a book of great value, as preserving admirable observations and reflections upon theological questions, and as casting much light upon the history of religion in Ireland during their time. Jebb's own works are of high merit. To him is due the full development of the theory originated by Bishop Louth, that parallelism, correspondency of thought, not of metre, is an essential element of Hebrew poetry.‡

---

\* Knox's *Remains*, vol. i. p. 306, ii. p. 13, iv. p. 375, and see, in relation to justification, also his letter to Mr. Parken (*Remains*, vol. i. p. 281); and compare with it his essays *On the leading design of the Christian dispensation, as exhibited in the epistle to the Romans*, and *On redemption and salvation by Christ, as exhibited in the epistle to the Romans and the Hebrews*. See further on the general question, Note CC of Appendix.

† In a letter of 5 Aug., 1828, Knox says "The Evangelicals (as they are called) have been the chief instruments of maintaining experimental religion in the Reformed Churches."—*Remains*, vol. iv. p. 501.

‡ See Jebb's *Sacred Literature*, 2nd edition, London, 1828.

About the time when Knox's *Remains* were published a movement originated with the High Church party at Oxford. Its leaders, in order to spread their ideas, issued a series of tracts, to which they gave the name of *Tracts for the Times*, whence their adherents were called "Tractarians." Knox, they alleged, both foresaw and contributed to the rise of this movement.* Its object was to revive the very high views in reference to apostolical succession, the sacraments, and the authority of the Church both in itself and as guardian of traditions from the early ages of Christianity, which had become popular among the English clergy in the latter part of the reign of James I. and in the reign of Charles I.; also to recommend reserve, when instructing the laity respecting some subjects, especially in connexion with the question of justification. These ideas found many supporters in England; and the Tractarian party there, not merely by their writings, but by numerous and conspicuous examples of zeal and piety, exercised much influence over the clergy. They found no followers in the Church of Ireland. Their system was by both the clergy and laity of that Church regarded as a mitigated form of all from which the Reformers dissented, and with which Protestantism was in Ireland contending. It was disapproved by the Bishops; in the charges of some of them decisively condemned; and it received from one of the Bench, Whately, then Archbishop of Dublin, assisted by other ecclesiastics of the Irish Church,†

---

\* See this asserted in an article on Church Parties in the *British Critic* for April, 1839, which Newman, in his *Apologia*, says was written by himself.

† Of this assistance the greatest and most valuable part came from

in the *Cautions for the Times*, an answer that, probably, of all which the controversy called forth was the most able.

In addition to his share in the *Cautions for the Times*, Archbishop Whately was the author of many treatises upon religious subjects, entitled to the highest place in theological literature. He was essentially a thinker, distinguished in his investigations, not more by the sagacity than the impartiality and judicial calmness with which they were conducted. He has been criticized as wanting in depth, and as being confined to a narrow round of topics. Neither observation is just. The notion that he wants depth arises from his clear and lucid style, not surpassed even by Paley, against whom a similar complaint was, for a like reason, urged; and the supposition that his range is limited is caused by a habit of repetition in the statement of his opinions, which he acquired at Oxford when as a tutor impressing instruction upon his pupils. It would be difficult to find essays more imbued with a philosophical spirit, or exhibiting more acuteness in the analysis of men's motives and conduct, than his *Bampton Lectures* "On the use and abuse of party feeling in matters of Religion," or the work which was termed *On the Errors of Romanism having their Origin in Human*

---

Dr. Fitzgerald, then Whately's chaplain, and afterwards Bishop of Killaloe, whose learning and sound judgment rendered him an invaluable ally in the controversy. A memoir of Bishop Fitzgerald has lately appeared, prefixed to an edition of *Lectures on Ecclesiastical History*, which he delivered in the University of Dublin. It is recorded of this eminent prelate that he was accustomed at times to write in his books the maxim, ἐν μέσῳ ἡ ἀρετή; and there is no doubt that his opinions were eminently characterized by its spirit.

*Nature*, but which, being of much wider scope than this title imports, might more appropriately have been called Errors inherent in Human Nature in connexion with religion.

The views of so eminent a person, in reference to some questions respecting which the opinions of other divines of the Irish Church have been stated, demand to be at least briefly noticed. In his *Essays on the Difficulties in the Writings of St. Paul*, he (as might from the subject he had proposed to himself for consideration be anticipated) discusses the predestinarian question. Referring to the opposite theories usually maintained in relation to election—one making it depend upon an immutable and unconditional decree arbitrarily determined upon, whereby a certain number are chosen, who, as a consequence, are influenced to a life of righteousness here and brought finally to eternal happiness hereafter; and the other admitting a choice, but treating it as not arbitrary; as, on the contrary, being founded upon the foreseen faith and obedience of those who are its objects—he shows that these alternatives by no means exhaust the views in reference to this subject which require to be examined. There may, he points out, be election without being election of the character suggested. The Jews were unquestionably as a nation elected, and elected arbitrarily: but it was an election not to blessings absolutely, but to a privilege, to the offer and opportunity of obtaining a peculiar blessing, such as was not placed within the reach of other nations. And so there is an election under the Christian dispensation, but of an analogous nature: an election not arbitrarily to salvation, but to privileges—the knowledge of the gospel, the aids of the Holy Spirit, and the offer of eternal life. Of these all are exhorted, but none compelled, to make a right use; and according as this is, or is not, the case, they will prove a blessing or a curse.*

In the *Cautions for the Times* apostolical succession, and the ideas upon this subject suggested in the Oxford *Tracts for the Times*, are considered. While the authors of the *Cautions* affirm that the three orders of bishops, priests, and deacons, were instituted by the apostles in the original platform of the Church; they also assert that no unalterable model of government is drawn for the Christian Church in Scripture, as there was for the Jewish. There has been an apostolical succession in the sense that there has been such an order of men as Christian ministers from the time of the apostles; but this is different from a succession in the individual minister, which these writers hold, could never be established as a fact.†

Whately is the fourth Irish prelate to whose opinions in relation to the episcopal and ministerial offices there has been occasion to refer; ‡ the series of authorities may well be closed by referring to a sermon upon the

---

\* See the second series of these essays, 7th edition, pp. 68-93. Whately is sometimes supposed to have held predestination to be of nations; in one sense he did, for nations may enjoy peculiar privileges; but the doctrine of *National Election* (properly so called) is not his, but Archbishop Sumner's, who considers rather who are called, whether nations or individuals, while Whately regards not so much who are called, but to what they are called, privileges or absolute blessings.

† See *Cautions for the Times*, pp. 301, 302, 315, 316, with which Whately's *Kingdom of Christ* may be compared.

‡ See the opinions of Bishop Downham at p. 107; of Archbishop Ussher at p. 130; of Bishop Taylor at p. 145. And see Appendix D D.

same subject, delivered by Professor Archer Butler, of the University of Dublin, which, like his other writings, exhibits a combination of profound thought with brilliant eloquence. The object of this discourse is to reconcile high views as to these offices with universal Christian sympathy. The preacher assumes the sacred right of the offices: that a divine commission was originally given: that it has been transmitted in direct and unbroken succession through and from the apostles. He admits that, nevertheless, there are Churches, where this organization does not exist and whose ministry cannot claim this transmitted authority, which have manifested examples of religious influences, of practical righteousness, and of devotional zeal. Does the *fact* refute the *theory?* No, it is replied; for, while the union of a divinely-appointed polity with a pure system of religion was intended, the latter by itself will produce these results. Besides, relaxations of a prescribed scheme might be permitted, and thus, or from special interpositions, the success of exceptions from it may be explained.*

Adhering to the limit already assigned for consideration of the theological writings of this period, it will be sufficient, in addition to those already noticed, to refer to the works of Laurence, Archbishop of Cashel (1822-1838), and of Mant, Bishop of Down (1823-1848). The *Bampton Lectures* of the former were designed to establish that the Articles of the Church of England were not framed to bear merely a Calvinistic sense;

---

* See *Sermons* by Rev. William Archer Butler: Dublin, 1849, p. 458.

and with that object he enters into an investigation of contemporary ecclesiastical history, and of the opinions of the authors of the Articles upon the subject of predestination. The writings of Bishop Mant[*] refer very much to questions which have been raised respecting the services, rules, and rubrics of the Church. In the controversy respecting education he took part with those who contended that religion should be the basis of education. But the literary work with which the name of Bishop Mant is likely to be most permanently connected is the *History of the Church of Ireland*, from the Reformation to the date of the Union. To this there has been occasion in the present treatise very frequently to refer: and to it every student of Irish Ecclesiastical History must continue to refer, as the most complete and accurate collection of the facts occurring within the period of which it treats.[†]

---

[*] A complete catalogue of the numerous writings of Bishop Mant, including his charges and sermons, will be found in Cotton's *Fasti*, vol. iii. pp. 213-218.

[†] Another history, also by a member of the Established Church of Ireland, the Rev. Robert King, ought to be studied in conjunction with Bishop Mant's. It commences from the introduction of Christianity into Ireland, and ends at 1622. Under the unassuming title of "A Primer," it contains the results of much research, especially as to the earlier periods.

# CHAPTER XVIII.

### DISESTABLISHMENT.

IN 1834 the first official inquiry into the number of persons in communion with the Established Church in Ireland was instituted.* In 1841 a census of the people was taken, and another in 1851; but in neither was any return required of religious profession. The census of 1851 disclosed a great diminution of the population generally; but in what degree this diminution affected the relative numbers of adherents to the different Churches and religious systems existing in Ireland was left uncertain. In 1861 was the next census; and then in Ireland the people were required to state of what religious denominations they professed to be members. When the enumeration was completed it disclosed the following result:—

| | |
|---|---:|
| Roman Catholics, | 4,505,265 |
| Members of the Established Church, | 693,857 |
| Presbyterians, | 523,291 |
| Other dissenting bodies (except Jews), | 76,661 |
| Jews, | 893 |
| Total, | 5,798,967 |

These figures, which were ascertained not from speculative estimates or other defective sources of in-

---

* See p. 229.

formation, but from the actual returns made of their religious profession by the people, placed beyond doubt the great disproportion existing between the number of members of the Established Church and the whole population.* The advocates of disestablishment at once saw the advantage which the facts thus proved gave them. They renewed the controversy, which had since 1838 been quiescent, and pointed out how it was then suggested that by the legislation of that period, directed, as it was, to conciliate the Roman Catholic portion of the people, all obstacles to the progress of the Church would be removed, and that only its success was to be expected.† These anticipations, it was urged, had obviously not been fulfilled, and their failure must, when taken into consideration for political purposes, assume the greater importance, because there was no demerit on the part of the Church, regarded merely as a religious institution, to account for it. On the contrary, its clergy were admitted to be, in every respect, worthy of their calling: foremost in works of benevolence, kind and generous, and encouraging kindness and generosity in others.

---

* In the inquiry of 1834 Commissioners were appointed to ascertain the number who in Ireland were in communion with "The United Church of England and Ireland." They had less perfect means of acquiring information than was provided by the mode in which the census of 1861 was taken. The Commissioners "were to ascertain the number in each parish on the spot, by the best evidence they could procure there or elsewhere." In comparing their estimates with the enumeration in 1861, it is to be remembered that they classed the Methodists with the members of the Church, while in the latter the Methodists were regarded as a separate religious body dissenting from it.

† See p. 238, *supra*.

Nor was it merely the Established Church which, it was said, must as a missionary Church be pronounced to have failed. Protestantism generally was open to the same reproach. The census showed that the members of the Presbyterian Church were not much less numerous than the members of the Established; its clergy were exemplary in conduct, and characterized by ability and energy. However they might differ from their episcopally-ordained brethren upon questions of Church government, they were their allies against the Church of Rome, and against its doctrinal teaching. There were also other Protestant dissenters in Ireland who took the same side. The Church of Rome and its religious system had successfully held their ground against all varieties of Protestantism, whether separately or in combination.

Previous to, and during the beginning of, the nineteenth century, there existed apathy and neglect on the part of Protestants in relation to the conversion of Roman Catholics. But this had long ceased. For more than fifty years before the census of 1861, energetic exertions were made for the purpose; societies formed to promote it were supported alike by Church Protestants and dissenting Protestants, and were supplied both in England and Ireland with ample contributions. Their agents penetrated every part of the country, bringing home to the inhabitants, by preaching, and by the books and tracts which they disseminated, a knowledge of the objections made to the authority and tenets of the Church of Rome. These efforts were not without results; but the results, it was admitted, were not sufficient of themselves to stay or even influence the course of political action.*

The topics which have been now referred to would suggest themselves upon even a cursory reference to the census of 1861, and to the events which preceded it. A more minute examination of the census disclosed other circumstances which, it was alleged, deserved to be at this time also taken into account. Three Churches —the Roman Catholic, Protestant Episcopalian, and Presbyterian—were seen to be pre-eminent in numbers; the same were also, all would allow, pre-eminent in intellectual cultivation, and in social power and influence. When the localities where the persons who returned themselves as in communion with these Churches came to be scrutinized, it was found that Protestants were numerous only in places where settlers had from time to time been introduced: the Episcopalian Protestants being in those where colonization was English, and the Presbyterian where it was Scotch. The portion of the people who were of Irish descent were seen to have almost all adhered to the Roman Catholic religion. So also did many of mixed native and English race, and a less number of pure English descent. Thus it was observed not only were there in Ireland three religious systems entitled to social pre-eminence, but,

---

* An account of the proceedings adopted in the nineteenth century for the conversion to Protestantism of Roman Catholics in Ireland will be found in a Paper read at the Church Congress held in Dublin in 1868, by the Hon. and Rev. W. C. Plunket, now Lord Plunket, and Archbishop of Dublin in the disestablished Church of Ireland.—See *Report* of this Congress, p. 115.

what seems to be without parallel in any other kingdom, each of these three derived its chief support from a distinct and different nationality.*

If the general result of the census was unfavourable to the continuance of the Establishment in Ireland, these, its more minute, details, were alleged to be equally so. Did it not seem, it was said, as if some inexplicable, but not the less insuperable, barrier opposed the introduction of Protestantism among the mass of the people? The experiment had been tried; it had not as yet succeeded. What reason was there to infer that the future would differ from the past? The people of Ireland, from the reign of Henry VIII. to that of James I., were subdivided into two religious denominations; and from the reign of James I. into three. None of them had in the intervening period gained ground against the others.†

Then as to reasons of a religious character, which thirty years before were offered in defence of the Establishment, these, it was contended, ought no longer to prevail. If the idea had once been entertained that the State should select for its favour an ecclesiastical system

---

\* Roman Catholics, Protestants belonging to the Church, and Presbyterians, according to the census of 1861, were distributed in the provinces as follows :—

|  | Rom. Caths. | Chur. Prots. | Presbyterians. |
|---|---|---|---|
| Ulster, | 966,613 | 391,315 | 503,835 |
| Leinster, | 1,252,553 | 180,587 | 12,355 |
| Munster, | 1,420,076 | 80,860 | 4,013 |
| Connaught, | 866,023 | 40,595 | 3,088 |
| Total, | 4,505,265 | 693,357 | 523,291 |

† Some writers of eminence seem to think that there are characteristics of the Celtic race which hinder the progress of Protestantism among them. But on this subject see Note E E of Appendix.

because it taught religious truth, this policy must, it was asserted, be held to have been for some time deliberately abandoned. An increased grant had been made to the College of Maynooth in order to provide instruction in Roman Catholic theological principles for students. After this measure the State, it was suggested, could not consistently allege an obligation, resting on the ground of duty, to maintain the Irish Church.*

In some respects, it was generally admitted, the State was benefitted by the existing Establishment: the union of the Churches strengthened the union of the kingdoms; the clergy promoted social improvement; but did these benefits, it was asked, counterbalance the difficulties in which the administration of government in the country was placed by local discontent originating from the ascendency of a Church which was unpopular with the great majority of the people?

Notwithstanding, however, that the arguments, which have been stated, were pressed with ability, and received with favour by many, six years elapsed after the census of 1861 before any move was made in Parliament to induce a decision in conformity with them. The adversaries of the Church were agreed in demanding its disestablishment, but not agreed as to the course to be

---

\* See Mr. Gladstone's *Chapter of Autobiography*, published in 1868, to explain his change of policy in reference to the Church of Ireland:—
"The moment," he says, "that I admitted the validity of a claim by the Church of Rome for the gift, by the free act of the Imperial Parliament, of new funds for the education of its clergy, the true basis of the Established Church of Ireland for me was cut away. The one had always been treated by me as exclusive of the other" (p. 30). Compare with these observations his former opinions, as they have been stated at p. 237, *supra*.

pursued in reference to its endowments. And, until they were united upon this point also, parliamentary action was thought to be both useless and injudicious.

The difference of opinion as to the endowments of the Church—if a measure of disestablishment were carried—was divided between the alternatives of total disendowment, or partial disendowment with a concurrent provision for the Roman Catholic and Presbyterian Churches. Which of these measures was to be preferred?

The answer to this question concerned other Churches besides the Established. The Roman Catholic and Presbyterian Churches were both in the receipt of assistance from the State: an annual sum was paid for the benefit of each from the Imperial revenues—to the College of Maynooth, about £26,000 a-year; to the Presbyterian Church, from £45,000 to £50,000 yearly.\*
If the Church were totally disendowed, these grants, it was certain, would not be continued. Thus total disendowment would eventuate in casting not only the Established Church but every other Church in Ireland solely upon voluntary support. In a country of limited means, the entire provision for educating, and afterwards for maintaining, the ministers of religion, must be supplied from that precarious source. This, it was argued, was to imperil grave interests.†

Nor would the effect of total disendowment be

---

\* See Mr. Gladstone's speech, March 1, 1869.
† See, in support of these views, *Letter of Earl Russell to the Right Hon. Chichester Fortescue*, Feb. 3, 1868; *Letter of Earl Grey to the Right Hon. John Bright*, March 26, 1868; *The Three Churches*, by Dean Stanley, London, 1868; and conversations of Nassau Senior with Archbishop Whately, in Senior's *Journals in Ireland*, vol. ii. pp. 129, 293.

confined to Ireland. What was now resolved upon for that country would form a precedent for other countries and other times. In every Christian kingdom in Europe there had been set apart, out of the general property of the community, a portion reserved as a fixed and permanent estate dedicated to the maintenance of religious teaching. Circumstances might in some or even in all of these kingdoms oblige a review of the arrangements connected with ecclesiastical endowments. Were they to be taught, by the example of the Parliament of Great Britain and Ireland, that the principle upon which to proceed was neither reform of the institutions in the enjoyment of these endowments, nor transfer to, nor redistribution among, other religious communities, but simple and absolute confiscation for purposes of a merely secular character?

At length, in 1867, Earl Russell, who was known to favour the concurrent endowment of the three Churches pre-eminent in Ireland in preference to their total disendowment, brought under discussion in the House of Lords, the question of the Irish Church. He moved that a Royal Commission should be issued to inquire into the property of the Church of Ireland, "with a view," as it was expressed in the terms of the motion, "to make the property more productive, and in order to its more equitable application for the benefit of the Irish people." This motion, with the omission of the reference to a more equitable application of the property, was acceded to by the Government of the day, and an undertaking was given that commissioners should be appointed to make the inquiry which was sought.

Accordingly, later in the same year such Commissioners were nominated. They were directed to inquire and report upon the whole organization and property of the Church in Ireland: as to its archbishoprics, bishoprics, dignities, benefices, and corporations aggregate, and the revenues of the same respectively; as to its several united and separate parishes and parochial districts; as to its churches and chapels; and as to the number of members of the Established Church of England and Ireland inhabiting the parishes or districts attached to the churches: also as to the property and emoluments vested in, and administered by, the Board of Ecclesiastical Commissioners for Ireland which had been constituted by the Church Temporalities Acts of 1833 and 1834, and their administration of the same; and lastly, to inquire and report whether any improvement should be made in the administration or distribution of the revenues, or in relation to the offices which were to be inquired into and reported upon.*

At the opening of the next Session of Parliament (1868), although the Commission thus appointed was engaged upon the inquiry committed to it, and had not then reported, the subject of the Irish Church occupied the attention of the House of Commons, and gave rise to considerable controversy. The Minister at this time in charge of Irish affairs in that House was the Earl of Mayo, remarkable then, as also afterwards in the

---

\* The Commissioners were Earl Stanhope (the historian); Earl of Meath; Viscount De Vesci; Sir Joseph Napier (Ex-Lord Chancellor of Ireland); Colonel Shafto Adair (afterwards Lord Waveney); E. P. Shirley; Edward Howes (one of the English Ecclesiastical Commissioners); George Clive, M.P.; and the author of the present treatise (then Vicar-General of the Province of Armagh).

more conspicuous office of Governor-General of India, for enlarged and generous views of policy. Objecting to the position of the Church of Ireland being made the subject of parliamentary controversy, before the Commission granted in consequence of Earl Russell's motion had reported, he, in the course of an elaborate speech dealing with the general condition of Ireland, expressed his unwavering hostility to any plan for total disendowment of the Church: "Of all the schemes that have been proposed," he said, "I object pre-eminently to that known as the process of levelling down." ... "I believe that in these matters, as in everything else, confiscation is the worst proposal."

But the Government of which Lord Mayo was a member were in a minority in the House of Commons. Their support of these views lent no additional weight to them in the estimation of that assembly; and the leaders of the Opposition determined to make the question of the Church the occasion of immediate party conflict. Resolutions, and then a Bill for the suspension of appointments in the Church of Ireland, were submitted to the House of Commons, with the avowal that they were preparatory to a complete measure of disestablishment being introduced when a new Parliament should meet, after the present had, in consequence of changes enacted in the representation of the country, been dissolved.

The justification offered for these proceedings was founded upon political reasons. Motives of expediency induced their adoption. No complaint whatever was made of the Church or of its Clergy; there was no allegation of any neglect or default on the part of either. "My belief," said Mr. Gladstone—who brought forward these measures—"is, that as far as abuses, in the common sense of the word, are concerned—that is, those which depend on the conduct of the bishops and clergy, and which are remediable by the wisdom and energy of the clerical body, or the purity of life of the lay members—it is my belief that the Irish Church is entirely free from such abuses. We must all accord to that Church this praise: that her clergy are a body of zealous and devoted ministers, who give themselves to their sacerdotal functions in a degree not inferior to any other Christian Church."

The Resolutions and Bill for suspending Irish ecclesiastical appointments passed through the House of Commons by considerable majorities; but the Bill was rejected in the House of Lords. Further parliamentary action in reference to the Church of Ireland was deferred until it was seen what, in reference to the Church question, would be the opinions of the members of the House of Commons to be returned at the general election, which was soon to take place.

Later in the same year (1868), the Commissioners appointed to inquire into the condition of the Irish Church made their Report. . . They calculated the area of the entire island at 20,701,346 acres. The whole (they stated) was included in and subdivided into parochial divisions. The Church population scattered over this extent had been, as has been already mentioned, ascertained by the Census Commissioners to be 693,357. From them the Church Commissioners obtained an account of its distribution over the country, according to the parochial districts under separate incumbents. These they reckoned at 1478; and of them there were 181 which had a Church population above 1000; 1096 with numbers varying from that amount down to 40 persons; 110 with under 40 and not less than 20; and 91 with less than 20. There were 2 Archbishoprics, 10 Bishoprics, 30 corporations of Deans and Chapters, 32 Deaneries, 33 Archdeaconries, and 1518 benefices.

The property of the Church, according to the Report, consisted of tithe rentcharges, lands let to tenants, and lands and houses in the occupation of ecclesiastical persons. The value of the last description of property the commissioners had no means of estimating, except what were furnished by the valuations for local taxation. It was therefore returned according to these valuations; but such estimates were, in accordance with the principles on which an official valuation was made, below the letting value. The net income from tithe rentcharge and from lands let to tenants was calculated to exceed £580,000, a-year.* Of this amount, more than £113,000 a-year was administered by the Ecclesiastical Commissioners for Church purposes, such as the building and repairing of churches, and providing requisites for the celebration of worship; about £19,000 a-year belonged to the capitular bodies, and was by them applied towards maintaining the cathedrals and their services; and the residue supplied the incomes of the bishops, dignitaries, and beneficed clergy.

The Commissioners made suggestions for improvement in the internal management of the Church and of its property. Among other things they recommended a reduction of the Episcopate to one Archbishop and

---

* See Note FF of Appendix.

seven bishops, accompanied by diminution of their salaries: the dissolution of all cathedral corporations, except in the cities where the residences of the Bishoprics retained were to be: and the abolition of cathedral dignitaries and officers in the dissolved cathedral corporations.*

At the general election which followed the dissolution of Parliament upon the termination of the Session of 1868, a majority of the members returned to the House of Commons were favourable to the disestablishment of the Irish Church. Early in 1869 a Bill intended to effect that object was brought forward by the Government which was then in office. This Bill, with some alterations, ultimately, under the name of the "Irish Church Act," became law.

The Act was founded upon the principle of the total disestablishment and disendowment of the Church of Ireland, and of the withdrawal of all assistance from the State to other Churches. The interests of incumbents of offices and benefices in the Church, and of other persons interested for life in the properties, or

---

* In a charge delivered in the autumn of 1868, after the publication of this Report, Archbishop Beresford observed:—"The proposition that the Church, after a severe scrutiny, has been shown to be not excessive in its general endowments, with no overgrown fortunes in its individual ministers, and free from the reproach of pluralities, has been established by this Report. What the clergy individually are (with rare exceptions), in character and conduct, and exemplary discharge of their duties, has been testified by their opponents; and by no one more freely and more fully than by Mr. Gladstone himself. If we are to fall, it is for no default of duty, no reasonable objection to our ecclesiastical system, nor to the constitution or condition of our Church: it is solely for external causes and reasons. Of this consolation we can never be deprived."

annual grants affected by the Act, were respected, and either preserved or made a subject of compensation.

For the purpose of this treatise it is at present only necessary to refer to some provisions of the Act:—On and after the first day of January, 1871, the union between the Churches of England and Ireland was, it was declared, dissolved, and the Church of Ireland was then to cease to be established by law. As of the same day, every Ecclesiastical Corporation in Ireland, whether sole or aggregate, and every Cathedral Corporation, was dissolved. Then also, subject only to such life estates and rights as were to be retained by ecclesiastical persons, and to such rights and compensation as were given to them in respect of any revenues taken from them, all the property of the Church, whether real or personal, was to vest in Commissioners, to be called "The Commissioners of Church Temporalities in Ireland," and by them to be converted and applied. Life estates in lands were preserved; but annuities were substituted for the incomes derived from tithe rentcharge, and were to be paid by the Commissioners. Power was given to create a corporation, to be termed "The Church Representative Body," which might hold and manage property for the disestablished Church. The churches in use at the passing of the Act were to be conveyed to this body, subject to the life interests of the incumbents; the same was to take place with such burying-grounds as adjoined these churches; and the Temporalities Commissioners were to sell to this corporation for the benefit of the Church the houses of residence and a suitable proportion of the glebes connected with them. As an equivalent for private endowments, which it was felt that it would be unjust to confiscate without compensation, a sum of £500,000 was to be paid to the Representative Body.

By the general law Convocation could not be summoned, nor could it proceed to business, without the licence of the Crown. There was also in Ireland an Act known as the Convention Act, which forbade representative assemblies, composed of delegates returned by election, from meeting. If the disestablished Church were to govern itself, these difficulties must be removed. It was therefore enacted that any law or custom whereby the archbishops, bishops, clergy, or laity of the Church of Ireland, were prohibited from holding assemblies, synods, or conventions, or electing representatives thereto, should be repealed, and that nothing in any Act should prevent them, by representatives meeting in general synod or convention, and therein framing constitutions and regulations for the general management and good government of the Church, and property and affairs thereof, and the future representation of the members thereof in diocesan synods, general convention, or otherwise.

It was also provided that, notwithstanding disestablishment, the existing ecclesiastical law, the existing articles, doctrines, rites, rules, discipline, and ordinances of the Church—but with and subject to such (if any) modification or alteration as should be made according to the constitution of the Church—should be deemed to be binding on its members in the same manner as if such members had mutually contracted and agreed to abide by and observe the same, and should be capable of being enforced in relation to any property vested in the Church under the Act, as if it had been conveyed upon trust to be enjoyed by persons who should observe such ecclesiastical law, and the said articles, rules, and ordinances.

As the annual grants from the State to the Presbyterian Church and the College of Maynooth were to cease, compensation was made to both by payment of sums of money which it was supposed would represent the value of the life interests of those who were then receiving and would have been benefited by the grants, if they had been continued.

The surplus, after answering all the compensations provided by the Act for the disestablished Church, for the Presbyterian Church, and for the College of Maynooth, was disposed of by a clause expressed in the following terms: . . . "Whereas it is expedient that the proceeds of the property (the subject of the Act) should be appropriated to the relief of unavoidable calamity and suffering, yet not so as to cancel or impair the obligations now attached to property under the Acts for the relief of the poor; be it enacted that the said proceeds shall be applied accordingly in the manner Parliament shall hereafter direct."

# CHAPTER XIX.

[1869–1871.]

THE Irish Church Act received the Royal Assent on the 26th of July, 1869. Under its provisions an interval of one year and five months was to elapse before the disestablishment and disendowment which it enacted would take effect. After the 1st of January, 1871, no valid appointment to any ecclesiastical office, benefice, or preferment, could be made in Ireland by the Crown, by any archbishop or bishop, or other ecclesiastical person, or by any lay patron. If the Church were to be continued, it was indispensable that in the meantime some constitution should be framed which would provide for the discharge of spiritual duties by successors to the existing incumbents of offices and benefices.

It was the intention of the Statute to confer upon the Church of Ireland complete freedom, and an unrestricted right to legislate in reference to its own internal arrangements. From the language of the provisions removing legal difficulties which prevented the meeting of a general Synod or Convention of bishops, clergy, and laity in Ireland, it was evident that those who framed them intended that measures requisite to meet the exigencies of the period should be enacted by an assembly of this character. These provisions came into immediate operation. In the statute no notice was taken of Convocation; however, the language used in reference to the meeting of a general Synod or Convention included within it Convocation also.

Convocation in Ireland was formed by the provincial Synods of the Archbishops meeting together.\* But without the permission of the Crown such a meeting was not lawful. From the reign of Queen Anne the Irish Convocation had never been either summoned or licensed to proceed to business by the Crown. Its sittings were therefore during the intervening period discontinued. The Church Act dispensed with the necessity of summons or licence from the Crown, and the archbishops could thenceforward act without this previous authority being given to them. It lay with them at their own discretion to assemble Convocation by summoning each his own provincial Synod to a joint meeting.

It is obvious that, when there existed within the Church a legally constituted body capable of discharging legislative functions, even although the laity were not members of it, it was in the highest degree advisable to ask its assistance and obtain its concurrence in whatever course was now to be pursued. If it were to recommend that its own meeting should be followed by the assembling of a Convention composed of laity as well as clergy, such a recommendation would lend additional sanction to an assembly of this nature, and probably remove the objections which

---

\* See as to Convocation in Ireland, pp. 19, 97, 169.

might by some be entertained to its assuming authority in reference to ecclesiastical affairs.

The number of Archbishops presiding at this time over the Church in Ireland was two—being the number retained under the provisions of the statutes which had been passed in 1833. These were the Archbishops of Armagh and of Dublin. Within the metropolitan jurisdiction of the former were included both the province of Armagh and the province of Tuam, as originally constituted in the system of the Church of Ireland; and within that of the latter the provinces of both Dublin and Cashel. The prelates who at this time filled these offices, after consultation with the other bishops, resolved, that in the circumstances in which the Church was placed, the first step that it was advisable to take was to summon their Synods so as to form a Convocation. They, accordingly, by mandates issued to their suffragan bishops, and by such other means as were in use upon the occasions when former Convocations were constituted, procured the attendance of their provincial Synods in the month of September, 1869, at St. Patrick's Cathedral, Dublin.

The assembly composed of these Synods, when it met, formed itself into a Convocation. It consisted of the archbishops and bishops, of all the deans and archdeacons, and of clerical persons elected, some by the chapters, and some by the clergy of each diocese, as their representatives.

The organization of the Episcopate at this time was as follows:—The number of episcopal persons to rule over the Sees of the Irish Church had, in consequence of the provisions of the Church Temporalities

Acts (1833 and 1834), been reduced to two archbishops and ten bishops.* Under them the Sees were incorporated, or united in the following manner:— Armagh with Clogher; Dublin and Glendalough with Kildare; Derry with Raphoe; Down with Connor and Dromore; Kilmore with Elphin and Ardagh; Tuam with Killala and Achonry; Ossory with Ferns and Leighlin; Cashel with Emly, Waterford, and Lismore; Cork with Cloyne and Ross; Killaloe with Kilfenora, Clonfert, and Kilmacduagh; Limerick with Ardfert and Aghadoe. Meath, in which Clonmacnois had been long merged, was not united with any other See.†

The Convocation, according to precedent, was composed of two Houses. The two archbishops and the ten Bishops formed the Upper House. As the Primacy of Armagh had, from the time of the decision of Strafford‡ in favour of this See, been always admitted, the Upper House was presided over by the Archbishop of Armagh. The Lower House, composed of the clergy, official and representative, elected as Prolocutor, Dr. West, Dean of St. Patrick's Cathedral, Dublin. Convocation sat for some days debating the various questions which arose for determination, and passed resolutions designed to provide for the altered position of the Church.

---

\* For the Sees of the Church of Ireland, *vide* Note Q of Appendix.

† The prelates who, at the time when this Convocation met, filled the two archbishoprics and the ten suffragan bishoprics were:—Beresford (Armagh); Trench (Dublin); Butcher (Meath); O'Brien (Ossory); Daly (Cashel); Knox (Down); Fitzgerald (Killaloe); Gregg (Cork); Graves (Limerick); Bernard (Tuam); Alexander (Derry); and Verschoyle (Kilmore).

‡ See p. 118 *supra*, and also Note Q of Appendix.

The first of these resolutions unanimously declared, "that they were now called upon, not to originate a constitution for a new communion, but to repair a sudden breach in one of the most ancient churches in Christendom." This was followed by another resolution inviting the co-operation of the laity—"That, under the present circumstances of the Church of Ireland, the co-operation of the faithful laity had become more than ever desirable." The mode in which this was to be obtained, and in which the future constitution of the Church might be most satisfactorily determined upon and framed, was held to be by the summoning of a general Convention, to consist, not merely as a Convocation or general Synod did, of bishops and clergy, but of bishops, clergy, and laity. And accordingly, in order to prepare the way for a Convention of this character being summoned, the Lower House of Convocation, with the concurrence of the Upper House, arranged what should be the number and nature of the representation of the clergy in such an assembly. They resolved that the representatives of the clergy in a general Synod or Convention of the bishops, clergy, and laity of the Church of Ireland, should be elected from the diocesan Synods; that the persons entitled to vote for these representatives in the diocesan Synods should be the beneficed clergymen, and also the licensed clergymen, provided they were of the order of priest in each diocese, and in any exempt jurisdiction out of the diocese; and that the persons qualified to be elected should be Presbyters, who had for five years been in Holy Orders. The number of representatives to this general Synod or Convention was to be in the proportion of one to every ten of the clergy entitled to vote in each diocese, together with an additional representative for any remaining number exceeding five. No dean or archdeacon was to have a seat *ex officio;* and no cathedral chapter was to return a representative.

So far, therefore, as the bishops and clergy assembled in Convocation were concerned, their decision was clearly announced to be, that a Convention or general Synod should be summoned, and that such Convention or general Synod should be composed, not only of bishops and clergy, but of laity also.

Similar views were in favour with the laity: and previous to the resolutions of Convocation, a meeting had been held of eminent laymen, who addressed to the two archbishops a request that they would convene a representative assembly under the name of a "Lay Conference," with a view to making arrangements for lay representation in a Convention or general Synod. The suggestion being approved by the Archbishops, they arranged that such "a conference" should take place in Dublin, and that representatives should be elected to attend it. For this purpose the following proceedings were then adopted:—In every parish a meeting of Church parishioners was held, at which parochial delegates were elected to the diocesan Synod. These lay parochial delegates having assembled in Synod in their respective dioceses, elected representatives to the lay assembly, which was to be convened by the archbishops. The number elected was one for every five of the parochial delegates. The total number was 417.

An assembly of laymen thus constituted, and representing the laity of the Church in every diocese, and thus in the entire island, met in Dublin, in October, 1869. At the first meeting the Archbishop of Armagh presided. Subsequently the Duke of Abercorn acted as chairman. This body resolved that the lay representatives to a Convention or general Synod, composed of both clergy and laity, should be to the clerical in the ratio of two to one : that the proportion of lay representatives to be allotted to the respective dioceses should be partly based on population and partly on the parochial system ; and they then fixed the number of laymen which, acting on that principle, should be allotted to each diocese. The entire number of laymen was to be 446. They also recommended that an organizing committee should be appointed, consisting of not more than four delegates from each Synod—two lay and two clerical; and that such delegates, with their respective bishops, and such other learned persons as the bishops and delegates might think it expedient to call to their aid, should frame a draft Constitution to be submitted to, and voted upon by, the future Convention of bishops, clergy, and laity.

The resolutions of Convocation and of the "Lay Conference," as to the Convention of bishops, clergy, and laity, were approved and adopted by the Episcopal Bench ; and, in conformity with their recommendations, a Convention or general Synod was summoned by the archbishops. Representatives to attend it, both clerical and lay, were elected by the diocesan Synods.

The matters which called for immediate decision were—What was to be the future legislative authority for the Church? In what manner questions, arising among its members in connection with their rights or duties under its system or in relation to its discipline, were to be decided? In whom was the right of appointing to bishoprics and benefices to be vested? In what manner was the Representative Body to be constituted? Neither doctrine, nor the former standards of faith, nor the services for divine worship, nor the polity and discipline of the Church of Ireland, had been in any way interfered with by the Church Act.*

On the 15th of February, 1870, the Convention of the bishops, clergy, and laity of the Church of Ireland met in St. Patrick's Cathedral, Dublin, and subsequently, by adjournments, at other places in Dublin, until the 2nd of April, when it was prorogued. In the autumn of the same year it again sat in Dublin, and then completed the enactment of a Constitution for the Church, and of a code of laws which defined the authority of the persons and bodies empowered to act in relation

---

* This was very clearly and forcibly pointed out, soon after the Irish Church Act was passed, in a Charge delivered to his clergy by the then Primate, Archbishop Beresford—a prelate whose statesmanlike qualities eminently fitted him to preside during a period of transition. In the same Charge he adverted to the temptations which beset the sudden acquisition of absolute powers of government, and of legislation, by bodies unaccustomed to such responsibilities; and cited, and impressed on his hearers the profound wisdom of, Bacon's well-known words—" It is good that men in their innovations should follow the example of time itself, which, indeed, innovateth greatly but quietly, and by degrees scarce to be perceived; it is good also not to try experiments unless the necessity be urgent, or the utility evident; and well to beware that it be the reformation that draweth on the change, and not the desire of change that pretendeth the reformation." (See *Charge*, published in Dublin, 1869, p. 17.)

to ecclesiastical affairs, and which also contained clauses designed to regulate the proceedings of these bodies. The Constitution having been subsequently amended, its provisions will be stated, not exactly as they were then expressed, but as they now (1886) stand.*

The Constitution deals with the Synods which were to represent the Church, the persons entitled to elect members to sit in them, and the qualifications of the persons who might be elected; also with their powers and duties. It provides for the episcopal, parochial, and cathedral organization; for the construction of tribunals; and for the frame of the Church Representative Body—the institution which, under the Church Act, was to receive and hold the property of the Church. But its legislation upon these subjects is preceded by a Preface of supreme importance, which it is proper first to notice.

This Preface is to the following effect:—It commences by affirming "That the Church of Ireland doth accept and believe the Canonical Scriptures of the Old and New Testament, as given by inspiration and as containing all things necessary to salvation; and doth continue to profess the faith of Christ as professed by the primitive Church;" it then proceeds to state that "the Church of Ireland will continue to administer the doctrine and sacraments, and discipline of Christ, as the Lord hath commanded; and will maintain inviolate the three orders of bishops, priests,

---

* The Journal of the Convention was published after it was dissolved. A preface to it states the events (*i.e.* the meeting of Convocation, and of the Lay Conference and the preliminary proceedings that have been referred to) which preceded the Convention.

and deacons; and that as a reformed and Protestant Church it re-affirms its constant witness against all those innovations in doctrine and worship, whereby the primitive faith hath been from time to time defaced or overlaid, and which at the Reformation this Church did disown and reject." It then proceeds to express the approval by the Church of "*The Book of the Articles of Religion*, commonly called the *Thirty-nine Articles*, which had been accepted by the bishops and clergy of Ireland, in the Synod holden in Dublin in 1634;" and also of "*The Book of Common Prayer*, and the form and manner of ordaining bishops, priests, and deacons, which had been approved in the Synod holden in Dublin, A.D. 1662."* This is followed by a declaration that the Church will maintain communion with the sister Church of England, and with all other Christian Churches agreeing in the principles of the declaration; and will forward, so far as in it lieth, quietness, peace, and love among all Christian people. A general Synod, consisting of the archbishops and bishops, and of representatives of the clergy and laity, is declared to be the authority to have chief legislative power in the Church, and such "administrative power as may be necessary for the Church and consistent with its episcopal constitution."

Following the declaration in the Preface, the Constitution provides a general Synod, composed of bishops, clergy, and laity. This Synod consists of two Houses —a House of Bishops, and a House of Representatives. The House of Bishops is formed of all the archbishops

---

* See pp. 118, 149, *supra*.

and bishops of the Church of Ireland for the time being; the House of Representatives of 208 representatives of the clergy, and 416 representatives of the laity. The representatives are returned from the dioceses in certain proportions specified in the statute, and are elected by the diocesan Synods. The members of the House of Representatives vote together, unless, upon a division being called, ten members shall by a requisition in writing require the votes to be taken by Orders, when they shall be so taken; the Orders then voting separately. Every proposed statute or canon is to be introduced as a Bill; and the procedure, in order that it should become law, must be in the manner prescribed. The bishops are to vote separately. And no question shall be deemed to be carried unless there be in its favour a majority of the bishops present, if they desire to vote, and a majority of the clerical and lay representatives present voting conjointly or by Orders; but if a question affirmed by a majority of the clerical and lay representatives, voting conjointly or by Orders, but rejected by the bishops, shall be re-affirmed at the next ordinary Session of the General Synod, by not less than two-thirds of the clerical and lay representatives, voting conjointly or by Orders, it shall be deemed carried, unless it be negatived by not less than two-thirds of the then entire existing Order of Bishops, the said two-thirds being then present and voting, and giving their reasons in writing. A Bill has to be read twice before going into Committee; then, when it has passed through Committee, in order to become law it must be read a third time. No modification or alteration can be made in the articles, doctrines, rites, rubrics, or (save so far as was rendered necessary by the Church Act) in the formularies of the Church, unless by a Bill. A Bill for any such purpose must be founded upon a resolution passed by the Synod, and no such Bill or resolution shall be deemed to be passed except by majorities of not less than two-thirds of each Order of the House of Representatives present and voting. The General Synod has power to alter existing provincial and diocesan territorial arrangements, which otherwise continue as they were.

Beside the general Synod, which legislates for the whole Church, it is provided that each diocese, or united diocese, shall have a Synod of its own. This consists of the bishop, the beneficed and licensed clergymen of the diocese, and of laymen; every parish is entitled to return two laymen for each of its officiating clergymen; and the lay representatives are to be elected by vestrymen registered as directed. The cathedrals are also represented; and, in the diocese of Dublin, Trinity College returns members to the diocesan Synod.

In the intervals between the meetings of the diocesan Synods the affairs of the dioceses are managed by diocesan Councils, composed of clergymen and laymen elected by the Synods; and over these Councils the bishops of the dioceses respectively preside.

Vestries composed of persons possessing certain qualifications prescribed by the Constitution meet annually, and elect churchwardens, and also a certain number of "select vestrymen": the latter during the year after their election have the control of parochial funds and contributions, and out of these provide the requisites for divine service, and defray the expense of keeping the church buildings in repair.

The regulations in reference to appointments to archbishoprics, bishoprics, and benefices upon vacancies, are as follows:—The archbishops and bishops (except in the instance of the archbishopric of Armagh) are elected by the diocese, or united dioceses (as the case may be) then to be filled, the voting being conducted according to prescribed rules. In the case of Armagh, upon vacancy the Synods of Armagh and Clogher elect an *ad interim* bishop. The bishops and the person chosen for this office then elect one of themselves to be Archbishop of Armagh. If the *ad interim* bishop is not selected, he takes the place of the bishop who is preferred. The incumbents of benefices are elected by Boards, each composed of the following persons, viz. :—Three laymen, elected by the vestry of the vacant parish, termed parochial nominators; two clergymen and one layman, elected by the diocesan Synod, termed the diocesan nominators; and the bishop of the diocese, who presides.

The tribunals are a Diocesan Court and an Appellate Court, called the Court of the General Synod. The former Court is composed of the bishop of the diocese, with his chancellor (who must be a barrister of ten years' standing) as assessor, of a clergyman, and of a layman, the two latter selected by rotation from a list of three clergymen and three laymen chosen by the diocesan Synod. The Court of the general Synod is composed of some of the bishops, and of a certain number of laymen, who hold, or have held, certain judicial offices, and who are elected by the general Synod to be members of the Court.

The provisions as to the Representative Body enact that it is to be composed of three classes—(1) the ex-officio; (2) the elected; (3) the co-opted. The ex-officio are the archbishops and the bishops; the elected are representatives from the dioceses, or united dioceses, chosen by their Synods (one clergyman and two laymen by each); the third class are persons co-opted by the other members of the body. The number of the ex-officio members is thirteen; of the elected, thirty-six; of the co-opted, twelve. Rules are laid down to define the powers of the corporation and to guide them in the management of the property vested in them.

Before the Convention had finally concluded its sittings, a Charter, dated 19th October, 1870, incorporating the Representative Church Body in accordance with the provisions contained in the Constitution, was granted by the Queen.

By the enactment of a Constitution, the continuance of the Church as an ecclesiastical organization was ensured; and by the incorporation of the Representative Church Body all difficulties in the way of the management and preservation of the property which, either under the Church Act it then received, or from donations and contributions it might afterwards receive, were removed.

As the enactments of the Convention are not final, as they are necessarily liable to be altered from time to time by the supreme legislative authority, that is by the general Synod, the provisions in relation to this assembly must be deemed to be of paramount importance. If they are examined, they will be found to combine in a remarkable manner elements which conduce both to progress and permanence—to be at once liberal and conservative. The former results are ensured by the representative character of the Synod; and the latter by the vote by Orders, by the proportion of each Order which, when the vote is taken by Orders, is required in order to enable any alteration in the articles, doctrines, and formularies of the Church to be made, and by the ultimate veto given under certain conditions to the House of Bishops.

## CHAPTER XX.

[1871-1885].

WHEN a supreme legislative authority over the affairs of the Church had been constituted, and a corporate body to hold its property and attend to its pecuniary interests had been formed, the matters which first claimed their attention were connected with the interests of the clergy in the emoluments of their benefices, and the provisions of the Church Act in reference to them.

The life estates of ecclesiastical persons were by the Act preserved in the case of their lands, and compensated for in the case of the tithe rentcharges by equivalent annuities. In connexion with their life interests in these annuities and in lands, it was provided that they might be commuted in the following manner: . . . The capitalized value of the incomes of ecclesiastical persons might, with the consent of the Representative Body and of the clergy, be paid over to the Representative Body, subject to, and charged with, the payment to the commuting clergy of their incomes for their lives. And as this proceeding would only have vested in the Representative Body the exact value of the annuities which they were in return to pay, it was, with a view to their safety in making such an arrangement, further provided that in all dioceses where three-fourths of the ecclesiastical persons should agree to commute, an addition of twelve pounds in the hundred was to be made to the commutation money.

The power conferred by these provisions being by the members of the Representative Body thought to be beneficial to the interests of the Church, as tending to promote the union and mutual co-operation of its members, rules were made by them to enable and encourage commutation. The rules were received with general approval; and ultimately the bishops and clergy (with only a few exceptions) commuted. The result has been that the Commissioners, in whom the property of the disestablished Church had been vested, in obedience to the Act of Parliament, have paid over to the Representative Body the capital sum of £7,581,470, charged with annuities to the amount of £596,751 yearly.

The Representative Body were thus possessed of a very large capital sum; and by means of the annuities, which they had to pay out of it, they were enabled to provide for spiritual duties in the parishes, so long as the clergy who were in office at the date of disestablishment should live. After their deaths there would be no resource except voluntary contribution. The needs of the existing generation were provided for without calling upon it; future generations would have to bear without assistance the burden of supporting their own ministers.

Under these circumstances it seemed just to ask those who had the advantage of an immediate provision for their parishes to contribute towards a future endowment for the Church; and the amount in the hands of the Representative Body afforded an opportunity for accomplishing this in an effectual manner. If subscriptions were during the lives of the commuting clergy sent to the Representative Body, the annual diminution of the fund from which their annuities had to be met might be lessened, and a considerable portion of the capital could be saved for the future.

Accordingly, in order to attain this end, the Representative Body entered into arrangements with all the dioceses, in pursuance of which immediate annual payments were to be made to them by the parishes, and they in return were to undertake to pay, according as vacancies occurred among the existing incumbents, a proportion of the incomes of the clergymen who might be appointed to succeed.

Still further to assist the accumulation of some endowment for the future, the Representative Body and the General Synod took advantage of another power contained in the Church Act, whereby the Representative Body was enabled to make terms with the commuting clergy in respect of their annuities; and they agreed that such of these clergy as desired to retire from the discharge of duty should receive a proportion of whatever then remained of the capital representing their annuities—the proportion being regulated by a fixed scale according to their ages.

These measures of the Representative Body have been attended with considerable success. In the period which has elapsed since disestablishment a very large amount of annual subscriptions has been received; and composition (as the division of the capitalized value of annuities payable to the clergy between them and the Representative Body is called) has resulted in profit.

It is, however, not merely in the arrangements connected with commutation and composition that the Representative Body have acted with judgment. Their general administration of the property of the Church has been most skilful. And their exertions to advance its interests have been zealously seconded by the laity generally. Much has been received from donations and bequests. Still, however, the great difficulty in the way of maintaining the clergy remains, that in a very large, if not the larger, part of the country, the numbers professing to be in communion with the Church are few, and on this account are often unable to supply the contributions which, if the parochial system is to be upheld, are required.

Beside the duties devolving upon the Representative Body that have been adverted to, they were empowered to purchase the houses of residence and portions of the demesne and glebe lands attached to them. The Act fixed the price to be paid for the houses, gardens, and curtilages, but left that which was to be paid for the lands to be settled by agreement. The Representative Body acted upon this power, and invested part of the funds in their hands in purchasing the houses and portions of the adjoining lands.

Much of the property in the hands of the Representative Body is impressed with peculiar trusts and obligations, either under the provisions of the Church Act or the directions of those who have bestowed it. What is not bound by trusts is subject to the control of the General Synod.

The General Synod and the Diocesan Synods meet yearly. The latter also, whenever vacancies occur in the Episcopal Bench, assemble to elect the future bishops. Of the present Bench seven were consecrated since disestablishment.*

In the organization of the Church there have been changes. Some parishes have been united, and the boundaries of others have been altered. The number of benefices has been diminished. In the case of the Episcopate there has been an addition of one bishop. The diocese of Clogher, which at the period of disestablishment was united to Armagh, having an unusually large number of members of the Church, has been again constituted a separate bishopric.

Of the legislation of the General Synod since disestablishment some enactments in relation to the Prayer Book, services for public worship, and formularies of the Church, are of importance. The Church Act left in force the then existing Articles, discipline, rules, rites, and doctrines of the Church, but gave the Church assembled in Synod power to modify and alter them. Propositions were therefore brought forward on several occasions in the General Synod in reference to these subjects, which led to a revision of the Prayer Book and of the services. A code of Con-

---

* The names of the Bishops from A.D. 1535 to 1841, according to their succession in the several Sees, is given by Bishop Mant in his *History*; from A.D. 1535 to the abdication of James II., in a Table in the Appendix to vol. i.; and from the abdication of James II. to November, 1840, in another Table in the Appendix to vol. ii. The appointments from the latter period to the present time will be found in Note G G of the Appendix to the present treatise.

stitutions and Canons, in many respects substantially new, was previously framed.

The Constitutions and Canons commence by enacting the forms of liturgy and of ordination to be used. The liturgy is to be the liturgy or divine service which is comprised in the Book of Common Prayer and administration of the sacraments, and ordination is to be according to the forms in the book of ordering bishops, priests, and deacons. In case other forms may be prescribed by the lawful authority of the Church of Ireland, they also are to be in force. The canons enjoin that "the Lord's day, commonly called Sunday," shall be duly observed "according to God's holy will and pleasure, and the order of this Church." Holydays authorized by the Church are also to be observed. Directions are given for the celebration of divine service. The dress to be worn by the bishops and clergy when engaged in the public ministration of the services of the Church is to be—for the bishops the customary ecclesiastical apparel of their Order; for the clergy a plain white surplice with sleeves; but bands may be worn, and upon the surplice the customary scarf of plain black silk, and the hoods representing university degrees are allowed. When preaching, the clergy may wear a black gown. Questions relating to dress are to be decided by the Ordinary, with an appeal to the "Court of the General Synod." The officiating minister is to speak audibly, and when offering up public prayer he is not to turn his back to the congregation: when saying the prayer of consecration in the Communion Service he is to stand at the north side of the table, by which it is explained is to be understood that side or end of the table which in churches lying east and west is towards the north. No minister or other person during the time of divine service shall make the sign of the cross, save where prescribed in the Rubric; nor shall he bow nor do any other act of obeisance to the Lord's Table or to anything there or thereon: no bell shall be rung during the time of divine service. The Ordinary may prohibit in the conduct of public worship any practice not enjoined in the Book of Common Prayer or in any Rubric or Canon enacted by lawful authority of the Church of Ireland. When the congregation consists wholly, or in part, of Irish-speaking people, the minister may use such portions of the service in the Irish tongue, and at such times, as the Ordinary shall direct. Directions are given for the clergy as to preaching, catechizing, obeying calls to christen or bury, solemnizing marriages, confirmation, and celebration of the Communion. The duties of Archdeacons, the qualifications and conditions required before admission to Holy Orders, are prescribed. The residence of incumbents is ordered, with, however, some exceptions, which are strictly defined. Power to deal with cases of negligence is given to the Bishops, and regulations affecting the conduct of clerical persons are made. The Communion Table is to be of wood, and to have such decent covering as the Ordinary shall approve; no lights are to be upon it or in the church, except when necessary for the purpose of giving light. No cross, ornamental or otherwise, is to be on the Communion Table, or on the covering thereof; nor shall a cross be erected or depicted on the wall or other structure behind the Communion Table. In the administration of the Lord's Supper any elevation of the paten, or cup, beyond what is necessary for taking the same into the hands of the officiating minister, the use of wine mixed with water, or of waferbread, and all acts, words, ornaments, or ceremonies other than those prescribed by the order in the Prayer Book, are prohibited. The use of incense, the carrying of crosses, banners, pictures, in any religious service or ceremonial, also processions through the church or churchyard in connexion with such services, are forbidden. No change is to be made in the structure, ornaments, or monuments of any church without the consent of the incumbent and select vestry, and the approval of the Ordinary. The duties of churchwardens and of the select vestry are prescribed. The authorities to construe and enforce obedience to the several canons are defined. In cases left to the decision of the Ordinary, any person aggrieved by his decision, or by his refusal to hear and determine the matter, may appeal to the Diocesan Court, and from it to the Court of the General Synod. Finally, the penalties which may be inflicted for wilful disobedience of the laws or canons of the Church, by persons holding office, are decreed.*

In 1878 a revised Prayer Book was published by authority of the General Synod of the Church of Ireland. It contained all alterations in the rubrics, services, and formularies which, down to that period, had received the sanction of the General Synod. Its use has been since that time enforced in the case of clergy-

---

* Additional canons in relation to the admission of intending communicants to the Lord's Supper were added in 1877.

men who, subsequently to the disestablishment of the Church, have been ordained, or have accepted a new appointment, or have by any other act become legally bound to obey the laws and canons of the Church.

In a Preface prefixed to the Prayer Book the circumstances which led to its revision are explained. Some changes in rubrics and services were indispensable by reason of the altered position of the Church consequent upon its disestablishment. Many desired that occasion should be taken to make a full review of the forms then in use. This suggestion, the Preface states, was the more readily acceded to, because it was perceived "that all men on all sides professed their love and reverence for the Book of Common Prayer in its main substance and chief parts, and confessed that it contained the true doctrine of Christ, and a pure manner and order of divine service, according to the Holy Scriptures and the practice of the Primitive Church; and that what was sought by those who desired such a review was not any change in the whole tenor or structure of the book, but the more clear deduction of what they took to be its true meaning, and the removing of certain expressions here and there which they judged open to mistake or perversion."

In order to guard against the supposition that either the fact of revision or the actual changes made implied any censure upon the former Prayer Book, the Preface points out that in the Convention of 1870 the book, as then in use, had been approved; also there is inserted an express disclaimer of any intention to suggest that, when rightly understood and equitably construed, it contained anything contrary to the Scriptures.

With respect to the reasons for the changes contained in the revised Prayer Book the preface states that they will for the most part appear upon a comparison of the two books. In some instances, however, " a further explanation why certain things have been altered and others retained" was deemed advisable, and has been given. The instances are the services for the Holy Communion and for Baptism, the office for the Visitation of the Sick, the form of Ordination for Priests, the Athanasian Creed, and the Lectionary. After stating what had been done, or deliberately left undone, in connexion with these subjects, the Preface ends with an admonition addressed to all who, for different and, it might be, opposite reasons, should object to the revision as it had been accomplished: . . . " And now (it proceeds) if some shall complain that these changes are not enough, and that we should have taken this opportunity of making this book as perfect in all respects as they think it should be made, or if others shall say that these changes have been unnecessary or excessive, and that what was already excellent has been impaired by doing that which, in their opinion, might well have been left undone, let them, on the one side and the other, consider that men's judgments of perfection are very various, and that what is imperfect, with peace, is often better than what is otherwise more excellent, without it."

With respect to the service for the Holy Communion, the Preface observes that some were at first earnest for the removal of expressions which they thought might lend a pretext for the teaching of doctrine concerning the presence of Christ in that sacrament repugnant to what was set forth in the Articles of religion; but that there had not been found in the formularies any just warrant for such teaching, and that therefore, in this behalf, no other change was made than to add to the Catechism one question, with an answer, taken out of the Twenty-eighth of the Articles.* In connexion with other errors in relation to this sacrament it is then added that canons (of which mention has been already made) were framed to prohibit such acts and gestures as might be grounded upon or lead to them; and that by the note which since the revision of Charles II. had been at the end of the Communion Service, and which was to be retained in the revised book, it is declared that the posture of kneeling, prescribed for all communicants, is not appointed for any purpose of adoration.

With respect to the "formularies relating to baptism" the Preface states that no substantial change had been made. At the same time it is declared that the liberty of expounding these formularies, hitherto allowed by the general practice of the Church, is recognized; and that, as concerning those points whereupon such liberty has been allowed, no minister of the Church is required to hold or teach any doctrine which has not been clearly determined by the Articles of religion.

With respect to the office for Visitation of the Sick, it is observed that the special absolution in this office

---

* The question and answer introduced in the Catechism are :—

*Question.*—After what manner are the Body and Blood of Christ taken and received in the Lord's Supper?

*Answer.*—Only after a heavenly and spiritual manner; and the mean whereby they are taken and received is Faith.

has been the cause of offence to many; and that as it is a form unknown to the Church in ancient times; and as no adequate ground for its retention was seen, and there was no ground for asserting that its removal would make any change in the doctrine of the Church, it was deemed fitting that in the special cases contemplated in this office, and in that for the Visitation of Prisoners, absolution should be pronounced to penitents in the form appointed in the office for the Holy Communion.*

With respect to "the formula for Ordination of Priests," the Preface states that no change was made: for that, upon a full review of the formularies, it is deemed plain that, save in the matter of ecclesiastical

---

\* The form of Absolution formerly in the office for the Visitation of the Sick, and now omitted, was in the following words : . . . " Our Lord Jesus Christ, who hath left power to His Church to absolve all sinners who truly repent and believe in Him, of His great mercy forgive thee thine offences; and by His authority committed to me, I absolve thee from all thy sins, in the name of the Father, and of the Son, and of the Holy Ghost." . . . This form with slight variations followed one in the Penitential of Egbert, Archbishop of York, in the eighth century (Wheatly *On the Book of Common Prayer*).

The form substituted is as follows: . . . " Almighty God, our heavenly Father, who of His great mercy hath promised forgiveness of sins to all them that with hearty repentance and true faith turn unto Him; have mercy upon thee: pardon and deliver thee from all thy sins: confirm and strengthen thee in all goodness: and bring thee to everlasting life: through Jesus Christ our Lord."

With both may be compared the form which Cardinal Newman in his *Apologia* states to be that in use in the Roman Catholic Church : . . . " Dominus noster Jesus Christus te absolvat : et ego auctoritate Ipsius te absolvo, ab omni vinculo excommunicationis et interdicti, in quantum possum et tu indiges. Deinde ego te absolvo a peccatis tuis, in nomine Patris, et Filii, et Spiritus Sancti."

censures, no power or authority is by them ascribed to the Church or any of its ministers in respect of forgiveness of sins after baptism, other than that of declaring and pronouncing on God's part remission of sins to all that are truly penitent, to the quieting of their conscience, and the removal of all doubt and scruple; that nowhere is it taught that confession to, or absolution by, a priest are any conditions of God's pardon: but, on the contrary, it is fully taught that all Christians who sincerely repent, and unfeignedly believe the Gospel, may draw nigh as worthy communicants to the Lord's Table, without any such confession or absolution: which comfortable doctrine of God's free forgiveness of sin is, it is added, more largely set forth in the Homily " of Repentance," and in that "of the Salvation of Mankind."

With reference to the Athanasian Creed, it is pointed out that the rubric directing its use on certain days has been removed; but that, in so doing, the Church has not withdrawn its witness, as expressed in the Articles of religion, to the truth of the articles of the Christian Faith therein contained.

As to the Lectionary, it is said, the English table of lessons was retained, with the exception that lessons from the Apocryphal Scriptures were omitted, and that the whole, instead of a part, of the Revelation of St. John was included in it.

The changes in the former Prayer Book, which are noticed in the Preface, seem to be those which are of most importance. The others consist of additional prayers and services for special occasions, and, in occasional instances, of amendments of the old forms.

Several rubrics are in some respects varied, and some new rubrics are added or substituted for others.*

With the account of the proceedings of the Church subsequent to the Irish Church Act, which has been given in this chapter and in the chapter immediately preceding it, I close the sketch of its history intended to be the subject of the present treatise.

There is no doubt that by disestablishment the Church was placed in circumstances of extreme difficulty. Accustomed, from the date of the Irish statute declaring the supremacy of the Crown, to act in union with the State, it was abruptly left to its own guidance without control. The right to legislate for its needs, and the authority to regulate its proceedings, became vested in a numerous body returned by a still more numerous constituency. The danger incident to the exercise of power by popular assemblies was at once imminent. There was reason to fear that change for the sake of change might be desired; that when it was effected it would reflect only the theological views with which the majority might happen to sympathize; and that thus the range of free thought would be narrowed. But these evils have been avoided. The Church has, so far, come forth in honour and safety; it has retained unity within itself and continuity with the past; it is still substantially the same in polity, in doctrine, in ritual, as it formerly was. It has not parted with

---

\* The changes made in the Prayer Book, as they appear in the revised Prayer Book published under the authority of the General Synod, are enumerated at more length in the Appendix, note H H.

its comprehensiveness; it permits every difference of opinion that was formerly allowed.

For a complete estimate of the effects of disestablishment upon its welfare the time has not arrived. The Church is not as yet cast upon its own resources. When separated from the State it still retained in its service a clergy of high excellence, educated and pious, bound, unless released by its own permission, to discharge for their lives their former duties. Its organization has been, and is still, maintained largely by their assistance; and its standard of theological teaching continues to be influenced by their example.

If it is too soon to forecast the effect of disestablishment upon the internal prosperity of the Church, it is certainly also too soon to judge of its effect upon other religious denominations. No substantial alteration has taken place in the relative numerical proportions of Roman Catholics, Protestant Episcopalians, and Presbyterians. Some provisions in the constitution of the Church as it existed before disestablishment, which were objected to by Protestant Nonconformists, and which therefore furnished reasons for their separation from it, have been removed. Thus the Church can no longer be charged with being controlled and secularized by the State; it is free and self-governed; appointments to bishoprics and benefices are not now in the power of the Crown; Bishops are elected by the Diocesan Synods, and incumbents of benefices by Boards; and of these bodies, both presbyters and laymen are, in addition to the Bishop of the diocese, members. In place of the coercive jurisdiction of ecclesiastical courts, formerly complained of, tribunals have been substituted which found themselves upon consent and voluntary submission. Yet it cannot be said that there is as yet apparent any nearer approach to union among Protestant ecclesiastical systems in Ireland; nor can such a result be predicted as likely to occur. Religious divisions survive their causes, and continue to exist long after the original grounds of difference disappear.

# APPENDIX.

## NOTES AND ILLUSTRATIONS.

I HAVE thought it better to defer to an Appendix the consideration of some subjects which, if introduced in the narrative, would have unduly interrupted its course. To the notes requisite for this purpose I have added others containing citations from original authorities which have ceased to be reprinted. For a correct estimate of transactions of remote date, we must note not only the fact, but the description of it, by those who record it—not only what is narrated, but how it is narrated.

### NOTE A.

The account given of the events connected with the arrival of Archbishop Browne in Ireland, and the introduction there by him of the principles of the Reformation, is (as has been mentioned in the note to page 18) based principally upon a letter of the Archbishop, which will be found extracted in the next note, and upon a *Life of Archbishop Browne*, written by Robert Ware, son of Sir James Ware. Although Sir James Ware's *Annals* comprise this period, they do not mention the proceedings in which Archbishop Browne was concerned. Robert Ware's *Life* is, however, partly founded upon papers which came to him from his father. (See p. 150 of the Dublin edition of Sir James Ware's Works, 1705.) There is another historian, who also treats of this period, Sir Richard Cox, Lord Chancellor of Ireland in the reign of Queen Anne, author of *Hibernia Anglicana*. He, however, seems to have derived his information in reference to this time from the two Wares. The *Annals of the Four Masters* do not allude to Archbishop

Browne. They refer in general terms to a law having been introduced under Henry VIII.: to the fact that opposition to the Pope arose; that new laws were made by the King and Council [Parliament(?)]; to the monastic orders having been expelled from their residences; and to the destruction of the images which had been in the churches.

It may be convenient to mention the editions from which Ware and other writers to whom there has been occasion frequently to refer in the present treatise are cited. Ware is cited from the Dublin edition of 1705, or Harris's edition of 1739, 1745, also published in Dublin. The works of Archbishop Ussher are cited from the edition in seventeen volumes, published by the University of Dublin (1847-1864). The life of Archbishop Ussher referred to is that by Rev. Dr. Elrington, contained in the same edition. The edition of Leland's *History of Ireland* used is the Dublin, in three volumes, octavo (1774); it is cited simply as "Leland." The edition of Swift's works cited is that edited by Sir Walter Scott, published in 1814. Hallam's *Constitutional History* is cited from the fourth edition; Froude's *History of England* from the edition in twelve volumes (1856-1870); his *English in Ireland in the Eighteenth Century*, from the edition of 1872. Sir John Davis's *Discovery*, &c., is cited from the Dublin edition, 1705; and Carte's *Life of Ormonde*, from the Clarendon Press edition. Calendars of the Patent and Close Rolls in Chancery in Ireland have been published for the reigns of Henry VIII., Edward, Mary, and Elizabeth. They were edited by Mr. Morrin, and are therefore referred to simply as "Morrin." The English State Papers were published by Royal Commission (1830-1852); they were edited by Mr. Lemon; vols. ii. and iii. (Part III.) relate to Ireland. There is also a Calendar of other State Papers relating to Ireland, marked by the years from 1509 to 1573. These are all referred to as "State Papers," or simply with the letters "S. P." Besides, there is also a Calendar of the Manuscripts of Sir George Carew, which are preserved in the library at Lambeth Palace; this is edited by Mr. Brewer. It is cited as "Carew MSS." *Original Letters*, &c., edited by E. P. Shirley (1851), are cited as "Shirley."

## Note B.

The letter of Archbishop Browne to Thomas Cromwell, then Lord Privy Seal, written in September, 1535 (which is referred to in the previous note, A, and at page 18, *supra*), is reported by Robert Ware, in the *Life of Archbishop Browne*, in the following words:—

"My most Honoured Lord,—Your most humble servant receiving your mandate, as one of his Highness's Commissioners, hath endeavoured almost to the danger and hazard of this temporal life, to procure the nobility and gentry of this nation to due obedience, in owning of his Highness their supreme head as well spiritual as temporal, and do find much oppugning therein, especially by my brother Ardmagh, who hath been the main oppugner; and so hath withdrawn most of his suffragans and clergy within his See and jurisdiction: he made a speech to them, laying a curse on the people whosoever should own his Highness's supremacy: saying that this isle, as it is in their Irish Chronicles, *insula sacra*, belongs to none but to the Bishop of Rome, and that it was the Bishop of Rome's predecessors gave it to the King's ancestors. There be two messengers by the priests of Ardmagh and by that Archbishop, now lately sent to the Bishop of Rome. Your Lordship may inform his Highness that it is convenient to call a Parliament in this nation to pass the Supremacy by Act; for they do not much matter his Highness's Commission which your Lordship sent us over. This island hath been for a long time held in ignorance by the Romish Orders: and as for their secular orders, they be in a manner as ignorant as the people, being not able to say Mass, or pronounce the words, they not knowing what they themselves say in the Roman tongue. The common people of this isle are more zealous in their blindness than the Saints and Martyrs were in the truth at the beginning of the Gospel. I send to you, my very good Lord, these things, that your Lordship and his Highness may consult what is to be done. It is feared O'Neal will be ordered by the Bishop of Rome to oppose your Lordship's order from the King's Highness; for the natives are much in numbers within his power. I do pray the Lord Christ to defend your Lordship from your enemies. Dublin, 4 Kalend, Septembris, 1535."

## Note C.

Sir John Davis says that before 33 Hen VIII. there were twelve counties beside the Liberty of Tipperary (see the next note, D); but in his treatise (*Discovery*, &c., p. 27) he makes Tipperary one of the twelve. He therefore seems to treat "the Liberty" as being, for parliamentary purposes, in addition to the county. Davis takes no notice of counties formed in Ulster under Edward I., which were afterwards, in the reign of Queen Elizabeth, united and formed into the modern county of Antrim, and some into the modern county of Down. These sent no members to Parliament in the reign of Henry VIII.

In 1556, under the Act 3 & 4 Philip and Mary, cap. 2, the King's County and Queen's County were formed (see p. 46). In 1565, under the same Act of Philip and Mary, but in the reign of Elizabeth, and by Sir Henry Sidney, then Lord Deputy, were formed the counties of Longford and Clare (the last from a territory before reputed in Munster, which he transferred to Connaught), Galway, Sligo, Mayo and Roscommon. Also in the reign of Elizabeth were formed by Sir John Perrot, L.D., in 1583, Leitrim, and in 1584, Armagh, Monaghan, Tyrone, Coleraine or Derry, Donegal, Fermanagh, Cavan (all under 11 Eliz., sess. 3, cap. 9); also Down and Antrim were finally defined and constituted by Perrot. In 1605, in the reign of James I., under the Act 11 Eliz., Wicklow was formed by Sir Arthur Chichester, L.D.

## Note D.

The account which I have given of the Parliament of Ireland in the reign of Henry VIII. follows that given by Sir John Davis, when Speaker of the Irish House of Commons, in his Address to the then Deputy, Sir Arthur Chichester (see page 96, *supra*). It is printed by Leland (vol. ii., App.), from the Journals of the House of Commons. On the subject of the admission of the natives to the House of Commons, Davis says: ... "Before the 33 year of King H. 8, wee do not finde any to have had place in Parliament, but the English of bloud, or English of birth onlye; for the mere Irish in those days were never admitted, as well because their countryes lying out of the lymittes of countyes, could send noe knights, and having neither cittyes nor boroughs in them, could send noe burgesses to the parliamente: besides that the State did not hold them fit to be trusted with the councell of the realm." ... As to the number of members of the House of Commons, he says:—"Before the 34 year of H. 8, when Meath was divided there were noe more but twelve countyes in Irelande besides the libertye of Tipperary; and the number of knights must needs have been fewe; and since the antient cittyes were but foure, and the boroughs which sent burgesses not above thirtye, the entire bodye of the whole house of commons could not then consist of one hundred persons; and though Queene Mary did add twoe shires, and Queene Elizabeth seaventeene more, to increase the number of knightes in that house, yet all did not sende knightes to the parliament, for the remote shires of Ulster returned none at all." ... As to the Lords temporal, he says:—"Though they are yet but fewe, yet was the number lesse before Kinge H. 8 was stiled Kinge of Ireland, for since that tyme divers of the Irish nobillitye, and some descended of English race, have been created both earles and barons. And lastly, for the bishops and archbishops, though their number was greater that nowe it is, in respect of the divers unions made of later years, yet such as were resident in the mere Irish countryes, and did not acknowledge the Kinge to be their patron, were never summoned to any parliament."

Davis in this Address does not mention Abbots and Priors as having ever had seats in the House of Lords; but Sir James Ware states that fourteen Abbots and ten Priors were entitled to be summoned; and he enumerates the names of the Religious Houses over which these abbots and priors presided. (See *Antiquities*, ch. 26, p. 116, and *Annals*, A.D. 1539, p. 100: Dublin edition, 1705.)

In Bagwell's *Ireland Under the Tudors*—a work which evidences much research, and is written with an impartiality not often to be found in Irish histories—a chapter is devoted to considering the Irish Parliament before Henry VIII. When parliamentary representation began to take shape in England, it was, he says, soon imitated in Ireland. But previously John had asked an aid from the archbishops, bishops, abbots, priors, earls, barons, justices, sheriffs, knights, citizens, burgesses, and freeholders of Ireland: "and in 1228 Henry III. ordered his justiciary to convoke the archbishops, bishops, abbots, priors, earls and barons, knights and freeholders, and the bailiffs of every county, and to read Magna Charta to them." (Vol. i. p. 94.)

## Note E.

The speech (mentioned at page 21) which Archbishop Browne is reported to have delivered in the Irish House of Lords, when he advocated before that assembly the Supremacy Act, is stated in Ware's *Life of Browne*. The report seems to be a summary. It is in the following words: ... " My Lords and Gentry of this his Majesties realm of Ireland, Behold your obedience to your King is the observing of your God and Saviour Christ ; for He, that High Priest of our souls, paid tribute to Cesar (though no Christian) ; greater honour surely is due to your Prince his Highness the King, and a Christian one : Rome and her Bishops in the Father's days acknowledged Emperors, Kings and Princes to be supreme over their dominions, nay, Christ's own Vicars ; and it is much to the Bishop of Rome's shame, to deny what their precedent Bishops owned ; therefore his Highness claims but what he can justifie the Bishop Eleutherius gave to Lucius the first Christian King of the Britains ; so that I shall without scrupling vote his Highness King Henry my supreme over ecclesiastical matters as well as temporal, and Head thereof, even of both isles England and Ireland, and that without guilt of conscience or sin to God ; and he who will not pass this Act, as I do, is no true subject to his Highness."

The story, alluded to in this speech, of a correspondence between Lucius, or more properly Llewer Mawr, who was said to have been in the second century a King of the Britons, and Eleutherius, then Bishop of Rome, is considered legendary. The genuineness of the letter to Eleutherius which is attributed to Lucius, is disproved by internal evidence. (See Canon Perry's *History of the English Church*, 1st ser., p. 3.) In the sixteenth century it seems to have been reputed of authority.

Dr. Reeves (who while this work was passing through the press, has become Bishop of Down, &c.), in addition to other valuable assistance contributed by him to its preparation, has called my attention to a citation of this correspondence by another Irish bishop of much later date than Browne. When Hampton, afterwards Archbishop of Armagh in the reign of James I., preached at Glasgow the sermon mentioned at page 106, *supra*, he referred to it, and pointed out that according to Eleutherius a King is God's lieutenant, vicar, and deputy, *vicarius Dei*. (As to this last title, see page 10, *supra*.) Wherefore he argues that the King is "a mixt person," and entitled to make laws for religion.

The idea, however, that a King is a mixed person, *persona mixta*, and so having temporal and ecclesiastical jurisdiction, did not originate with Hampton. It will be found mentioned in a discussion in the Year-Books (10 Hen. VII., 18) : . . . "Brian said that a sage Doctor of Laws said one time to him that priests might be tried at common law, 'car il dit, quod rex est persona mixta, car est persona unita cum sacerdotibus Saint Eglise.'" (And see Bishop Stillingfleet's *Works*, vol. iii. p. 782.)

Burnet, when commenting on the Article which relates to the Supremacy (XXXVII.), refers to the fictitious correspondence of Eleutherius and Lucius; and observing that it is probably a forgery, he adds the just remark, that being unquestionably very old, and having for many ages passed for true, it is, though not genuine, of value, as showing the ideas of a remote age, "for a forgery is calculated to the sense of the age when it is made."

## Note F.

The State Paper referred to in the note (page 24), as containing the names of the Irish chieftains and of the Anglo Irish lords (who in effect ruled the greater part of the island), is in the *Calendar of State Papers, Tempore, Hen. VIII.*, vol. ii. p. 11. It professes to describe "all the noble folk, as well of the King's subjects and English rebels, as of Irish enemies." . . . "There be (it says) more than sixty counties called regions in Ireland inhabited with the King's Irish enemies, some regions as big as a shire, and some a little less; where reigneth more than sixty chief captains (whose names and descriptions are afterwards given), whereof some calleth themselves kings, some king's peers in their language : some princes, some dukes, some archdukes, that liveth only by the sword, and obeyeth no other temporal person, but only to himself that is strong : and every of the said captains maketh war and peace for himself, and holdeth by sword, and hath imperial jurisdiction within his room, and obeyeth to no other person, English nor Irish, except only to such persons as may subdue him by the sword."

Of the English noble folk the names of thirty are given, who are described as "following the same order as the Irish chiefs, and keeping the same rule, and every of them maketh peace and war for himself, without any licence of the King, or of any other temporal person, save to him that is strongest and of such that may subdue them by the sword."

The effect of this subdivision of power may be seen in the constant wars between the chiefs, as recorded in the *Annals of the Four Masters*. Taking their account, Mr. Richey has computed that between A.D. 1500 and A.D. 1534 there were, principally in Ulster and Connaught, which were the districts then most owned by the Irish, besides hostilities against the English, which are omitted from the calculation, one hundred and fifteen battles and incursions for plunder; that in the same time, of Irish gentlemen there were one hundred and two killed in battle, and one hundred and sixty-eight murdered. (*Lectures on Irish History*, 2nd series, p. 11.)

These constant wars creating general insecurity, and turning the attention of the population to martial pursuits and exercises in preparation for them, hindered civilization and improvement. They also led to new and additional oppressive exactions being levied on agriculture, in order thereby to maintain them. (See in Mr. Bagwell's *Ireland under the Tudors*, already referred to, vol. i. p. 131, an enumeration of the taxes and impositions levied by the chieftains, English and Irish.)

## Note G.

The account of the Pale under Henry VIII., as it is given in the paper sent to him in 1535 (mentioned in the note to page 24), is most unfavourable. The paper must be regarded as of high authority, for it was prepared and subscribed by the Archbishops of Armagh and Dublin (Cromer and Browne), by the Bishops of Meath and Kildare (dioceses in the Pale), by some abbots and peers residing in the Pale, and by other persons of station, and was sent to Henry, in the care of Allen, Master of the Rolls. It describes "the great decay of this land" (which term was then used to denote the Pale); that neither the English order, tongue, nor habit has been used, nor the King's laws obeyed above twenty miles in compass: that the old exactions were levied on the people, and that there be other "like abuses and oppressions practised;" also it relates the discouragement of the English settlers, and the admission of the Irishry as tenants, "which can live hardily without bread or other good victuals;" submitting to more rent and other impositions than English husbandmen be able to give.

The Pale at this time extended from Dublin to Dundalk about fifty miles to the north of Dublin; from Dundalk to Kilcullen about twenty miles west; and from that round under the Wicklow mountains to Dalkey, about eight miles south of Dublin. At an earlier period it had extended as far south of Dublin as Waterford.

In considering the state of society in Ireland in the reign of Henry VIII., even in the Pale, it is to be noted that the first mention of a printing-press in Ireland is in the next reign (Edward VI.), when the first prayer-book of this King and proclamations were printed for the Government by a person named Humfrey. (See page 40, *supra*.) The date at which first a Latin book is known to have been printed in Ireland is 1626. (See *Life of Ussher*, p. 123, *note*.) Before this date, however, in 1618, according to Ussher (*Works*, vol. xv. p. 135), the "Company of Stationers" erected "a factory for books and a press" in Dublin. Ussher says they were to begin with printing the statutes of the realm, and then to come to some of his own writings.

## Note H.

According to Ussher, about the beginning of the twelfth century the Roman use for liturgical purposes was brought into Ireland by Gillebertus, legate from the Pope, and it was afterwards confirmed by Malachias and Christianus, also legates. Gillebertus speaks of "diversi et schismatici illi ordines, quibus Hibernia pene delusa est," thus evidencing that before him there were varieties of procedure. Of Malachias, St. Bernard in his life says: " Consuetudines sanctæ Romanæ ecclesiæ in cunctis ecclesiis statuebat. Hinc est quod hodieque in illis ad horas canonicas cantatur et psallitur juxta morem universæ terræ: nam minime id ante fiebat, ne in civitate quidem."

Christianus presided over the Council of Cashel (1172) when the rule (cited at page 32, *supra*) was made as to *omnia divina* proceeding *juxta quod Anglicana observat ecclesia*. This rule, with the other statutes of that Council, was confirmed by the authority of King Henry II. *Regiæ sublimitatis authoritate firmata* is the expression of Giraldus Cambrensis (See Ussher's *Religion professed by the Ancient Irish: Works*, iv. 274.

Archbishop de Loundres came over in the next century (1212). He also was a legate. By him the collegiate church of St. Patrick, Dublin, was erected into a cathedral; and it is stated that " he took care to conform it to the statutes of Sarum Church." It is very improbable that he would have neglected to require, or at least to encourage, the Sarum use to be observed in Dublin, and wherever else his jurisdiction extended.

### Note I.

The account of the proceedings of the assembly of the clergy, convened by Sir Anthony St. Leger in 1551, is contained (as is mentioned in the note to page 86, *supra*) in Robert Ware's *Life of Archbishop Browne;* and from the importance of the meeting, the exact words of it are now cited. . . . . " Before proclamations were issued out (*i.e.* proclamations to bring the new English Prayer Book into use), Sir Anthony St. Leger upon his (*i.e.* the King's) order called an assembly of the archbishops and bishops, together with other of the then clergy of Ireland, in which assembly he signified unto them as well His Majestie's order aforesaid, as also the opinions of those bishops and clergy of England, who had adhered unto the order, saying that it was His Majestie's will and pleasure, consenting unto their serious considerations and opinions, then acted and agreed on in England as to ecclesiastical matters, that the same be in Ireland so likewise celebrated and performed." Ware then continues : . . . " Sir Anthony St. Leger having spoken to this effect, George Dowdall, who succeeded George Cromer in the primacy of Ardmagh, stood up, who (through his Romish zeal to the Pope) laboured with all his power and force to oppose the liturgy of the Church, that it might not be read or sung in the Church; saying, 'then shall every illiterate fellow read service (or mass), as he in those days termed the word service.' To this saying of the archbishop, Sir Anthony replied, ' No ; your Grace is mistaken, for we have too many illiterate priests amongst us already, who neither can pronounce the Latin, nor know what it means, no more than the common people that hear them ; but when the people hear the liturgy in English, they and the priest will then understand what they pray for.' Upon this reply, George Dowdall bade Sir Anthony beware of the clergie's curse. Sir Anthony made answer, 'I fear no strange curse, so long as I have the blessing of that Church which I believe to be the true one.' The archbishop again said, 'Can there be a truer Church than the Church of St. Peter, the Mother Church of Rome?' Sir Anthony returned this answer, 'I thought we had been all of the Church of Christ; for He calls all true believers in Him his Church, and Himself the Head thereof.' The archbishop replied, 'Is not St. Peter's the Church of Christ?' Sir Anthony returned the answer, 'St. Peter was a member of Christ's Church; but the Church was not St. Peter's; neither was St. Peter, but Christ the head thereof.' Then George Dowdall, the Primate of Ardmagh, rose up, and several of the suffragan bishops under his jurisdiction, saving only Edward Staples, then Bishop of Meath, who tarried with the rest of the clergy then assembled, on the kalends of March, according to the old style, 1551, but if we reckon as from the Annunciation of Our Lady, which was the 25th of March, it was 1550. Sir Anthony then took up the order, and held it forth to George Browne, Archbishop of Dublin, who (standing up) received it, saying, 'This order, good brethren, is from our gracious King and from the rest of our brethren, the fathers and clergy of England, who have consulted herein and compared the Holy Scriptures with what they have done, unto whom I submit, as Jesus did to Cæsar, in all things just and lawful, making no question, why or wherefore, as we own him our true and lawful King.' After this, several of the meeker, or most moderate of the bishops and clergy of Ireland, cohered with George Browne, the Archbishop of Dublin, amongst whom Edward Staples, Bishop of Meath, who was put out from his bishopric for so doing in Queen Mary's days, on the 29th of June, 1554; John Bale, who on the 2nd of February, 1552, was consecrated Bishop of Ossory for his fidelity, and afterwards by Queen Mary expulsed; also Thomas Lancaster, Bishop of Kildare, who was at the same time put from his bishopric, with several other of the clergy, being all expulsed upon Queen Mary's coming to the Crown."

## Note K.

Another matter, in respect of which it seems to be advisable to cite the exact narrative from Robert Ware's *Life of Archbishop Browne*, is the account there given of the Commission said to have been sent by Queen Mary " to call the Protestants in question" in Ireland, and of the abstraction of it from the messenger at Chester. (See page 45, *supra*.) It is in the following words:—" Queen Mary, towards the end of her reign, granted a Commission to call the Protestants in question here in Ireland, as well as they had done in England; and to execute the same with greater force, she nominated Dr. Cole, sometime Dean of St. Paul's in London, one of the Commissioners; and so sent the Commission by this said doctor; and in his journey coming to Chester, the mayor of that city, hearing that Her Majesty was sending Commissioners into Ireland, and he being a churchman, waited on the doctor, who in discourse with the mayor took out of his cloak-bag a leather box, and said unto him, ' Here is a Commission that shall lash the heretics of Ireland,' calling the Protestants by that title. The good woman of the house being well affected to the Protestants and to that religion, and also having a brother named John Edmonds, a Protestant, and a citizen in Dublin, was much troubled at the doctor's words; but she, waiting her convenient time, whilst the mayor took leave of the doctor, and the doctor complimenting him down the stairs, she opened the box and took the Commission out, and placed in lieu thereof a pack of cards, with the knave of clubs faced uppermost, and wrapt them up. The doctor coming up to his chamber, suspecting nothing of what had been done, put up his box as formerly. The next day going to the water-side, wind and weather serving him, he sailed towards Ireland, and landed on the 17th October, 1558, at Dublin; then coming to the Castle, the Lord Fitz-Walters, being at this time Lord Deputy, sent for the doctor to come before him and the Privy Council, who coming in, after he had made a speech relating upon what account he came over, presented the box to the Lord Deputy, who causing it to be opened, that the secretary might read the Commission, there appeared nothing save a pack of cards, with the knave of clubs uppermost; which not only startled the Lord Deputy and the Council, but the doctor, who assured them he had a Commission, but knew not how it was gone. Then the Lord Deputy made answer, 'Let us have another Commission, and we will shuffle the cards in the meanwhile.' The doctor, being troubled in his mind, went away, and returned into England, and coming to the Court, obtained another Commission; but staying for a wind at the water-side, news came to him that the Queen was dead. Thus God preserved the Protestants in Ireland from the persecution intended."

Ware refers to Boyle, the celebrated Earl of Cork, and Primates Henry and James Ussher, as authorities for this story. He also says that Queen Elizabeth gave the woman who abstracted the Commission a pension of £40 a-year. A similar narrative will be found in Sir Richard Cox's *History;* but it seems to be by him derived from Ware.

Among the Carew MSS. Mr. Bagwell has found a passage in " instructions from Philip and Mary to the Lord Deputy, 28th April, 1556," which, in addition to the circumstantiality with which the story has been told, tends to confirm its credibility . . . " Lord Cardinal Poole, being sent unto us from the Pope's Holiness and the said See Apostolic, Legate of our said realm, mindeth in brief time to despatch into Ireland certain his Commissioners and officials to visit the clergy and other members of the said realm of Ireland."—*Ireland Under the Tudors,* i. 418, *note.*

It will be observed that this extract tends to confirm the opinion I have expressed at page 45, that if the Commission was sent, it originated in England, without suggestion from anyone in Ireland.

---

NOTE L.

In considering the legislation of the English Parliament as to the supremacy in the reign of Queen Elizabeth, we must keep in mind (what is often overlooked) that the Acts of Henry VIII. in relation to the subject were repealed under Queen Mary; and that neither the Supremacy Act of Henry, nor any other of his enactments, giving the title of "supreme head" was (with one exception) revived under Queen Elizabeth. The exception is an Act entitled, "A Bill that Doctors of the Civil Law, being married, may exercise ecclesiastical jurisdiction" (87 Hen. VIII., chap. 17). This was probably owing to the Queen's objection to be called "Supreme Head." (See p. 51, *supra.*)

There is no title in Queen Elizabeth's Acts defining the ecclesiastical position of the Crown, except in the Oath of Supremacy, and there the title is, " Supreme Governor of this realm, and of all other Her Highness's dominions and countries, as well in all spiritual or ecclesiastical things or causes, as temporal: " but the title " supreme head " is, nevertheless, given to the Sovereign by legal writers as a title to which the Crown is by the common law entitled. Thus Blackstone says, " the King is considered by the laws of England as the head and supreme governor of the National Church."—Book i. ch. 7.

Beside the support which the declaratory form of the Act of Henry VIII. (framed not as if enacting a new law, but as if declaring an existing law) gave to the idea that the common law asserted the supremacy, there was an express decision of the English judges in its favour. In Caudrey's case, reported by Lord Coke (5 Rep.)—a case which came to be decided on the common law, not on statutable law—it was resolved that " by the ancient laws of this realm, this kingdom of England is an absolute empire and monarchy consisting of one head, which is the King, and of a body politic, compact and compounded of many, and almost infinite several, and yet well-agreeing members : all which the law divideth into two several parts, that is to say, the clergy and the laity both of them, next and immediately under God, subject and obedient to the head: also the head is instituted and furnished with plenary and entire power, prerogative, and jurisdiction, to render justice and right to every part and member of this body, of what estate, degree, or calling soever, in all causes ecclesiastical or temporal; otherwise he should not be a head of the whole body."

The judgment in Caudrey's case professes to found itself upon a series of authorities, commencing with the words in the laws of the Confessor, which have been already cited (page 10, *supra*), which describe the King as *vicarius summi regis*, and as ruling and defending the Church. An argument to the same effect, and very probably following the judgment in that case, is said to have been on one occasion delivered in Ireland. In the reign of James I. Sir John Davis is stated to have, at the Castle of Dublin, made a speech designed to show that the prerogative claimed for the Crown in ecclesiastical affairs by Henry, Edward VI., and Elizabeth, was no new thing, but " a flower of the Crown from the beginning," and that the acts of these Sovereigns against appeals to Rome, and in confirmation of the regalia of the

Crown, were affirmations of the common law as it had been used and practised in the courts of their royal progenitors. (Carte's *Life of Ormonde*, vol. i. p. 79.)

The nature of the Supremacy, as it is by the Church of England, and as it was by the established, and is now by the disestablished, Church of Ireland acknowledged, must be ascertained from Article XXXVII. (which being one of the Articles required by an Act of Parliament to be subscribed by the clergy, must, it is to be observed, be held to have parliamentary sanction). This Article declares " that Her Majesty hath the chief power in the realm and other her dominions, and that unto her the chief government of all estates of the realm, whether they be ecclesiastical or civil, doth appertain, and that she is not subject to any foreign jurisdiction."

There seems no reason to think that statesmen of the age of Henry VIII. intended to claim more for the Crown than it is admitted was conceded by the Supremacy statute of Queen Elizabeth, and by Article XXXVII. Henry may himself have wished to be a Pope as well as a King, but he took care publicly to negative this meaning for " the headship." Thus, in a letter which he addressed to Tunstall (Bishop of Durham) in connexion with the meeting of the Convocation of York, when the proposition of " the headship " (*supremum caput ecclesiæ*) was to be brought forward, he points out that it is " as persons, and as to property, acts, and deeds, the clergy are under the King as head ; and that as to spiritual things, as sacraments, they have no head but Christ." (See summary of the letter in a very learned paper of Bishop Stubbs, printed in the Appendix to the Report of the Royal Commission on Ecclesiastical Courts, 1883.) A like repudiation of the notion that a spiritual character is claimed by the supremacy appears in an authoritative document drawn up at the time of the Supremacy Act, which says " the King, as supreme head, has only such power as to a king of right appertaineth by the law of God, and not that he should take any spiritual power from spiritual ministers that is given them in the Gospel." (See Froude's *History*, vol. ii. p. 327, where the entire paper is cited.)

Article XXXVII., applying in its language to a King or Queen (*Regia Majestas* in the Latin version), could not be adopted by the Protestant Episcopal Church in the United States of America. Accordingly, in lieu of it, the following Article has been substituted by that

Church : . . . " The power of the civil magistrate extendeth to all men as well clergy as laity, in all things temporal; but hath no authority in things purely spiritual. And we hold it to be the duty of all men who are professors of the Gospel to pay respectful obedience to the civil authority, regularly and legitimately constituted."

## Note M.

The Irish Parliament of 1560 having been that which passed the Supremacy Act, and passed also the Act introducing in the Church of Ireland the English Prayer Book, and being in this way the means of giving to the Church, as then established, a Protestant character, it becomes a matter of much interest to ascertain of what persons it was composed. A record which throws light upon the subject has fortunately been preserved. This record is in the Rolls Office in Chancery in Dublin. It is headed, " Nomina Dominorum spiritualium et temporalium ac Communium in quodam Parliamento dominæ reginæ apud Dublin die Veneris proxime ante festum Sancti Hilarii viz XI° die Januarii, anno regni reginæ Elizabethæ secundo . . . summonito et tento." This record has been recently printed in the Appendix to Hardiman's edition of the Statute of Kilkenny, in the *Tracts relating to Ireland*, published by the Irish Archæological Society, vol. ii. pp. 134-8.

The Domini spirituales (twenty in number) are enumerated as follows : . . . " Hugo Dublin, Hiberniæ Primus, Dominus Canc.; Rolandus Cassil; Chris. Tuam; Willielmus Midensis; Patr. Wat. and Lismor.; Rogerus Cork and Clon.; Alexr. Fern.; Thomas Darensis (i. e., Kildare); Thomas Leghlin; Johannes Ossorien. Imolacensis (Emly); Hugo Lymericen; Rollandus Clonfert et Elph.; Eugenius Dunen (Down); Eps. Rossensis; Eps. Laonensis (Killaloe); Eps. Coranensis (Achonry); Eps. Aladensis (Killala); Eps. Ardfertensis; Eps. Ardacadensis (Ardagh)."

It will be observed that the Christian names of thirteen of these bishops are given, and that of seven merely the titles are mentioned. The reason for this is not stated by any contemporary, nor even by any old authority; but it has recently been suggested that in those instances where Christian names are recorded, the bishops named attended, and that the others did not. The insertion of the Christian names in the one case, and the omission in the other, is by Mr. Bagwell thought (and not unreasonably) to indicate that the Dublin officials knew little about the latter. (Vol. ii. p. 368.)

The names of the thirteen Bishops whose Christian names are given were, Dublin, Curwin; Cashel, Fitzgerald, or Le Baron; Tuam, Bodkin; Meath, Wm. Walsh; Waterford, Patk. Walsh; Ferns, Devereux; Kildare, Leverous; Leighlin, Field; Ossory, Thonery; Limerick, Lacy; Clonfert, De Burgo; Down, Magennis. The names of the seven bishops whose titles only are given were: Emly, De Burgo; Ross (it is doubtful if this was filled; see Ware); Killaloe, O'Brien; Achonry (who was bishop seems doubtful; Dr. Brady, in his pamphlet on the *Conversion of the Bishops*, Dublin, 1886, says O'Coyne or Quin); Killala (Ware has not the name; Dr. Brady says O'Gallaher); Ardfert, Fitz Maurice; Ardagh, MacMahon.

There were then eight other bishoprics, and these are not at all mentioned in this record, viz., Clogher, Clonmacnoise, Kilmore, Dromore, Derry, Raphoe, Killaloe, Kilfenora.

The Domini temporales (twenty-three in number) mentioned in this record are, Earl of Ormond (Butler); Earl of Kildare (FitzGerald); Earl of Desmond (FitzGerald); Earl of Thomond (O'Brien); Earl of Clanricarde (De Burgo); Lord of Buttevante (Barry); Lord of Fermoy (Roche); Lord of Atherney [Athenry] (Breminghame); Lord of Kinsale (Courcey); Viscount of Gormanston (Preston); Viscount of Baltinglass (Eustace); Viscount of Mountgarret (Butler); Baron of Delvyn (Nugent); Baron of Slane (Fleming); Lord of Killyen, or Killeen (Plunket); Lord of Howth (St. Laurence); Lord of Trimleston (Barnewall); Baron of Lacksnaway, or Licksnaw, commonly called Baron of Kerry (FitzMorishe, or FitzMaurice); Lord of Dunsany (Plunket); Baron of Dunboyne (Butler); Baron of Louthe (Plunket); Lord of Currahmore (Poer); Upper Ossory (Fitzpatrick).

For the House of Commons twenty counties are mentioned. The names of the members for ten are given (two for each). They are Dublin, Meath, Westmeath, Louth, Kildare, Catherlow, Kilkenny, Waterford, Tipperary, Wexford. The other ten are, Cork, Kerry, Limerick, Connaught, Clare, Antrim, Ardes, Down, King's County, Queen's County; but for these ten no names of members are stated.

There are twenty-nine cities and boroughs mentioned, and the names of the members returned for them are given, except in one instance—Kilmallock. The twenty-eight for whom both the names of the cities and boroughs, and of their burgesses (two for each) are stated, are Dublin, Waterford, Cork, Lymerick, Drogheda, Galway, Youghill, Cragfergus, Kilkenny, Kinsale, Wexford, Rosse, Dundalk, Carlingford, Clonmell, Fideteh (Fethard), Thomastown, Athenry, Nase, Kildare, Kells, Tryme, Athboy, Navan, Athird (Ardee), Mullingar, Athie, Dungarvan.

It will be observed that Connaught, not being yet subdivided, is treated as one county; that only two towns situate in that province (Galway and Athenry) returned members; that from Ulster are named only one bishop (Down), no temporal peer; but three counties (Down, Ardes, and Antrim), and one borough (Carrickfergus). Peers and Commoners are, with few exceptions, of Anglo-Irish race.

Ware's notice of this Parliament is merely . . . "12 Jan. 1559 (O.S.), began the Parliament to sit in Christ's Church, which also ended in the beginning of February following, having enacted the Act of Uniformity and several other laws." . . . "At the very beginning of this Parliament, her Majestie's well-wishers found that most of the nobility and Commons were divided in opinion about the ecclesiastical government, which caused the Earl of Sussex to dissolve them, and to go over to England, to consult her Majesty about the affairs of this kingdom." (*Annals*, A.D. 1559.)

## Note N.

The account given by Ware of the meeting of ecclesiastical persons (mentioned at page 60, *supra*) which took place after Lord Sussex's return from the journey to England, which is related in the last note (M), is as follows: . . . "The Earl of Sussex having been in England some months, returned again and took his oath as Lord Lieutenant of Ireland. Within three weeks after which came letters from her Majesty to him, signifying her pleasure for a general meeting of the clergy of Ireland, and the establishment of the Protestant religion through the several dioceses of the kingdom. Among bishops, William Walsh, then Bishop of Meath, was very zealous for the Romish Church; not content with what offers her Majesty had proposed, but very much enraged (after the assembly had dispersed themselves), he fell to preach against the Common Prayer (in his diocese at Trim), which was newly come over, and ordered to be observed; for which the Lord Lieutenant confined him, till he acquainted her Majesty with it, who sent over her orders to clap him up in prison." (*Annals*, A.D. 1559.)

### Note O.

It is admitted by all writers who have discussed the conduct of the bishops at the accession of Elizabeth, that Archbishop Curwin not only conformed, but took an active part in carrying into operation the new ecclesiastical system. There seems also no doubt that Field, or O'Fihel (Leighlin), conformed. In a State Paper (dated 28th May, 1559), it is stated that he took the oath of allegiance and of abjuration of all foreign jurisdiction and authority (Shirley, p. 93, and *Cal. S. P. Eliz.*, p. 154); and on the 6th October, 1564, he was appointed along with Archbishop Loftus, Bishop Brady of Meath, and Bishop Daly of Kildare (all nominated to their bishoprics by the Queen, and all decided Protestants), upon a Commission for inquiry into heretical opinions, into charges of not using the proper Church services, and other ecclesiastical offences."—Morrin, vol. i. p. 489.

Others of these bishops beside Field are named in Commissions dated after the Queen's Supremacy Act. The seventh section of this Act prescribed the oath of supremacy, and required it to be taken by every archbishop, bishop, and all and every other ecclesiastical person and minister, and all and every temporal judge, justice, mayor, and other lay or temporal officer and minister. Forfeiture of office *ipso facto* as if the party were dead, and disability to retain their offices, were penalties attendant on the refusal of these persons to take the oath (sec. 8). It is, therefore, in the highest degree improbable that bishops named in Commissions, if they had not already taken, did not before acting take, the oath.

The bishops who are thus named in Commissions are Archbishop FitzGerald, or Le Baron (Cashel), who was one of the Commissioners in a Commission of gaol delivery for Munster and Thomond, dated 2nd August, 1560 (Morrin, vol. i. p. 433); Archbishop Bodkin (Tuam), who was a Commissioner in 1567 (for as such he signed an injunction to the sheriff of the county of Connaught (Morrin. vol. i. p. 505); Devereux (Ferns), who is named in Commissions dated May, 1559, and 13th April, 1562-3, for administering civil and military affairs in

Wexford county (Morrin, vol. i. pp. 412, 477). Patrick Walsh (Waterford), is named in a Commission dated November, 1566, for arbitrating between Ormond and Desmond (*Cal. S. P.* 320); Lacy, or Lees (Limerick), in one for gaol delivery in Munster and Thomond, dated 2nd August, 1560 (Morrin, vol. i. p. 483); his name also appears in a decree made by the members of another Commission dated 29th September, 1564 (Morrin, vol. i. p. 492); and he seems to have acted again on one in 1568 (*Cal. S. P.* Eliz. 360).

The inference to be drawn from bishops being Commissioners is not to be extended beyond outward conformity. Thus it comes out in an examination (17th March, 1564-5) of Creagh, the Roman Catholic Archbishop of Armagh, that Lacy, notwithstanding that he in this way politically helped the Government, gave twelve marks to the nuncio who about four years previously came over from the Pope. (Shirley, p. 173). Ware says Lacy resigned in 1571. Others say he was deprived. In the note at page 42, *supra*, it has been erroneously assumed that he retained the See of Limerick until his death. Whether he resigned or was deprived, he is said afterwards to have been in communion with Rome. Lacy's place was filled by the restoration of Casey, who had been displaced under Mary. Leverous and Thonery, not Protestant, were at first in commission. (Morrin, i. 412.)

With respect to Devereux, it is to be noted that he came into office under Henry VIII., and after the Supremacy Act of 1537; and that he continued under both Edward VI. and Mary. In 1566 a dispatch to Cecil, signed by Sir H. Sidney and others, complains of Devereux granting his lands to his sons. It does not say whether they were legitimate or illegitimate. If legitimate, Devereux had married, and must be held to have been a Protestant; if illegitimate, it is unlikely that unless he at least professed Protestantism more proceedings than complaining would not have been taken by the Deputy.

With respect to the other bishops at the accession of Elizabeth (sixteen in number), in the case of two of them some incidents are stated which would suggest their conformity. De Burgo (Clonfert), uncle of Lord Clanricarde, was in 1561 on sufficiently good terms with Queen Elizabeth to recommend that a clergyman named Laly should be confirmed in the Deanery of Tuam (Morrin, vol. i. p. 448). Eugene Magennis (Down) was one of the prelates at the consecration of Goodacre and of Bale in the time of Edward VI. (see pages 39, 40, *supra*).

he received a pardon from her in 1559; and it is not likely that he then disobeyed her. Ware expressly states that Magennis was present at the Parliament of 1560. Of the rest nothing is recorded that can be considered to bear upon the question, except that on Magennis's death, in a petition from (it is supposed) Pierres, Constable of Carrickfergus, praying that some worthy, learned man be promoted to the bishopric of Down, it is said that "certain Irish prelates near adjoining were very zealously affected."—Shirley, *ibid.*, p. 135.

It has been said by some modern writers that the oath of supremacy could not have been enforced except from bishops in the Pale (Meath and Kildare), and that in fact it was not attempted to be enforced. But why not from those who were prelates in the dioceses bordering on the Pale? Also why not from those who were Commissioners, or who happened to attend Parliament? A Roman Catholic writer of authority, Rothe, Bishop of Ossory, in the reign of James I., states that the oath was directed to be enforced:—" Quisquis (he says) refugeret illud (juramentum) suscipere, ex toto cuneo Prelatorum statim excideret a suâ dignitate et prelaturâ." By the same authority it is related that Sussex reproached Leverous for his refusal to take the oath, when so many doctors and prelates in England and Ireland had recognized the Queen's supremacy:—" Quorsum negaret. Reginam esse caput ecclesiæ, quod tamen recognoscebant tot magni et illustres viri, tot doctores et præsules tam in Anglia quam in ipsâ Hibernia."

The suggestion, therefore, which has been lately made, that the consecration of Elizabeth's first bishops (Craik, Loftus, &c.) was by Curwin alone, is in the highest degree improbable. By the Act regulating appointments, and by the ordination service, it was intended that the canonical number should attend; the Queen's collation was ordered to be signified to the prelates who were to officiate at the consecration, and obedience was required under the penalties of the *premunire* statute (2 Eliz., chap. 4, secs. 2, 3, 5).

It is worthy of remark in connexion with this subject, that Bramhall, when asserting the regularity of the first consecrations of bishops under Elizabeth in England, uses as an argument the fact that there was no need of irregularity, as, if there were any want of English bishops, Irish bishops could have been had recourse to: ... " If it had been needful, they might have had seven more out of Ireland, archbishops and bishops; for such a work as a consecration, Ireland never wanted stores of ordainers; nor ever yet did any man assert the want of a competent number of consecrators to an Irish Protestant bishop. They who concurred freely in the consecration of Protestant bishops at home would not have denied their concurrence in England, if they had been commanded." (*Works*, Ang.-Cath. Libr., vol. ii. p. 52.)

It has also been asserted that the power of Queen Elizabeth over the Irish Episcopate during the rest of her reign was confined to the Pale. But there are more than forty patents abstracted by Morrin dated within the Queen's reign which relate to bishoprics; appointing and translating to them, and in some instances permitting other preferments to be held *in commendam*. This does not seem consistent with the Queen having no power. The English Government was certainly able to influence the dioceses near the Pale, and probably more. Against the writers who limit the extent of the Queen's power may be set the authority of Mr. Brewer, the able editor of the State Papers, whose views in reference to all historic questions connected with the reigns of the Tudor princes deserve great respect. He has expressed his opinion that "unless Elizabeth's Deputies and Council were so negligent and ignorant as never to complain, and never to betray the emptiness and vanity of the Queen's commands, as well as the impossibility of complying with them, we must admit that from the first year of her reign, and all through to the close of it, she exercised her jurisdiction far beyond the limits of the English Pale." (*Preface to Carew MSS.*)

Those who desire to pursue further the subject of this note may be referred to the pamphlets on the subject of Dr. Brady, Archdeacon Lee, and Dr. Alfred Lee, published in Dublin and London, 1866 and 1867; and see also Bagwell's *Ireland Under the Tudors*, chap. xxxv.

---

NOTE P.

Fuller, in his *English Church History*, makes a curious digression to Trinity College, Dublin. He enumerates in it the different benefactors to whom the College was indebted, numbering them in the ollowing order:—(1) Henry Ussher, then Archdeacon of Dublin, afterwards Archbishop of Armagh, and uncle of James Ussher, "who (he says) took a journey to England, and procured the mortmain from (2) Queen Elizabeth." (3) Lord Burleigh, the first Chancellor. (4) Sir William Fitz William, the Deputy. (5) Mr. Luke Challoner, "who (he says) received and disbursed the moneys." (6) The Mayor and Aldermen of Dublin, who bestowed on the College the site, "with some accommodations (of considerable grounds) about it." (7) Archbishop Adam Loftus, who was the first Master "holding it as an honorary title, though not so much to receive credit by, as to return lustre to, the place." (8) Sir Warham St. Leger, who " was very bountiful in paying yearly pensions to the students before the College was endowed with standing revenues." (9) Sir Francis Shane, whom he describes as "a mere Irishman, but a good Protestant, who kept this infant foundation from being strangled in the birth thereof." (10) Robert Devereux, Earl of Essex, who gave " a cannoneer's pay and the pay of certain dead soldiers, to the value of well-nigh £400 a-year, for the scholars' maintenance." (11) King James, " who (he says) confirmed the revenues *in perpetuum*, endowing the College with a great proportion of good land in the province of Ulster." " Nor (he afterwards adds) is it to be forgotten that what Josephus reports of the temple built by Herod : κατ ἐκεῖνον τὸν καιρὸν οἰκοδοωουμένου τοῦ ναοῦ, τάς μὲν ἡμέρας οὐχ ὕειν, ἐν δὲ ταῖς νυξὶ γίνεσθαι τοὺς ὄμβρους, ὡς μὴ κωλῦσαι τὸ ἔργον—' During the time of the building of the temple it rained not in the daytime, but in the night, that the showers might not hinder the work.' I say, what by him is reported hath been avouched to me by witnesses above exception, that the same happened here, from the founding to the finishing of this college ; the officious heavens always smiling by day (though often weeping by night) till the work was completed."

The first stone of the College was laid 19th March, 1592, of the present style, or 1591–2 of the style then in use.

## Note Q.

According to the Report of the Royal Commissioners on Ecclesiastical Revenue and Patronage, dated 1st March, 1833, the Sees of the Church of Ireland were thirty-five—Armagh, Dublin, Glendalough, Cashel, Emly, Ardagh, Meath, Clogher, Clonmacnois, Down,

Connor, Derry, Raphoe, Kilmore, Dromore, Kildare, Ossory, Ferns, Leighlin, Limerick, Ardfert, Aghadoe, Waterford, Lismore, Cork, Ross, Cloyne, Killaloe, Kilfenora, Elphin, Clonfert, Kilmacduagh, Killala, Achonry, Elphin.

Before 1536 Dublin and Glendalough, Down and Connor, Ardfert and Aghadoe, Waterford and Lismore, were incorporated or united permanently together. The others could at that time be held separately or in union.

With respect to the union of the others, the Report states that by Act 11 Eliz. Cashel was united with Emly, and Clonmacnois with Meath; that from 1744 Ardagh had been held *in commendam* with Tuam; that Ferns was permanently united with Leighlin at the beginning of the seventeenth century: so also was Clonfert with Kilmacduagh, and Killala with Achonry; that from 1660 Limerick was united with Ardfert and Aghadoe; that from the Restoration Cork and Ross were accustomably united; and from 1750 Killaloe and Kilfenora.

In 1536 four of the Sees were Archbishoprics, viz., Armagh, Dublin, Cashel, and Tuam.

Among the Sees of the Irish Church Armagh was from a remote date conceded the Primacy. It is claimed for it in the "Book of Armagh," a MS. of the ninth century: and Bishop Reeves has found even older authorities in its favour. (See Report of Royal Commission, 1868, App., p. 99.) "Armagh," he says, "owed its dignity to the supposed choice of St. Patrick, which again may have been influenced by its proximity to Emania, the ancient capital of Ulster." Among the suffragan bishoprics Meath had precedence: it does not appear why. Ware merely says that Meath was formed, not long after the coming of the English, out of the old Sees of Clonard, Kells, and Duleek, and that in the order of sitting among the suffragan bishops of Ireland in councils and elsewhere the bishop of Meath had the first place, the bishop of Derry the second, and the rest took their places according to the time of their ordination. (*Antiquities*, Dublin edition, 1705, pp. 39, 40.)

The number of suffragan bishoprics at the date of the Report of 1833 was eighteen. The number at the date of the Reformation Mant reckons to have been twenty-six. (*History*, vol. i. p. 8.)

The alterations in the arrangements as to bishoprics made by the

Act of 1833 (see p. 229) had all taken effect before the Royal Commission of 1867 (see p. 266). Then the arrangements as to the archbishoprics and bishoprics, and the Sees united together, were as follows:—The archbishoprics were—(1) Armagh, which was united with Clogher, and had provincial jurisdiction over the old province of Tuam; (2) Dublin, which was united with Glendalough and Kildare, and had provincial jurisdiction over the old province of Cashel. The bishoprics were—(1) Meath; (2) Down, Connor, and Dromore united; (3) Derry and Raphoe united; (4) Kilmore, Elphin, and Ardagh united; (5) Tuam, Killalla, and Achonry united; (6) Ossory, Ferns, and Leighlin united; (7) Limerick, Ardfert, and Aghadoe united; (8) Cashel, Emly, Waterford, and Lismore united; (9) Cork, Cloyne, and Ross united; (10) Killaloe, Kilfenora, Clonfert, and Kilmacduagh united. The first five were suffragan to Armagh; the last five suffragan to Dublin.

## Note R.

Ware gives a list of the monasteries and convents which were founded, exclusive of those which, having been erected in the first times of the Irish Church, had been afterwards converted into parish churches. The religious houses enumerated by him numbered 362, of which 142 were in Leinster, 90 in Munster, 82 in Connaught, and 48 in Ulster. (See *Antiquities*, Dublin edition, 1705.) Harris, in his edition of Ware, increases the number.

The Augustinian Order (so called from a monk to whom their discipline was due), including the Aroasians, seem to have had the largest number of these houses; the Cistercians some of the greatest, as Mellifont, near Drogheda, and Holy Cross, in Tipperary. The Mendicant Orders had a considerable number. At Kilmainham and Clontarf were great establishments of the Hospitallers, or Knights of St. John.

According to the State Paper of 1515, which has been cited in a previous note of the Appendix (F), the preachers at that time were "the begging Friars." From this and some other authorities Brewer, in his preface to the State Papers, and following him Richey, regard these monastic persons favourably. But, on the other hand, Ussher (*Works*, iv. p. 302) and Bishop Bedell (Mant, i. 436) speak severely of them. Ussher cites Fitz Ralph, Archbishop of Armagh in the fourteenth century—a prelate unquestionably of the highest eminence—to testify against them. It is, however, to be remembered, that in an appeal of the Mendicant Friars to Pope Innocent VI. against Fitz Ralph they were successful; also that Fitz Ralph was opposed in principle to the system of monastic mendicancy, and so was unfavourably predisposed towards it when he came to examine its practice. Thus he distinctly says:—Dominus Jesus nunquam mendicavit: docuit nec debere homines mendicare: nullus potest prudenter et sancte spontanee mendicitatem super se perpetuo assumere asservandam. (See Ussher's *Works*, vol. iv. p. 302.)

With respect to the moral conduct of the religious orders in Ireland generally, in the time of Henry VIII., the opinion of recent historians has been divided. Dr. Killen speaks of them with censure. (See his *Ecclesiastical History of Ireland*, vol. i. pp. 336-339.) Dr. Richey takes the opposite side. (See his *Lectures on Irish History*, 2nd series, p. 78.) Mr. Bagwell adopts somewhat of an intermediate view—"That some monks were immoral or useless is (he says), doubtless, true;"... but "there is ample evidence that the monks were not all bad." (See *Ireland Under the Tudors*, vol. i. p. 299.)

The chief authority, in addition to some recorded instances of actual delinquency, to support the charges against the monks is Robert Cowley, Master of the Rolls. He expressed to Cromwell, then Henry's chief adviser, the opinion that "the religious houses in Ireland were less continent and virtuous than those in England." (*S. P.* ii. 371.) But if Cromwell and Henry found Cowley's report of their general character affirmed by others, or themselves believed it, it is difficult to understand why in no Irish Statute or Commission relating to the monks are charges of this kind made against them, especially as in one of the Commissions there are accusations of a different nature, viz., that the religious houses were addicted to "their own superstitious ceremonies," and to the "doctrines of the Roman Pontiff.". (Morrin, vol. i. p. 55.) This observation is entitled to the more weight, because Henry, in his Act in relation to the smaller monasteries in England, puts forward their vicious living in justification of their suppression. (27 Henry VIII., c. 28.)

In the case of six religious houses, of which one was a nunnery, the council petitioned that they should be spared, upon the ground that "in default of inns, which are not in this land, the council and officers, also Irishmen and others resorting to the king's deputy, are most commonly lodged in them at the cost of the said houses, and that in them young men and children, both gentlemen's children and others, both of mankind and womankind, be brought up in virtue, learning, and in the English tongue and behaviour, to the great charges of the said houses." (*S. P.*, Ireland, vol. iii. p. 130.)

## Note S.

The state of the clergy in 1515 is described in the same State Paper (*Cal. S. P.*, vol. ii. p. 11) which has been already cited (Notes F and R), in the following terms. . . . "There is no archbishop nor bishop, abbot nor prior, parson or vicar, nor any other person of the Church, high or low, great or small, English or Irish, that useth to preach the Word of God, saving the poor friar beggars." . . . "The Church of this land use not to learn any other science but the law of Canon (*i. e.* Canon Law) for covetyce of lucre transitory: all other science whereof grows none such lucre the parsons of the Church doth despise. They hold more by the plough rustical than by lucre of the plough celestial, to which they have stretched their hands, and look always backwards. They tend much more to lucre of that plough whereof grows slander and rebuke than to lucre of the souls—that is, the plough of Christ."

In 1528, Inge, Archbishop of Dublin, and Chief Justice Birmingham, wrote to Wolsey:—"Your Grace, we doubt not, heareth the sorrowful decay of this land, as well in good Christianitie as other laudable manners, which hath grown for lack of good prelates and curates in the Church"—curates used in the same sense as in the Collect for bishops and curates. "The diocese of Meath" (the most civilized in Ireland) they afterwards say "is far in ruin, both spiritually and temporally, by the absence of the bishop there." (*S. P.* ii., pt. 3, p. 126.)

Archbishop Browne, in his letter of September, 1535 (App. B), draws a distinction between the monks and the clergy. The former, he says, "keep the people in ignorance; the latter are as ignorant as the people, being not able to say Mass, or pronounce the words, they not knowing what they themselves say in the Roman tongue."

Again, in a later letter to Cromwell, Browne says:—"Those of the clergy as your Lordship hath had from me before, being ignorant and not able to speak right words in the Mass or Liturgie, as being not skilled in the Latin grammar; so that a bird may be taught to speak with as much sense as several of them do in this country." (*Life of Browne* by Ware, letter 3, Kal. April, 1538.)

In articles exhibited by Lord Kildare against Lord Ormonde he speaks of the churches in the counties Kilkenny and Tipperary being in such extreme decay that no divine service is kept there. . . . "If the king do not provide a remedy, there will be no more Christentie than in the middle of Turkey." (*Cal. Carew MSS.*, vol. i. p. 23.)

## Note T.

A translation of the New Testament into Irish is said to have been made by Archbishop Fitz Ralph in the fourteenth century. (See Ussher's *Historica Dogmatica*, Works, vol. xii. p. 345.) But if there was, it has not been preserved. The first which was ever printed seems to have been commenced by Nicholas Walsh, successively Chancellor of St. Patrick's Cathedral, Dublin, and Bishop of Waterford (1577-1585), assisted by Nehemiah Donnellan, afterwards Archbishop of Tuam, and John Kerney, Treasurer of St. Patrick's. It was completed by William Daniel or Donnellan, Archbishop of Tuam (1595-1628). This version was first printed in 1602, accompanied by a dedication to James I., in which the archbishop says that " in the translation I tied myself, as of duty I ought, to the original Greek." The same prelate subsequently translated the English Prayer Book into Irish, and had his version printed in 1608-9, with a dedication to the Lord Deputy. This was ordered to be read in the shire towns of every diocese. (See the notices of Walsh and Daniel in Ware's *Bishops*; Richardson's *History of the Attempts to Convert the Native Irish*: London, 1712, pp. 14, 15; Mant's *History*, vol. i. pp. 292-3.)

The Old Testament in Irish was first published in 1685. Its publication was in a great degree due to the exertions of Robert Boyle, then well known from his philosophic studies: it was superintended by Archbishop Narcissus Marsh. The version adopted in it seems to have been commenced under the care of Bishop Bedell, and to have been perfected about the time of its publication. (Mant's *History*, vol. i. pp. 468, 671.)

## Note U.

Of the bishops in 1613, Meiler Magrath (Cashel); Lyon (Cork); Crosby (Ardfert and Aghadoe); Linch (Clonfert), were appointed by Queen Elizabeth. The others were appointed by James I. They were—Hampton (Armagh); Montgomery (Meath); Echlin (Down); Moygne (Kilmore); Buckworth (Dromore); Knox (Raphoe); Turner (Derry); Jones (Dublin); Pilsworth (Kildare); Wheeler (Ossory); Ram (Ferns); Adams (Limerick); Lancaster (Waterford); Rider (Killaloe); Daniel (Tuam); and King (Elphin). None of James's bishops were Irish by race or birth.

## Note V.

The clause in the Irish Articles of 1615, which is stated at page 102, and which appears to me to have been intended to mitigate the severity of the propositions in relation to election and reprobation that were introduced into them from the Lambeth Articles, has received less attention from those who have commented upon the Irish Articles than it merited. They generally speak of the Irish Articles as repetitions upon this subject of the Lambeth. On the other hand, with the qualification expressed in this clause, the Irish seem to me not to go beyond what Hooker, in the treatise mentioned in the note to page 102, describes as St. Augustine's "latter judgment." To illustrate this, I extract one passage from Hooker's summary of this judgment: . . . "The whole body of mankind, in the view of God's eternal knowledge, lay universally polluted with sin, worthy of condemnation and death: over the mass of corruption there passed two acts of God—an act of favour, liberality, and grace, choosing part to be made partakers of everlasting glory; and an act of justice, forsaking the rest, and adjudging them to endless perdition; *these* vessels of wrath, *those* of mercy."

The view of the question of predestination which is put forward in the words I have cited, has, by some writers, been termed Augustinianism, in order to distinguish it from the Calvinistic scheme of predestination, of which reprobation is an essential element. It would seem to have been that most in favour in the Church before the Reformation—at least I am not able to find any solid distinction between it and the teaching of Thomas Aquinas, the highest authority among the

schoolmen, as it appears in the extracts from his writings given by Sir James Macintosh in his *Introduction to Ethical Philosophy*. Thus:—
" Prædestinatio est causa gratiæ et gloriæ ... Deus inclinat ad bonum administrando virtutem agendi et monendo ad bonum. Sed ad malum dicitur inclinare in quantum gratiam non præbet, per quam aliquis a malo retraheretur."

The Article of the Church of England which relates to the subject of predestination (XVII.) was composed by divines who held in reference to the question discordant opinions. There seems no doubt that the language used in it was designedly of a character which might admit of its being consistently subscribed not only by persons holding Calvinistic or Augustinian views, but also by those who, like Arminius and his followers, dissented from both these systems.

At the date of the Irish Articles the English Seventeenth Article was accepted by English clergymen, who agreed in every respect with the Irish Articles. If therefore the Irish Convocation had sought only liberty for their own ideas, they could have had that by adopting the Thirty-nine Articles. It seems evident that what they desired went farther, and aimed at excluding all who did not hold in reference to predestination, at least Augustinianism.

## Note W.

The bishops at the time of the Convocation of 1634, beside Ussher, Martin, and Bramhall, were: Spottiswoode (Clogher), by birth Scotch; Echlin (Down), Scotch (succeeded by Leslie in 1635, also Scotch); Bedell (Kilmore), by birth English; Richardson (Ardagh), English; Buckworth (Dromore), English; Leslie (Raphoe), Scotch; Bulkeley (Dublin), English; Pilsworth (Kildare), English (but in 1635 succeeded by Robert Ussher, Irish); Wheeler (Ossory), English; Ram (Ferns and Leighlin), English (succeeded, in 1635, by Andrew, English); Hamilton (Cashel), Scotch; Webb (Limerick), English; Steere (Ardfert and Aghadoe), English; Michael Boyle (Waterford and Lismore), English (succeeded, in 1635, by Atherton, also English); Richard Boyle (Cork), English; Jones (Killaloe), English; Barlow (Tuam), English; King (Elphin), English; Dawson (Clonfert), English; Adair (Killala), Scotch.

## Note X.

The first accounts of the loss of life in the Rebellion of 1641 were, there seems no doubt, much exaggerated, and especially as to the loss at the commencement. Sir William Petty (*Political Anatomy*, ch. iv.) thought that 37,000 were massacred in the first year of the tumults. Warner, one of the Fellows of Trinity College, Dublin, after examining the depositions of witnesses in relation to the subject, which are preserved in the library of his college, reduced the estimate of loss of life, directly and indirectly, during the first two years, to 12,000; but he seems to have rejected some evidence which he should have acted upon. A recent re-examination of these depositions has led to an estimate of the number " murdered by the sword, gun, rope, drowning, &c., in the first three or four years, not including those killed in battle, at 25,000." (See Miss Hickson's *Ireland in the Seventeenth Century*.) In this book for the first time some of the most important of the depositions are printed. The question of the number of lives lost in the first year of this rebellion is also discussed by Hallam (*Const. History*, ii. 352); by Froude (*English in Ireland*, ii. 96–113); and by Lecky (*Hist.*, ii. 125–170); but it is to be noted that their observations were written before Miss Hickson's work was published.

## Note Y.

The sections of the Irish Uniformity Act (17 & 18 Car. II., ch. 6) which require incumbents of benefices to be episcopally ordained are the 8th and 9th. The eighth deprived any person then an incumbent, and in possession of any benefice, &c., who was " not already in holy orders by episcopal ordination, or should not before 29th September, 1667, be ordained priest or deacon according to the form of episcopal ordination," *i.e.* the form in the then revised Prayer Book. The ninth clause enacted that no person should thenceforth be capable of being admitted to any benefice, &c., before such time as he should be ordained priest, according to the form and manner in the said book (*i.e.* the then revised Prayer Book) prescribed, " unless he have formerly been made priest by episcopal ordination," upon pain of pecuniary penalties, and of disability to take or to be admitted into the order of priest, by the space of one whole year. These clauses are identical with the 13th and 14th clauses of the English Act of Uniformity, except that in the English Act the date at which deprivation was to take effect was "the feast day of St. Bartholomew" (August 24), 1662. The object in both countries seems to have been the same—to declare invalid orders conferred by presbyters, and to recognize those conferred by Roman Catholic bishops.\*

It was, however, in the interval between the Restoration (1660) and the Irish Act of Uniformity (1665) that the clergy in possession of benefices in Ireland, who had not been episcopally ordained, and of whom most had orders from presbyters, were held not entitled to retain them. The view at that time taken of the law applicable to them seems to have been somewhat as follows:—There had then been no statute ever passed by an Irish Parliament repealing the Irish Uniformity Act of Elizabeth. Cromwell never even summoned an Irish Parliament. Whatever was done under the Commonwealth in relation to the Irish Church was regarded as a mere exercise of arbitrary will, of no force or effect when the usurping authority had passed away. The Uniformity Act of Elizabeth would, therefore, operate after the Restoration, just as it did under Charles I. This Act did not contain the clauses now cited from the Acts of Charles II., but it contained provisions which seem to have been thought to have much the same effect. It imposed the obligation to use the Prayer Book as then revised, and as part of it the Ordination Service, in the Preface to which it was expressly declared that "no man shall be accounted or taken to be a lawful bishop, priest, or deacon, in the Church of Ireland, or suffered to execute any of the said functions, except he be called, tried, examined, and admitted thereto, according to the form hereafter following, or hath had formerly episcopal consecration or ordination."

The practice in England was not, however, strictly consistent with this view of the law. After Elizabeth's Prayer Book came into use, there were ministers officiating in the Church of England who had

---

\* The words "formerly made priest by episcopal ordination" seem to me not confined in their operation to the date of the Act. And in this construction is probably to be found the reason why a Roman Catholic priest, conforming to the Church of England or the Church of Ireland, has been allowed to officiate without re-ordination. Of this practice the great preacher, Kirwan, is perhaps the most celebrated example in Ireland. (See on the question Phillimore's note to Burns' E. L., ed. 1842, p. 70.)

not been episcopally ordained. Keble says that they were numerous. "Nearly," he says, "up to the time when he (*i.e.* Hooker) wrote, numbers had been admitted to the ministry of the Church in England, with no better than Presbyterian ordination." (Preface to his edition of Hooker's *Works*, vol. i. p. lxxvi.) Keble mentions that their admission was attributed to a construction placed upon a statute of 13 Elizabeth, which permitted persons not ordained according to the prescribed form to subscribe the Articles: otherwise their ecclesiastical promotions to be void, Most of such persons had foreign orders. (See Keble's Preface, p. lxxvi.).

## Note Z.

The question agitated by Molyneux in the reign of King William III.—whether the English Parliament could bind Ireland by its statutes—had been previously raised—(1) in the English Courts; (2) in the Irish Parliament; (3) in a celebrated treatise ascribed to an Irish Lord Chancellor, Sir Richard Bolton, but more probably, Harris thinks, written by Patrick D'Arcy, an eminent Irish barrister.

(1). The first reference to the question in the English Courts seems to have been in a case reported in the *Year Books*, 2 Ric. III., fol. 12. There it is stated to have been laid down in the English Exchequer Chamber that the Irish have a Parliament, which makes and changes laws for them, and that they are not bound by statutes made in England, because they do not send here knights of Parliament (*non obligantur per statuta in Anglia, quia non hic habent milites Parliamenti*); but this, it is added, is to be understood concerning lands and affairs in that kingdom, and matters affecting them: *sed hoc intelligitur de terris et rebus in terris illis*. It is, however, added that, these being subjects of the King, as such are bound to anything to be done out of Ireland, &c., like those who dwell in Calais, Gascony, Guienne, &c.

A directly opposite opinion is reported to have been pronounced in the reign of Henry VII. by Chief Justice Hussey: *le chief justice disoit que les statutes faits en Engleterre liera ceux d'Irland;* and this, it is added, was then not denied by the other Justices, although they had been of a contrary opinion in the preceding Term, when the Chief Justice was absent. (*Year Books*, 1 Hen. VII., fol. 2.) Another case in the *Year Books* also bears upon the question (20 Hen. VI., fol. 8).

There Justices Fortescue and Portington laid down that if a tax of a tenth or fifteenth were granted in England, this should not bind them in Ireland, the latter giving as his reason that "the Irish do not receive commandment by writ to come to our Parliament."

In this way the question stood when *Calvin's Case* (as to the status of subjects born in Scotland after the accession of James I. to the throne of England) was brought before the English Judges. The position of Ireland relatively to England being discussed in illustration of the question in the case, the dictum in the *Year Books*, 2 Ric. III., already cited, was referred to; and, in reporting it, Lord Coke, who was himself one of the Judges, after the words denying the binding effect of English law in Ireland, inserts the words, " unless it (Ireland) be specially named " (Coke's *Reports*, pt. 7, fol. 22); for which the reason is afterwards assigned, that although Ireland was a distinct dominion, yet " the title thereof being by conquest, the same by judgment of law might by express words be bound by Act of the Parliament of England."

(2). The reference to the question in the Irish Parliament was in two statutes—19 Edw. IV., and 29 Henry VI. These statutes are not in the Statute Book, but exemplifications of them were preserved in the Treasury at Waterford. (See Bolton's and Mayart's Tracts, afterwards referred to.) These Acts affirmed, that in order to bind Ireland an English statute or law should be confirmed by the Irish Parliament.

(3). Bolton's Tract is written to refute the dictum in *Calvin's Case*, and to assert the independence of Ireland. He was answered by Mayart, who is described by Harris as Sergeant and Second Judge of the Common Pleas.

Molyneux in his treatise repeats much that was in Bolton's. He meets with express contradiction the statement upon which the dictum in *Calvin's Case* was founded—that Ireland was a conquered country. He holds that it voluntarily submitted. Ireland, too, he urges, was a kingdom just like Scotland, and in the same position as Scotland after the accession of James I.; and therefore the law as to both countries must be the same. But no one had ever alleged that the Acts of the English Parliament could bind Scotland.

## Note A A.

The statement of Lord Chancellor Bowes as to the growing discontent caused in the Irish House of Commons by its subordinate position, which has been referred to at page 216, is in the following words : . . . " Formerly, Protestant or Papist were the key-words; they are now court or country, referring still to constitutional grievances . . . They have considered your House (*i.e.* the English House of Commons) as the model, and in general think themselves injured in the instances in which theirs, upon the legal constitution, must differ."

At a later date Grattan, when urging on the Irish Parliament to assert its independence, held up for their imitation the example of the English Parliament in exacting the Petition of Right, and the Bill of Rights. (Speech, 19th April, 1780.)

It was at the time remarked that if the apprehension then were, that the example of England would excite an emulation of freedom in Ireland, the converse had been the case in the days of the Roman Empire. Agricola thought that if the Irish were not subdued—*et velut e conspectu libertas tolleretur*—the Britons would revolt.

## Note B B.

The evidence of Mr. Blake, referred to at page 237, is in the following terms : . . . " I should not wish to see any settlement of the Catholic question effected in which the rights of the Established Church were not preserved. I gave expression to the same feeling when I was examined before the House of Lords. I think what I stated then in substance was, that I should not be favourable to any settlement, or that I should object to any settlement, which went to disturb the Protestant Establishment; that I considered it a main link in the connexion between Great Britain and Ireland, and that with that connexion I was satisfied the interests of Ireland were essentially identified. I understand it has since been imputed to me, that in uttering this sentiment I indulged in a peculiar latitude of expression in order to make a show of liberality. I wish, therefore, now most unequivocally and most solemnly to reiterate the same feeling . . . .
The Protestant Church is rooted in the Constitution ; it is established by the fundamental laws of the realm ; it is rendered, as far as the

most solemn acts of the legislature can render any institution, fundamental and perpetual; it is so declared by the Act of Union between Great Britain and Ireland. I think it could not now be disturbed without danger to the general securities we possess for liberty, property, and order; without danger to all the blessings we derive from being under a lawful government and free constitution. Feeling thus, the very conscience which dictates to me a determined adherence to the Roman Catholic religion, would dictate to me a determined resistance to any attempt to subvert the Protestant Establishment, or to wrest from the Church the possessions which the law has given it."

Not long before this evidence was given by Mr. Blake, Mr. (afterwards Lord) Plunket, in a debate in the House of Commons on a motion for an inquiry into the Church of Ireland (6th May, 1825), thus expressed himself: ... "I consider the Protestant Establishment necessary for the security of all sects; and I think that there should not only be an Established Church, but that it should be richly endowed, and its dignitaries enabled to take their stations among the nobles of the land. But speaking of it in a political point of view, I have no hesitation in stating that the existence of the Protestant Establishment is the great bond of union between the two countries. If ever the unfortunate moment shall arrive, at which the legislature shall rashly lay hands upon the property of the Church, that moment will seal the doom of the Union, and terminate for ever the connexion between the two countries."

## Note C C.

The proposition that justification is by faith only may be concurred in by persons who yet disagree widely: the proposition being, of course when this occurs, explained by them in different ways. This diversity of interpretation arises from the various meanings attributed to the words faith and justification. Thus, by some divines faith is in the proposition understood to signify mere trust, while others think that it is used to express what has been termed *fides formata*, faith informed and perfected by charity, &c.: and justification has, on the one hand, been restricted in its sense to acquittal from the consequences of sin, the person justified being then counted righteous; and, on the other hand, it has been extended to include that he is not only counted, but made righteous, and counted because he is made.

The Irish divines who explain faith as trust, and justification as acquittal, derive their opinions from the German Reformers. With them faith was *fiducia*, and justification (in the words of the Augsburg Confession) *remissio peccatorum et imputatio justitiæ*. The ideas of the opposing school of thought, as represented by Jeremy Taylor and Alexander Knox, may be traced distinctly in some of the Fathers; (with perhaps a slight difference) in eminent Roman Catholic divines, and in at least one great Protestant writer, Grotius. (See Bishop Browne on Article XI., and a tract by Bishop Fitzgerald, entitled *Episcopacy*, &c., published in Dublin in 1839.)

The Thirty-nine Articles having been re-affirmed by the disestablished Church of Ireland (see page 284), the Eleventh Article, which treats "of justification," has, in the system of this Church, an authority equal to that which it possesses in the Church of England. This Article speaks of justification by faith only as a "doctrine most wholesome and very full of comfort," and refers to one of the Homilies (called in it the Homily of Justification, but in the Homilies called "a Sermon of the salvation of mankind") as more largely expressing this comment. The following extract from the Homily may be compared with the writers to whom reference has been made: . . . "The true understanding of this doctrine—we be justified by faith without works, or that we be justified by faith in Christ only—is not, that this our act, to believe in Christ, or this our faith in Christ, which is within us, doth justify us and deserve our justification unto us; for that were to count ourselves to be justified by some act or virtue that is within ourselves. But the true understanding and meaning thereof is, that although we have faith, hope, charity, dread and fear of God within us, and do never so many good works thereunto, yet we must renounce the merits of all our said virtues of faith, hope, charity, and all our other virtues and good deeds, which we either have done, shall do, or can do, as things that be far too weak, and insufficient, and unperfect to deserve remission of our sins and our justification; and therefore we must trust only in God's mercy, and in that sacrifice which our high Priest and Saviour Christ Jesus, the Son of God, offered for us upon the cross, to obtain thereby God's grace and remission, as well of our original sin in baptism, as of all actual sin committed by us after our baptism, if we truly repent and turn unfeignedly to Him again . . . Great and godly a virtue as the lively faith is, yet it putteth us from itself, and remitteth or appointeth us unto

Christ, for to have only by Him remission of our sins or justification. So that our faith in Christ, as it were, saith unto us thus: It is not I that take away your sins, but it is Christ only; and to Him only I send you for that purpose, forsaking therein all your good virtues, words, thoughts, and works, and only putting your trust in Christ."

## Note DD.

The theories in reference to Episcopacy, which have been put forward by divines of the Protestant Churches of England and Ireland, seem to be reducible to the three following propositions, and to have been advanced in the order in which they are now stated:—

(1) No one precise form of Church government is absolutely prescribed in the Scriptures. A regular ministry was constituted, but no specific order of pre-eminence or distribution of office and authority was laid down. A right to choose among systems of ecclesiastical government resides, according to some, in the State, and according to others in the national Church of the country. (2) The order of Bishops is of apostolical institution. (3) The order of Bishops is of divine institution, a mode of government not resting upon mere practice or usage, but enjoined as of universal and perpetual obligation in the Christian religious system.

Those whose opinions are represented in the first proposition (1) point out the advantages which accrue from ecclesiastical government being, like the civil government, not bound by one inflexible model. In each the end—the order and well-being of the community—remains always the same, but the means by which it is to be attained can be varied so as to adapt them to the vicissitudes of time and occasion, and bring them into harmony with the condition, circumstances, and dispositions of the people among whom they are to be introduced.

The theologians who support the second proposition (2) in general consider that what is *apostolici juris* is *divini juris* also, since we may assume the Apostles to have been guided by a divine impulse, or at least controlled by a divine superintendence. They do not, however, in general hold Episcopacy to be *divini juris* in the same sense as ordinances (*e.g.* the sacraments), which were established by our Lord, and the institution is, therefore (they concede), not, as such ordinances are, either indispensably necessary or immutable.

The advocates of the third proposition (3) regard Bishops as direct successors of the Apostles. Most of them interpret the commission implied in the words of our Lord after His Resurrection—" As the Father hath sent me, even so send I you "—to be one conferred not generally, but upon the Apostles, and regard the accompanying act— " He breathed on them "—as done in analogy with the original gift of " the breath of life ; " the effect in each case not being restricted to the immediate recipients of the benefit, but designed to be transmitted through them in a perpetual series of successors.

## Note E E.

Among those authors who (as has been mentioned at page 263) think that the character of the Celtic race disinclines them to Protestant systems of religion is Motley. In his *History of the Dutch Republic*, vol, iii. p. 82, he assigns as one of the reasons why in some provinces of the Netherlands Protestantism did not extend itself, " the greater infusion of the Celtic element always keenly alive to sensuous and splendid manifestations of the devotional principle."

In any race which (like the Celtic) is fervid, emotional, easily affected through the imagination and the feelings, tendencies of this nature may be expected to exist, and, where existing, to predispose the people to favour ritualistic and ceremonial systems of religion. *Natio est omnis Gallorum* (and Galli Galatæ and Celtæ are but varieties of the same race), *admodum dedita religionibus*, says the historian of antiquity through whom the Celtic character is best known. (B. G. vi. 16.)

But tendencies do not necessarily always prevail ; and race is not an altogether overpowering influence in the social system : it is only one of several agencies which operate at the same time, and the result is the representative of the reciprocal action of all, not of the exclusive action of any one: nor, when it is in connexion with religion that the future is to be predicted, may we forget that higher impulses, such as a conviction that particular doctrines have been divinely taught, are liable to intervene and disturb calculations based upon mere probability.

While it may be true as a general rule that Protestantism has not been successful with Celtic nations, still there are remarkable exceptions from the rule. The inhabitants of Wales, of the Highlands of Scotland, and of the Isle of Man, are of Celtic origin, and they are all now Protestant.

Another historian, Macaulay, thinks that it is only in communities where the tongue is Teutonic Protestantism makes way. "Wherever," he says, "a language derived from ancient Rome is spoken, the religion of modern Rome prevails to this day." From this he deduces the inference that the Reformation was "not only an insurrection of the laity against the clergy, but also an insurrection of the great German race against an alien domination." (*History*, vol. i. p. 67.)

And no doubt there was in the German people, and from the period when they resisted the dominion of ancient Rome had been, a free and independent spirit, which aided the progress of Protestantism, and predisposed those among whom it was at first originated, or to whom as of like or kindred race with themselves it most speedily travelled, to sympathise with it. But that it spread no farther is due, probably, not so much to anything in the character of the nations among whom it did not penetrate, as to internal improvement in the character of the Church, which continued its connexion with Rome, and to the consequent removal of the sources of discontent with its condition which, far more than doctrinal controversies, led to the Reformation. The external movement for reform, as has been pointed out by Ranke, was met and stayed by counter-reform from within (*History of the Popes*, vol. ii. books 5, 7). Of the nations which at the end of the sixteenth century adhered to the Church of Rome, however much they differed in race or language, none has since seceded from it.

## Note FF.

In the Report of 1868, the annual revenues of the Established Church of Ireland (exclusive of the value of houses of residence and lands in the occupation of ecclesiastical persons), after deducting an allowance for the proportion of poor-rates, which the persons paying rents and tithe rentcharge were entitled to deduct from ecclesiastical owners, and after deducting the expenses of collection and quit-rents were estimated to be : . . . From the rents of lands let to tenants, £204,932 19s. 7d.; from tithe rentcharge, £364,224 16s. 11d.; from other sources, £15,530 6s. 1d.; making in all, £584,688 2s. 7d. In this estimate the amount actually deducted on account of poor-rate for the year 1866, was taken as a measure of the allowance made on that account. In the same Report the value set on the houses of residence and the lands connected with them, which were actually in the occupation of ecclesiastical persons, was derived from the official valuation for the purposes of local taxation. It amounted to £50,237 yearly. This, of course, was subject to the taxes which affect occupiers of land, such as poor-rate, &c., which in the year 1866 came to £18,086. The building charges due in respect of the houses were returned at £232,335. The net revenues seem to have been distributed among their ecclesiastical owners in the following manner: the bishops owned about £58,000 a-year; the capitular bodies about £19,000 a-year; the Ecclesiastical Commissioners about £113,000 a-year; and the beneficed incumbents the remainder. Of the benefices with incumbents, the emoluments—after deducting for poor-rate, &c., and making an allowance for actual payments to curates in 1866, and for the rent of a house when there was no glebe-house—seem to have been much as follows: ... Of about 300 under £100 a-year; of about 420 between £100 and £200 a-year; of about 355 between £200 and £300 a-year; those of the remainder were more than that amount, but in only seven instances did they equal or exceed £1000 a-year. (See Tables annexed to the Report: viii. as amended in Appendix, p. 249, ix., x., xx., xxi., xxii., xxvi., xxviii.)

The Commissioners were directed to report suggestions for improvement in the system of the Church (see page 267); but they interpreted the words in which this was expressed to confine them to alteration and redistribution within the limits of the Church, and to require them to assume that the Establishment would be continued. This being so, the matter which then appeared to them most to need reform was the inadequate remuneration of many of the incumbents of parishes, and the disproportion between payment and work—the former being frequently in an inverse ratio to the latter. It was in order to remedy this state of affairs, and to obtain a fund for the purpose, that the Commissioners (as has been mentioned at page 270) proposed to reduce the number of bishops, of cathedral capitular bodies, and of cathedral dignitaries. With the same object they desired " a readjustment of parochial arrangements and endowments, based upon a consideration of the circumstances proper to be taken into account, such as area, Church population, and Church accommodation." In this way in places where there were few Protestants the number of distinct districts to be provided with incumbents could be diminished, and the revenues of those suppressed be set free for general use.

The policy, advocated in the Report, of adjusting the internal arrangements of each locality to the extent of resident Church population, and of endeavouring adequately to provide for the clergy in charge of the parishes, even if it were necessary to reduce their number in order to do so, seems still more suitable to the circumstances of the Church, when it is, as now, dependent upon voluntary support. Accordingly, so far as reducing the number of incumbencies, it has been, and as the opportunities open by vacancies probably will in the future be, still further carried out. But no change has been as yet made in the number of cathedral dignitaries, although numbers of them have neither cathedral duties to discharge, nor salaries to receive.

The Representative Body submit to the General Synod yearly reports of the financial condition of the Church. The last report (1886) brings their accounts down to 31st December, 1885. The amount of subscriptions, legacies, and donations, which they received in the year 1885 was £137,167. They had then £3,732,686 remaining of the commutation money paid over to them by the Commissioners of Church Temporalities as the capitalised value of the annuities of the ecclesiastical persons who commuted their incomes under the provisions of the Irish Church Act (see page 291, *supra*). The original amount of annuities charged on the commutation money had by deaths, composition, &c., been then reduced to £130,810 a-year, which continued to be charged on and payable out of the remaining capital sum. Beside this capital sum, and the glebes purchased, the Representative Body then had in investments about £2,742,309; of which the sum of £500,000 had been paid to them as a substitute for private endowments under the Act of Parliament, and the rest was derived from bequests, donations, &c.

In 1881 a Census was taken, which ascertained the religious profession of the people, and the number of persons who classed themselves as of each Church or persuasion. The following Table contains the returns of this Census, and also of the Census of 1861, which was the last before disestablishment :—

| A.D. | Roman Catholics. | Prot. Epis-copalians. | Presby-terians. | Methodists. | All other Persuasions except Jews. | Jews. | Total. |
|---|---|---|---|---|---|---|---|
| 1861 | 4,505,265 | 693,357 | 523,291 | 45,399 | 31,262 | 393 | 5,798,967 |
| 1881 | 3,960,891 | 639,574 | 470,734 | 48,839 | 53,796 | 472 | 5,174,306 |

## Note GG.

The following Table enumerates the Bishops of the Church of Ireland appointed subsequently to November 1840, the date when Bishop Mant's Tables, recording episcopal appointments made after A.D. 1585, end:—

| See. | Bishop. | Date of Consecration. | Vacancy. |
| --- | --- | --- | --- |
| Meath, | Charles Dickinson, D.D., | 1840 | 1842 |
| Ossory, Ferns, and Leighlin, | James Thomas O'Brien, D.D., | 1842 | 1875 |
| Meath, | Edward Stopford, | 1842 | 1850 |
| Cashel, Waterford, Lismore, and Emly, | Robert Daly, | 1843 | 1872 |
| Cork, Cloyne, and Ross, | James Wilson, | 1848 | 1857 |
| Down, Connor, and Dromore, | Robert Knox, | 1849 | 1886[1] |
| Limerick, Ardfert, and Aghadoe, | William Higgin, | 1849 | 1853 |
| Meath, | Thomas S. Townsend, | 1850 | 1852 |
| Meath, | James H. Singer, | 1852 | 1866 |
| Derry and Raphoe, | William Higgin, | 1853 | 1867 |
| Limerick, &c., | Henry Griffin, | 1854 | 1866 |
| Kilmore, Elphin, and Ardagh, | Marcus Gervais Beresford, | 1854 | 1862[2] |
| Cork, Cloyne, and Ross, | William Fitzgerald, | 1857 | 1862[3] |
| Killaloe, &c., | William Fitzgerald, | 1862 | 1884 |
| Cork, Cloyne, and Ross, | John Gregg, | 1862 | 1878 |
| Dublin and Kildare, | Richard C. Trench, | 1864 | 1885 |
| Meath, | Samuel Butcher, | 1866 | 1876 |
| Limerick, &c., | Charles Graves, | 1866 | — |
| Tuam, Killaloe, and Achonry, | Hon. Charles Bernard, | 1867 | — |
| Derry and Raphoe, | William Alexander, | 1867 | — |

### Subsequent to Disestablishment.

| See. | Bishop. | Date of Consecration. | Vacancy. |
| --- | --- | --- | --- |
| Kilmore, | Charles Leslie, | 1870 | 1870 |
| Kilmore, | Thomas Carson, | 1870 | 1874 |
| Cashel, &c., | Maurice F. Day, | 1872 | — |
| Kilmore, Elphin, and Ardagh, | John R. Darley, | 1874 | 1884 |
| Ossory, Ferns, and Leighlin, | Robert S. Gregg, | 1875 | 1878[4] |
| Meath, | Lord Plunket, | 1876 | 1885[5] |
| Ossory, &c., | William Pakenham Walsh, | 1878 | — |
| Cork, &c., | Robert S. Gregg, | 1878 | — |
| Killaloe, | William Bennett Chester, | 1884 | — |
| Kilmore, | Samuel Shone, | 1884 | — |
| Dublin and Kildare, | Lord Plunket, | 1885 | — |
| Meath, | Charles Parsons Reichel, | 1885 | — |
| Armagh, | Robert Knox, | 1886 | — |
| Down, Connor, and Dromore, | William Reeves,[6] | 1886 | — |
| Clogher, | Charles M. Stack, | 1886 | — |

[1] Translated to Armagh.   [2] Translated to Armagh.   [3] Translated to Killaloe.
[4] Translated to Cork.   [5] Translated to Dublin.
[6] Previously, on vacancy in the See of Armagh, elected Interim Bishop of Armagh and Clogher.

## Note H H.

The Prayer Book published by the General Synod differs from that which was formerly used in the United Church of England and Ireland, and is still used in the Church of England, in the following particulars:—

i. In the Prefaces, a new Preface is inserted (see page 298, *supra*), and the dates are put to the former Prefaces. The entire of the addendum to the Preface which is entitled, "concerning the Services of the Church," and which is in fact a Rubric, has been omitted. This takes away the direction that "all Priests and Deacons are to say daily the Morning and Evening Prayer either privately or openly, not being let by sickness or some other urgent cause."

ii. The direction how the Psalter is to be read is placed at the head of the Psalter; the order how Holy Scripture is appointed to be read is, in some respects, altered, and the Lectionary which follows varies from the English, principally by omitting all Lessons taken from the Apocrypha, and by inserting additional Lessons from the Apocalypse (see page 302, *supra*).

iii. After the Table of Vigils, &c., there is inserted power for the Archbishops and Bishops to appoint Days of Humiliation, and Days of Thanksgiving, to be observed by the Church of Ireland, and to prescribe special services for the same. Here also there is introduced a Note on the Golden Numbers.

iv. In the Order for Morning and Evening Prayer, in the title the words "to be said and used," before "daily," are omitted, also the direction as to dress is omitted, and this is hereafter to be regulated by the Canons (see page 295, *supra*). Then are introduced powers to enable selections from the Services, with approval of the Ordinary, to be used; also for the use of the Morning and Evening Prayer, the Litany, and the Order for the Administration of the Lord's Supper, as separate Services, or in any combination, subject to the control of the Ordinary. And if the use of full Services be found seriously inconvenient, the Ordinary may dispense with one or more of them. With his permission a sermon may, on special occasions, be preached without the use of morning or evening prayer, some prayers from them being used. The Archbishops may vary the prayers relating to the Royal family. It is explained that though all things set forth are to be read or sung in the English tongue, this is not to prevent the Irish language, or any other the people may understand better, being substituted.

v. In the Order for Morning Prayer, the cxlviii. Psalm (*Laudate Dominum*) is introduced as an alternative to the *Te Deum* or *Benedicite*. When the Litany is said, the Lord's Prayer and three versicles after the *Te Deum* may be omitted.

vi. The Rubric directing the use of the Athanasian Creed is omitted; and the Creed remains without alteration, but with no direction as to its use (see page 302, *supra*).

vii. There is a new Rubric before the Litany directing what is to be read with it, when it is read either as a separate Service or in combination with the Communion Service.

viii. In the occasional prayers and thanksgivings there is introduced from the Service for the 20th June a prayer for Unity; also the following new prayers—(1) for a sick person; (2) for Rogation days; (3) for New Year's Day; (4) for Christian Missions; (5) for the General Synod while it is in Session; (6) for use in Colleges and Schools; (7) a thanksgiving for recovery from sickness. The prayer for use in time of plague, &c., is altered in some respects; so also is the prayer for Parliament, in which for the words " most religious and gracious Queen," are substituted the words " our Sovereign Lady the Queen."

ix. In connexion with the Collects, Epistles, &c., there are three Rubrics providing, among other things, for the case of a holyday falling upon a Sunday. If on Christmas Day or Easter Day there are two celebrations of the Holy Communion, a new Collect, Epistle, and Gospel, are provided, which may be used at the first. For the Sunday after Easter Day there is a new Epistle.

x. In connexion with the Order for Administration of the Lord's Supper the preliminary Rubric is altered in some respects; so also are the Rubrics before the Offertory. In the Offertory sentences the two from Tobit are omitted. The Rubric about the collection of the Offertory is altered, to enable it to be before the sermon. In the Nicene Creed, in the words "I believe in the Holy Ghost, the Lord and Giver of life," a comma has been inserted after Lord, to bring the sense more to the Greek form, viz., τὸ Πνεῦμα τὸ ἅγιον, τὸ κύριον, καὶ τὸ ζωοποιόν. The Rubric before the exhortation to those who come to the Communion contains an insertion of the words "those who do not intend to communicate, having had opportunity to withdraw." The exhortation is slightly altered. It may be omitted at the discretion of the minister, the consent of the Ordinary having been first obtained, but provided that it shall be read once a month at least, and at all great festivals. In the Rubric before the prayer of consecration the words "standing at the North side of the table" have been introduced (and see the canons on this head, page 295, *supra*). At the end of the office some additional Collects are introduced; one of which may be used after the Offertory when "the prayer for the Church Militant" is not read. In the Rubrics which follow these Collects provisions are added which enable the minister to dispense with the "prayer for the Church Militant"; prohibit the administration of the Communion unless two at the least are present; and permit on occasions sanctioned by the Ordinary the service to begin with the Collect, Epistle, and Gospel. The direction as to the nature of the bread is now imperative—"shall be," not as before, "it shall suffice that it be." When by reason of numbers it is inconvenient to address each communicant separately, the words, on delivering the elements, may, with the consent of the Ordinary, be said once to as many as shall together kneel at the Holy Table; but they are to be said separately to any communicant desiring it.

xi. In the Service for Public Baptism of Infants alterations are made in the Rubrics, the effect of which is to permit parents to be sponsors for their own children; and when three sponsors cannot be found, to allow two; and if two cannot be found, to allow one. Also some alterations are made as to the times for administration of the rite. In the exhortation at the beginning of the service, in place of the words "except he be regenerate and born anew of water and of the Holy Ghost" are substituted the words "except a man be born of water and of the Spirit." Also the Rubric before the words "I baptize thee" has been altered, and now reads, "he shall dip it (the child) in the water discreetly and warily, if they shall desire it, and he shall be certified that the child may well endure it; otherwise it shall suffice to pour water upon it." At the end of the service a new Rubric is added, which explains the use of the sign of the cross: "that it is not thereby intended to add any new rite to this sacrament as a part of it, or necessary to it; or that the using of that sign is of any virtue or efficacy of itself, but only to remind all Christians of the death and cross of Christ, which is their hope and their glory; and to put them in mind of their obligation to bear the cross in such manner as God shall think fit to lay it upon them, and to become conformable to Christ in his sufferings." In the Public Baptism of Adults the opening exhortation is modified, as in the Service for Infants, and a new Rubric states that persons of riper years may, upon great and urgent cause, be baptized in private.

xii. In the Catechism a question and answer having relation to the Sacrament of the Lord's Supper have been introduced (see page 300, *supra*). In the Rubric directing the curate to catechise, for the words "on Sundays and Holydays" are substituted "at such times as he shall think convenient." The direction in another Rubric that everyone shall have a godfather or godmother as a witness of their confirmation has been omitted.

xiii. In the Order for Confirmation is inserted a question asking those baptized in riper years if they renew the promise of their baptism. The Rubric as to admission to the Holy Communion is now changed into "every person ought to present himself for Confirmation (unless prevented by some urgent reason) before he partakes of the Lord's Supper."

xiv. In the Form of Solemnization of Matrimony the first Rubric recognizes the use of Licences, and gives directions as to Banns. In the opening exhortation there are some verbal changes. Directions are given for procedure when more than one couple are married. The prayer beginning "O merciful Lord!" is verbally altered. At the end of the Service there are added the third of the Collects after the Offertory, and the benedictory prayer for grace (2 Cor. xiii. 14).

xv. In the Visitation of the Sick there is a new Rubric, permitting the minister to edify and comfort the sick as he shall think meet by instruction or prayer; but if the sick person requires the office to be used, the minister shall use it. A precatory form of absolution is substituted for the former (see page 301, *supra*); and in the Rubric before it the words "the sick person shall be moved to make confession" are changed into "if the sick person feel his conscience troubled with any weighty matter," and the words "he shall absolve him" into the words "the minister shall say thus." There are added a new alternative Collect after the absolution, and a new prayer for a sick person when his sickness is assuaged. In the Communion of the Sick the Rubric before it is modified, to allow the Collect, Epistle, and Gospel of the day to be used in place of those prescribed. Power is given to shorten the office if the person is sick; and the last Rubric is in some respects varied.

xvi. In the Order for Burial of the Dead the first Rubric is enlarged, and allows in certain cases a portion of the office to be used for unbaptised persons: an alternative Lesson from 1 Thess. is added to the former one from 1 Cor. xv. In the words said at the grave, beginning "For as much," &c., the words "of His great mercy" are left out. In the prayer beginning "Almighty God, with whom do live the spirits of them that depart this life," for the words "we give Thee hearty thanks for that it hath pleased Thee to deliver," &c., are substituted the words "we bless Thy holy name for all Thy servants departed this life in Thy faith and fear."

xvii. In the Commination Service the first exhortation has been modified; and in the long exhortation "fruits of penance" have been changed to "fruits of repentance."

xviii. Rubrics are placed before the Psalter taken out of the old prefaces.

xix. In the Ordination and Consecration Services Church is instead of Realm, and also of Church and Realm.

xx. In the Form for the Anniversary of Her Majesty's ascension there are some unimportant variations of Rubrics, and some Collects are omitted.

xxi. Some emendations are made in the former Irish Service for Visitation of Prisoners: in the Absolution in this Service the same change is made as in the Visitation of the Sick.

xx. There are the following new Services:—(1) "to be used on the first Sunday on which a minister officiates in a church to which he has been instituted;" (2) "A form of thanksgiving for the blessing of harvest;" (3) "A form for the consecration of a church;" (4) "A form of consecration of a churchyard or other burial-ground."

THE END.

# ERRATA.

### PAGE 41.

It is erroneously stated that in the second Prayer Book of Edward VI. the Prefatory Sentences, the Exhortation, &c., were introduced in the Evening Prayer. They were not introduced in the Evening Prayer until the revision of Charles II.

### PAGE 42.

The person in whose place Casey was restored was not, as stated in the note, then dead: he had either resigned or been deprived. (See Appendix, page 326.)

### PAGE 55.

It should have been noticed that in the clause defining what should be deemed heresy, the words of the English Supremacy Act, which required that the determination of Parliament should be with the assent of the clergy in their Convocation, were in the Irish Supremacy Act omitted.

### PAGE 212.

Instead of the words "the Union of the Kingdoms and Churches of Great Britain and Ireland," the words should be "the Union of the Kingdoms of Great Britain and Ireland, and of the Churches of England and Ireland."

---

Chapters XV., XVI., XVII., XVIII., XIX., have been erroneously numbered XVI., XVII., XVIII., XIX., XX.

www.ingramcontent.com/pod-product-compliance
Lightning Source LLC
Chambersburg PA
CBHW020304240426
43673CB00039B/697